LOCAL ACTIONS

D1564431

LOCAL ACTIONS

Cultural Activism, Power, and Public Life
in America

EDITED BY

MELISSA CHECKER AND MAGGIE FISHMAN

COLUMBIA UNIVERSITY PRESS

NEW YORK

COLUMBIA UNIVERSITY PRESS
PUBLISHERS SINCE 1893
NEW YORK   CHICHESTER, WEST SUSSEX

Library of Congress Cataloging-in-Publication Data
Local actions : cultural activism, power, and public life / edited by
    Melissa Checker and Maggie Fishman.
        p.   cm.
    ISBN 0-231-12850-9 (cloth: alk. paper) — ISBN 0-231-12851-7
    (pbk.: alk. paper)
        1. United States—Social conditions. 2. Social change—United States.
    3. Social participation—United States. 4. Community life—United States.
    5. United States—Politics and government. I. Checker, Melissa.
    II. Fishman, Maggie.

    HN57.L585 2004
    306'.0973—dc22
                                                                    2003059554

Columbia University Press books are printed on permanent and durable
acid-free paper.
Printed in the United States of America

c 10 9 8 7 6 5 4 3 2 1
p 10 9 8 7 6 5 4 3 2 1

To social change, large and small

Contents

Foreword

FAYE GINSBURG

In their introduction to this groundbreaking collection of ethnographic studies of "local actions" in contemporary America, editors Melissa Checker and Maggie Fishman invoke the crisis of collective identity that many Americans experienced after September 11, 2001. The crisis they identify—the tension between unity and diversity in the U.S.—escalated in the early months of 2003 as America moved toward and entered into war. For many American researchers, both in and outside of the academy, these events also provoked us to reexamine the purpose of our own practices. How can our work help us better grasp, analytically, the complex transformations of everyday life around us and their theoretical as well as political significance? Is it possible to produce ethnography that simultaneously expands the intellectual scope of the field while also entering productively back into the lives of those we study and providing interventions into the broader public sphere(s) that we share with our subjects?

While these kinds of concerns may be newly underscored at this historical moment, clearly they are not new for the authors represented here. Nor are they entirely new for the field of anthropology, which for many years has developed in tandem with a left-liberal politics in American intellectual life. This preface will discuss some of the anthropological precedents and genealogies that have led to the kinds of research agendas, models, and practices presented in this volume. The emerging generation of ethnographers writing in this volume launched their research in the 1990s, hoping both to understand and sometimes contribute to the efforts of people in local communities—organized along a range of vectors—to transform their worlds through collective action. They also decided to work in the United States as their first commitment rather than as a second project after a first fieldwork stint "elsewhere." These choices are strategic in two ways.

First, the authors' attention to situations of cultural transformation has enabled them to include, as part of their analysis, a sophisticated and nuanced understanding of what is driving certain kinds of social change as well as the dilemmas that are facing social actors in these circumstances. These include a range of styles of social action from progressive movements to multicultural initiatives as imagined (if imperfect) programs for community building to conservative religious practices. In many of the studies the researchers share the concerns and even the identities of the people they are studying—while also attending to inherent fault lines in their projects—ranging from the divisions of race and class in the environmental justice movement, the utopian goals of the beleaguered field of arts education, or the identity struggles of Korean American adoptees. Others have chosen to study groups that are more challenging to the subject position of the researcher, such as conservative Christian megachurches attracting American middle-class congregants, the religiously based "ex-gay" movement, or Hasidic Jews whose insistence on insular cultural practices in the racially charged neighborhood of Crown Heights reveals the contradictions in superficial efforts at "multicultural exchange."

Second, the authors' have made self-conscious decisions to work in the U.S. as an empirically, theoretically, and politically productive area for ethnographic work. While anthropologists have often committed themselves to ongoing support for communities they have worked with abroad, such an approach has been optional at best, despite ethical guidelines established by the American Anthropological Association. As researchers "working at home," we are far more complicit in the worlds we study, as citizens who have a stake and a say in the cultural policies shaping our own and our informant's lives and as writers whose work will enter into their discursive world as well as that of the academy. The anthropologists writing here carefully thought through these implications in ways that engage with ongoing discussions about doing anthropology in the U.S.

These discussions began at least three decades ago, breaking a dichotomous deadlock of an earlier era in which work was either "scientific" (and therefore significant primarily to a community of scholars, but not necessarily of more general interest) or "applied" (and therefore meant to be of practical use to the community being studied, but assumed to be of lesser intellectual value).

In the 1970s, for example, the anthropologist Barbara Myerhoff, after many years of work with Huichol Indians in Mexico, began her research with elderly Jews in southern California, work that resulted in her prize-winning book, *Number Our Days*. She defended her (at that time unusual) choice to carry out research in the U.S. based on her existential relationship with the different worlds of her subjects. "I will never be a Huichol Indian, but I will become a little old Jewish lady," she told filmmaker Lynne Littman in the documentary on her work—also called *Number Our Days*—that won an Oscar in 1977 (though Myerhoff's untimely death in 1985 lends a posthumous tragic irony to her statement). In the book Myerhoff elaborated on the obligations this kind of identification with a community entails for a researcher. She describes the ongoing claims members were able to make on her as a Jew and as a "lady professor" whose work eventually rendered them visible and significant to the world, while also helping to raise badly needed resources for these people living in financially marginal circumstances. As with Myerhoff's work, the quality of the *Local Actions* collection demonstrates that the boundaries between "here" and "there" and "us" and "them" are ever more permeable. Clearly, this can have a salutary effect, rather than compromising the objectivity of researchers, as was the common disciplinary wisdom until recently. As anthropologists George and Louise Spindler pointed out in a prescient review article that in 1983 recognized the U.S. as a legitimate ethnographic area, "When we write about our own culture we are ourselves expressions of what we are writing about" (49). Indeed, this kind of research raises to a new level of self-consciousness questions about its impact on the lives of those we study who inevitably "read what we write"(Brettell 1993), sometimes far more quickly than we could have imagined. This, of course, raises questions about the burden of representation carried by ethnographers.

Accordingly, in the 1980s, American anthropology was preoccupied with experimentation with ethnographic writing as a stylistic intervention into modes of imagining other cultural worlds, a prosodic tendency that has been both enlivening and, at times, made ethnographies increasingly inaccessible to even highly literate informants (Clifford and Marcus 1986).

This collection, written over a decade later, pushes this experimentation into the realm of the social. Authors ask not only about the possibilities of writing and different modes of address but also about potential representational violence created by the objectification of people's lives in texts. At the same time, they are concerned with how their work renders visible and significant the everyday reality of the lives we study in ways that contribute to broader arenas of cultural production and analysis.

In their introduction the editors suggest that their approach expands on the tradition of cultural critique that has characterized American anthropology for the last century, as George Marcus and Michael Fischer argued compellingly in their 1986 book exploring that topic. This strategy used the authority of social science to demonstrate the value of alternative possibilities to those of the dominant American system through the empirical realities of other cultural lives. One can track this approach from the nineteenth-century writings of Lewis Henry Morgan on the Iroquois, people he admired for their "natural democracy," to Boas's efforts to use scientific measurement of the crania of recent immigrants to contradict racist claims about their intellectual abilities in the early twentieth century; to Margaret Mead's popular efforts to use the insights of cultures "elsewhere" to argue for more relaxed and sensible approaches to child rearing and adolescence in the U.S. Other predecessors, such as Robert and Helen Lynd, were more direct in the ways that critique and research came together. They used Americanist ethnography to engage directly with public debates on the impact of consumer capitalism on daily life (Veblen et al.), in their seminal and widely read books *Middletown* (1929) and *Middletown in Transition* (1937), ethnographic studies of Muncie, Indiana, considered the quintessential middle American city at the time for its supposed homogeneity. By 1939 Robert Lynd wrote *Knowledge for What? The Place of Social Science in American Culture*, an indictment of the increasingly insular and quantitative scientific discourse in social science, which he felt removed such work from the realm of public debate. There are many more examples of this legacy; this skeletal sketch is simply meant to show how questions about the possible critical engagement of ethnographic work with contemporary concerns are perennially present. This is particularly the case in the U.S., where the relationships and commitments established by fieldwork are accompanied by the reality of "natives" looking over our shoulders as we fashion our representations of their worlds.

The focus in this volume on *cultural activism* indicates a distinctive re-framing of the legacy of "cultural critique" by recognizing the productivity of the cultural imagination of social actors themselves. As a heuristic tool, cultural activism calls attention to the way that people engage in *self-conscious mobilization of their own culture practices* in order to defend, extend, complicate, and sometimes transform both their immediate worlds and the larger sociopolitical structures that shape them. Examples are all around us, from the creation of institutions such as the Studio Museum in Harlem, to the development of Native American cinema, to the world-changing activism of Christian evangelicals. These kinds of culture-making activities are especially characteristic of American social life since the 1970s—what some have called the postcivil rights era, a period strongly associated with the emergence of identity politics, consumer capitalism, and the rise of neoliberal politics. Differing from more overtly politicized forms of activism that characterized much of the 1960s and seventies, in these formations "culture" increasingly has been objectified and deployed as a powerful vehicle for collective self-production in an era when "the politics of recognition" (Fraser 1997) shapes the claims of people who find themselves rendered marginal by an exclusionary public sphere. In a classic Foucauldian manner certain groups have been able to claim and shape those forms of identification that had been used, in some cases, to contain or stigmatize them. They are used instead to assert their presence in the polities that encompass them by entering into broader movements for recognition, human rights, and social transformation. The resignification of the term *queer* as part of a broad movement for equity and justice for gay men and lesbians is exemplary of this kind of semiotic transformation of a negative category into a positive one through activist efforts.

In the framework of this volume, subjects and researchers alike share desires for a more capacious and equitable polity, in registers that can both diverge and overlap. Many of the authors are simultaneously studying communities and working on behalf of them either as at least partial members (Abdulhadi, Fishman, Shankar, Spilde) or as sympathetic fellow travelers (Checker, Kim,Valentine). Others, (Elisha, Erzen, and Goldschmidt) work in settings with those with whom they differ, despite their sympathetic engagement with and analytic comprehension of the worlds of their subjects. These researchers find themselves playing a kind of translational role, helping those outside these worlds to understand what motivates these kinds of social actors. For example, Henry Goldschmidt acknowledges his "grudging agreement" with his Hasidic informants' rejection of a homogenizing multiculturalism, much as Elisha finds himself drawn to the critique of materialism offered by some of the leaders and parishioners carrying out servant evangelism. Because of these crosscutting identifications and commitments, as well as the strong interest in the cultural possibilities represented by the social worlds they share with their subjects, a number of the authors work outside the academy as policy makers and consultants (Fishman, Spilde), and occasionally journalists and even political representatives (Abdulhadi).

At the same time, the authors are wary of presenting such formations as homogeneous and are constantly alert to the complexity and diversity *within* different categories of identification. Thus they bring compelling evidence for the analytic effectiveness of the ethnographic method, which inevitably reveals the fault lines in communities, social movements, and institutions that run along class, race, and generational lines. These fault lines, picked up by the inductive approach of anthropological research, might easily be missed by the more deductive and quantitative methodologies associated with contemporary sociology, for example. This is due to the intimacy and length of time typical of anthropological work, as well as the fact that the method *requires* reflexivity: the self is, in fact, the site of knowledge production, as each of the articles demonstrates with elegance and insight, often produced by the fabled generativity of "mistakes" in the field, which Valentine poignantly makes clear in his efforts to bring together two of his informants. The project of building theory out of everyday life, in turn, produces rich, compelling, and deeply contextualized narratives that reproduce in some dimension the way that knowledge arises from "being there."

Ethnography is also particularly suited to track the impact of global capital, the increasing flow of bodies and information, and the accelerating transformations in biomedicine, media, and information technologies in everyday life. In the subtle interactions of the quotidian one sees how the production of cultural identity is a highly contested process, whether in the relatively contained debates in the worlds of arts education or culturally diverse high schools, the violence experienced by those who violate normative gender categories—violence that works on a continuum from actual murder to job discrimination to personal pronoun choices, or the discomfort with computers and internet communication that Checker found among African Americans engaged in fighting environmental discrimination in their neighborhood, making her aware of the impact of racial and class stratification on access, literacy, and comfort with these technologies. More generally, this book makes a compelling case for how a focus on *cultural activism* can be theoretically and epistemologically catalyzing, invigorating a sense of the potential worldly purpose of this kind of work.

Finally, in the interests of full disclosure, I am delighted to acknowledge that I had the great pleasure to have the editors and seven of the ten contributors as graduate students in a seminar on ethnography in the U.S. called "Constructing America" that I regularly teach at New York University. The course integrates students in the Departments of Anthropology and American Studies, a program that has been particularly interested in ethnography under the leadership of Andrew Ross during the 1990s. The majority of the research projects discussed here first took shape in papers for that seminar, and I was privileged to serve as an adviser on six of the Ph.D. projects that developed from that work. A number of the authors were also in a dissertation writing group that emerged at NYU and expanded to accommodate fellow travelers from the Anthropology Department at the University of California at Santa Cruz who were living and working on the East Coast.

It is more than coincidence that this collection reflects these particular departments and institutions. The course "Constructing America" actually grew out of a seminar of that name that my colleague and friend Susan Harding ran at the NY Institute for the Humanities during the early to mid 1980s. (She is now an anthropology professor at UCSC who helped mentor contributors to this volume.) We were each engaged in ethnographic research with conservative social movements identified with the rise of the New Right. Susan was studying new forms of Christian fundamentalism, and in particular the work and impact of Reverend Jerry Falwell, founder of the Moral Majority, a project that culminated in *The Book of Jerry Falwell* (2000), while I was working with women activists on both sides of the abortion debate, through the lens of a prolonged battle over an abortion clinic in Fargo, North Dakota, resulting in the book *Contested Lives: The Abortion Debate in an American Community* (1989, 1998). At that time many fewer anthropologists were working in the U.S. as a primary site, and even fewer were studying these kinds of social activists, who were seen by many in the academy to be anathema to American cultural life. In response we formed the "Constructing America" seminar to provide an interdisciplinary space that could bring together anthropologists, historians, and cultural critics carrying out social research in the U.S. A central concern of that seminar (and eventually the course I taught at NYU) was to examine the ways that anthropologists (and others) studying American culture are simultaneously engaged (along with their subjects) in constructing it, in part because of the rapid circulation of writing back into the communities being studied. Unsurprisingly, our students found the sense of a shared intellectual framework a decade later, when "Constructing America" became the title of a panel at the 2000 American Anthropological Association meetings organized by Melissa Checker and Maggie Fishman from which this book grew.

The synergy of the intellectual camaraderie that developed in these different contexts is strikingly evident in the ways that the research and ideas addressed in this book cascade from one essay to the next. It is the closely guarded secret of teaching that it can be among the greatest pleasures of academic life, particularly when it helps to launch so vibrant a set of new scholars as those who have made this book; they have demonstrated a clear sense of their own intellectual identity as well as the contributions that their work can bring to the field—and to the world.

WORKS CITED

Brettell, Caroline B., ed. 1993. *When They Read What We Write: The Politics of Ethnography*. Westport, Conn.: Bergin and Garvey.

Clifford, James and George Marcus, eds. 1986. *Writing Culture: The Poetics and Politics of Ethnography* . Berkeley: University of California Press.

Fraser, Nancy. 1997. *Justice Interruptus: Critical Reflections on the "Postsocialist" Condition*. New York: Routledge.

Ginsburg, Faye. 1989. *Contested Lives: The Abortion Debate in an American Community*. Berkeley: University of California Press.

—— 1998. *Contested Lives: The Abortion Debate in an American Community*. 2d ed. Berkeley: University of California Press.

Harding, Susan. 2000. *The Book of Jerry Falwell*. Princeton: Princeton University Press.

Lynd, Robert. 1939. *Knowledge for What? The Place of Social Science in American Culture*. Princeton: Princeton University Press.

Lynd, Robert and Helen Lynd. 1937. *Middletown in Transition: A Study in Cultural Conflict*. Harcourt Brace and Jovanovich.

—— 1959 [1929]. *Middletown: A Study in Modern American Culture.* Harcourt Brace and
    Jovanovich.

Marcus, George E. and Michael M. J. Fischer. 1986. *Anthropology as Cultural Critique:
    An Experimental Moment in the Human Sciences.* Chicago: University of Chicago
    Press.

Spindler, George, and Louise Spindler. 1983. Anthropologists View American Cul-
    ture. *Annual Review of Anthropology* 12:49–78.

Acknowledgments

The creation of this book was inspired by our appreciation for the diverse group of activists that we have encountered through our research and through the work of our colleagues. For both of us, coming of age in an era of critique and questioning of the history and dominant models of social science research, the opportunity to study, write about, and contribute to activist efforts has grounded us as anthropologists. We thank all the activists who gave hours of their time to share with us their perspectives and their work. As coeditors, we had the opportunity to read each of these essays numerous times and to develop a deep appreciation for the rich and thoughtful work of our contributors. We thank our contributors for their hard work and support for a project that was off the beaten tenure track. The production of this volume has also benefited from the contributions of colleagues and friends. The following is only a partial list of those to whom we extend our gratitude.

We would like to thank the Department of Anthropology at New York University, where many of the ideas in this book were incubated. The critical perspective, commitment to anthropology as a discipline, and faith in fieldwork "at home" transmitted to us there were crucial to the genesis of our perspective and that of many of the contributors. We are especially grateful to Faye Ginsburg, upon whose rigorous creative and critical anthropology of America this book is grounded and who has been a great support to the project since its inception as a panel at an annual meeting of the American Anthropological Association. Wendy Lochner of Columbia University Press offered her faith, enthusiasm, and experience as our project grew from proposal to manuscript. CUP editors Suzanne Ryan and Susan Pensak brought their expertise and dedication to its final stages. Omri Elisha has offered his intelligence, creative thinking, insightful comments, and general support from the get-go, and David Valentine and Henry Goldschmidt provided much needed wit and morale boosting throughout the project.

Our introduction benefited immeasurably from the comments of anonymous reviewers. We thank Linda Bennett, Owen Lynch, Steve Albert, Peter Zabielskis, Jessica Winegar, Wendy Leynse, Shalini Shankar, Tanya Erzen, Yiftach Resheff, Pia Moos, Katie Fishman, Julie Rogers, and Shanti Crawford for contributing incisive suggestions and input to the introduction. We are also grateful to Pia Moos, Kate Spilde, Henry Goldschmidt, and David Valentine for their contributions to the book's cover.

Our families and friends have lived with the demands, the trials, and the tribulations that go along with any project of this nature. Words cannot convey our appreciation for their time and patience. Finally, this project has taught us as coeditors the degree to which two heads are better than one. And for that as well as the friendship that has grown out of this collaboration we are especially grateful.

LOCAL ACTIONS

Introduction

MELISSA CHECKER AND MAGGIE FISHMAN

"*Americans for once came together.*" Over and over we heard undergraduates utter this common refrain as we struggled to help ourselves and our students come to grips with the terrible events of September 11, 2001. Indeed many of those Americans determined to construe something positive from that disastrous day have pointed out that, for the most part,[1] it brought Americans together. For most of that autumn Americans took a break from their individual commitments and took collective national action—giving copious amounts of blood and sending countless donations to New York City. Time and again we hear that such unity is all too rare in our society. In particular, we are often told that the absence of unified social action is swiftly diminishing the potential for Americans to effect large-scale changes that will improve their lives. But how can America, the world's oldest continuous democracy, reconcile this desire for "unity" with the vast diversity for which it is known?

Such questions resonate with a long-told tale decrying American factionalism and atomization. For example, in 1963 sociologist Roland Warren wrote that community in America was changing drastically, in part because of the "development of differentiated interests among local people who thus associate more often on the basis of specialized interests than on the basis of merely living in the same place" (1963:5). For Warren, these specialized interests translated into a dismal lack of desire and ability to effect communitywide changes. Thirty-seven years later, in his highly popular work *Bowling Alone*, sociologist Robert Putnam (2000) decried a decrease in American civic engagement. Putnam updated Warren's argument about specialization by pointing out that "cyberbalkanization" has caused people to confine their communications to those who share precisely the same interests, limiting chances for real-world, place-based, diverse interactions. In recent years a number of popular critics have similarly claimed that by separating themselves into categories based on race, gender, ethnicity, sexual orientation, environmental awareness, or religion, special interest groups in the U.S. competitively grab for power, undermine a sense of an American collectivity, and threaten the opportunities of others.[2] Manifestations of such complaints can be seen in English Only movements, efforts to repeal affirmative action, and a backlash against various multicultural agendas, including diversity education in public schools.

In this volume we leave behind arguments about the relative merits of identity politics and American self-interest. Our research reveals that, all too often, the very concept of identity politics obscures the diversity within activist groups, the kinds of change they are hoping to effect, and the degree to which they do not separate themselves. Instead, we examine particular activist projects as they unfold on the ground. We find instances of activism across the country, in such seemingly unlikely places as urban areas that have for years been branded as "ghettos," at backyard barbecues, and at suburban megachurches. We find that people *do* grapple with issues of large-scale social change through channels available to them. Understanding the significance of these efforts means expanding the definition of what we consider political—for some a high school dance performance or filming an autobiography counts as socially transforming work.

From this perspective we propose to reframe identity politics as "cultural activism" and present ten very different groups of activists who are working to change dominant discourses and to stake their claims in an ever evolving public sphere. Rather than isolating themselves, these groups are reaching out to an American public, and often to each other, as they demand to be recognized, counted, and heard. Although organized around identity, such groups have a public orientation that is by definition not separatist. As Fraser argues, "After all, to interact discursively as a member of a *public*—subaltern or otherwise—is to attempt to disseminate one's discourse into ever-widening arenas" (1992:17). Thus in this volume we contend that identity-based organizing actually offers a multitude of possibilities and promises for coalition building and for harnessing collective power.

The essays in this volume, then, tackle such questions as: Given particular historic circumstances, how do people come together to define a problem and form agendas? What kinds of public routes do they take to criticize those aspects of social life that they find limiting or unjust? On what basis do people reach across boundaries, form coalitions, and increase their constituencies? How do they establish group solidarity and also form the alliances and networks necessary to effect social change? How do individuals engage with existing institutions? When do they compromise, and when do they rebel? Finally, given the fact that characterizing "Americanness" is an admittedly difficult task, is there anything in these forms of organizing and activism that is peculiar to the American system? We answer these questions through the wide variety of ethnographic case studies that make up this volume.

In the midst of such activist-oriented vitality, American academics are rethinking and reshaping their own roles in public life. Thus the chapters in this volume offer not just fine-grained analysis of the ways in which Americans resist, alter, and appropriate public discourse but also an awareness of the multiple roles that academics might play in the activist efforts they study. For most of the last century many academics have perceived their job to be one of dispassionate analysis. In the past twenty years, however, the same factors that produced a new multiplicity of activist forms have shifted the terms of academic practice, encouraging the questioning of old stances, posing challenges to former ways of doing business, and raising new possibilities for engaging with public issues through our research. As a result it has become possible for social scientists to explicitly relate our research to political, ethical, and critical concerns.

In this vein we take up our own agenda as editors. Our goal is not to judge the paths taken by cultural activists in terms of prognoses for future mass actions but rather to gain a better understanding of how diverse groups of people across America conceive of, and take steps toward, social change. To do so, we have gathered together case studies by anthropologists that use the formidable tools of ethnography to explore vital issues in American society. We believe ethnography is a particularly effective method of doing research and making sense of the actions, motivations, structures, and settings that lead to social change. At a time when instantaneous public surveys update us daily about mass opinion, when the results of focus groups and questionnaires are presented as reports on what our nation is thinking and feeling, issues in the public sphere are often reduced to simplified polarized positions. Long-term, in-depth research projects that seek to understand the complexities of events as they unfold on the ground in real time offer us a crucial, alternative view. Thus the case studies selected for this volume were not meant as an all-inclusive representation of activist Americans but rather as a compelling *sample* of the vast and various work being done by activists and anthropologists today.[3] Moreover, we believe that the methods of ethnography not only lend themselves to informing public debates about the issues we research—they demand that we get involved. Thus our contributors comment on their own agendas, and in some cases the various ways they are participating in the struggles for social change they study. By framing these projects as cultural activism, we suggest that activism is alive and well in America: In fact, for many Americans (including academics), engaging in political practice is an essential part of their everyday lives.

CULTURAL ACTIVISM AND AMERICAN CULTURE

Anthropologist Faye Ginsburg first coined the term *cultural activism* to interpret the very public efforts of various groups who use music, visual arts, and film to articulate a political agenda (Ginsburg 1997).[4] In this work we also use the term to highlight public efforts to challenge and reconfigure aspects of our society that people perceive as oppressive. Here we extend Ginsburg's concept by drawing on the broader anthropological definition of "culture" as the full range of social practices and historical processes that people draw upon to conceive of and constitute their lives (see Mahon 1997:47). Thus cultural activism comprises multiple kinds of public actions, both formal and informal, that people use to alter the circumstances of their lives—such as teaching art to public school children, interpreting Scriptures, staging public protests, and lobbying Congress.

Recent studies of "resistance" have drawn attention to the host of everyday ways that people express their dissatisfaction with the status quo. These studies illustrate how individuals transform basic and undramatic acts of life, such as choosing what to eat or wear, into moments of protest (for instance Comaroff and Comaroff 1991; Ong 1987; Scott 1985; Taussig 1980). Similarly, cultural activists often do not work through political channels but develop their activism around cultural forms that are more immediately available to them. The crucial difference, however, in this volume is that our contributors analyze situations in which people move beyond individual acts of resistance and join with others to engage in public, shared acts of opposition. For we contend that it is only through *collective* social action that resistance develops the potential for political transformation. As Steven Gregory writes, "The exercise of political power and resistance consists precisely of those social practices that enable or disable people from acting collectively as political subjects" (1998:12).

At the same time, as we mentioned above, not all groups of cultural activists can be considered part of organized movements with specific agendas, goals, and memberships. In addition, cultural activists do not necessarily speak about their projects in conventionally political terms. As scholars Arturo Escobar and Sonia Alvarez argue, contemporary social movements "do not restrict themselves to traditional political activities, such as those linked to parties and state institutions. Rather, they challenge our most entrenched ways of understanding political practice and its relation to culture, economy, society and nature" (1992:7). Thus, the "political" activities in which cultural activists engage encompass a wide range of arenas where people contest the circumstances of their lives and challenge dominant discourses. Moreover, like individual acts of resistance, the collective and public acts of cultural activists are often embedded in everyday life (see Melucci 1988). Indeed we find these activists in different niches, bearing different relationships to traditional or formal activism, variously organized and structured according to the diverse circumstances that produced them. In most cases we find that people pursue activism through avenues that are already available, and sometimes these avenues do not lead to large-scale change. In short, we define cultural activism as the range of collective and public practices and strategies that people use to alter dominant perceptions, ideas, and understandings for the sake of social change.

By looking at such instances of cultural activism together, we can analyze the various ways in which Americans draw on the resources available to them to effect social change. For example, Shalini Shankar's South Asian teenagers create dances for their high school's Multicultural Day that expand people's ideas of South Asian culture. These teens do not refer to themselves as "activists," and they organize formally only during the three-month period prior to the performance. However, Shankar argues that if we see Multicultural Day as the one available space for these teens to take an active role in representing themselves, we can view the brief period in which they seize the stage as a distinctly political moment. On the other end of the organizational spectrum, David Valentine looks at transgender New Yorkers who strongly identify themselves as activists. Like the teens, they struggle to alter dominant ideas about who they are and what they are capable of achieving as a group. Yet, as these activists work to change their public image, they must also rely on and participate in a legal system whose terminology emphasizes their victimhood. While South Asian teens and transgender activists do not share a political language to define their projects, both groups must find ways to use existing discourses, spaces, and systems to instigate change.

We emphasize that in many cases the activists described are aware of the degree to which their actions sometimes reinforce systemic institutions of power. As anthropologist Anthony Giddens has pointed out, social actors think critically about the structures and systems they inhabit and that constrain their actions (see Giddens 1990). Such constraints are particularly prominent for activists who wrestle with the idea that, as black feminist poet and critic Audre Lorde famously noted, "The master's tools will never dismantle the master's house" (1984:112). In all the cases presented in this book, activists must make painful choices about whether and to what extent they should work within the systems they are trying to change. Each choice to pick up or discard the "master's tools" is complex, historically contingent, and culturally specific. For instance, Melissa Checker looks at recent efforts of African American grassroots environmental justice activists in a small neighborhood in Augusta, Georgia to work with professional environmentalists. Traditionally the environmental movement has left out the needs of minority groups and has in some cases even exacerbated the environmental hazards they face. However, partnering with professional environmentalists presented these minority activists with opportunities to increase their power and resources. Thus they faced difficult decisions about how to pursue alliances with a movement that in many ways symbolized their historic exclusion from mainstream American life.

Indeed all the cultural activists described here must navigate complicated relationships with common public discourses and legal, political, and economic institutions. Although the vast diversity in the U.S. has led many scholars to question the very notion of "American-ness," we find certain similarities in activists' goals, methods, and strategies for altering public discourse. In fact, as we see it, a propensity toward cultural activism in the U.S. derives from a form of organizing first noted as quintessentially American by Alexis de Tocqueville. In writing about "voluntary associations," this early nineteenth-century French observer of American society pointed to the crucial connection between social action and identity formation in America. He argued that Americans were joiners who created a sense of belonging by forming committees and joining voluntary associations. De Tocqueville writes, "At the head of any new undertaking, where in France you would find some territorial magnate, in the U.S., you are sure to find an association" (1988 [1842]:513). For de Tocqueville it is primarily through group affiliations that the American individual defines who he or she is.

One hundred and sixty years after de Tocqueville put his observations on paper, we argue that contemporary cultural activism in America emerges from a tradition of collective attempts at self-definition through group affiliation. As Faye Ginsburg notes, Americans continue to construct American society and their own identities together:

> The [American] cultural system requires that the individual constitute himself or herself in order to achieve a social identity, and that the means available for achieving identity are through voluntary affiliations with others in a group that offers a comprehensive reframing of the place of the self in the social world. (1989:221)

This is not to say, however, that cultural activism is merely about finding a place to belong or a way to identify oneself; rather, we find that for many Americans becoming part of a collectivity incorporates imperatives to social action. In addition, the most pressing social issues in the U.S. often present themselves to individuals in the form of identity questions. Thus the cultural activists in this volume are joining together publicly to assert collective identities that reflect their lived experiences more accurately. In so doing, they are redefining themselves as more powerful members of society *and* they are attempting to reshape mainstream ideas about who they are and what they are capable of. The activists in this volume, therefore, share a characteristic American desire to join collectivities in order to define themselves and to redefine society at the same time.

Rather than envisioning these groups as atomized and mutually exclusive, we emphasize the ways in which they are continually reaching out, forming networks, and associating with one another. Rabab Abdulhadi, for example, describes the multiple changes that Palestinian American activism has undergone over the past several decades. Combining ethnographic and historical analysis, she demonstrates that since the late 1960s Palestinian Americans have defined the very notion of "Palestinianness" through the processes of identification and coalition building with groups of African Americans, feminists, Latino/a, and Jewish activists.

Through the following ethnographic analyses of communities and collectivities that may at first blush seem isolated, self-contained, or unique, we are able to see some of the possibilities in identity-based organizing. We believe that outlining the steps that lead to such organizing, and making explicit the potential for individual groups to expand their organizing bases, is itself a tool for activism. It is therefore our hope that the essays in this volume exemplify the myriad ways in which a new generation of anthropologists is developing its commitments to activism and moving toward a more active engagement in public life.

NAVIGATING NEW DIRECTIONS FOR ACADEMIC ENGAGEMENT

If you can, please make a statement identifying yourself as a member of society as well as a "social scientist" who undertakes research not just for the sake of the scientific record.
—FISHMAN AND CHECKER, 2002, email to contributors

The creation of *Local Actions: Cultural Activism, Power, and Public Life* was motivated by our excitement over new trends in academia (and more specifically, anthropology) that have opened the door for more explicit academic activism. The papers we have chosen for this volume provide excellent examples of how a new generation of anthropologists is using ethnography to better understand and speak about issues in our own society. Although it is possible to identify a legacy of explicitly committed American scholarship that dates back to an earlier period of American intellectual life, only recently has it become imaginable that publicly engaging with political issues could be integral to American academic practice in the future. This new openness stems from critiques of the objective research paradigm that have prevailed in academia's recent history. In this section we will briefly outline some of the factors that have led to this shift in academic practice.

In *The American Evasion of Philosophy: A Genealogy of Pragmatism* Cornel West calls for American academics to build on the influential tradition of American pragmatism and assume the role of public or "organic" intellectuals.[5] West argues that American pragmatists conceived of philosophy "as a form of cultural criticism [that] attempts to explain America to itself at particular historical moments" (West 1989:5). Eschewing esoteric questions about the nature of reality that preoccupied post-Kantian European scholars, American pragmatists combined historical consciousness with an emphasis on social and political matters, providing a model for scholars today.[6] West argues that by rooting their insights in social movements public intellectuals might create "a new and novel form of indigenous American oppositional thought and action" that combines academic study with an agenda for real-world change (1989:8).[7]

How did American academics lose touch with their historic commitment to public issues? As American academia developed into a profession, the pursuit of intellectual expertise was increasingly promoted as a goal for academics over the sharing of knowledge with the public outside the academy (Bender 1993). In addition, as a result of growing specialization within the academy, the social sciences were increasingly distinguished from the humanities on the basis of a research paradigm involving the ideals of "objectivity" and "pure science."[8] Professional standards required that research be presented in a scientific style and that researchers present themselves as impartial observers reporting the facts. Scholars increasingly chose to mute ethical or political concerns in order to adhere to such standards. Anthropology—the disciplinary home of ethnography and of most of the contributors to this volume—exemplifies this trend.

Anthropologists had to negotiate particularly puzzling relationships with ideals of objectivity because ethnographic research depends on developing personal relationships and integrating oneself in particular communities. American anthropology evolved as a discipline that specialized in researching the alternative ways of life of Native Americans and other "primitive" small-scale societies around the world. Anthropologists posed different questions and developed different methods than American sociologists, for example, who specialized in societies like their own, which they studied with the new technologies and methods of statistics and questionnaires. In order to understand people whose lives were so different, anthropologists developed and refined an ethnographic methodology. Ethnography generally entailed at least twelve months of fieldwork, which began with a long period of "hanging out"—living and working in a community and participating in community events so that daily life became comprehensible. Only after integrating themselves into a particular society could anthropologists communicate with people from a common basis of assumptions and then understand and interpret what those people were doing and how they explained their actions.

Because the distinction between "native" and "researcher" was central to the paradigm of anthropological research, academic anthropologists did not study their own society—at least not directly. However, by presenting and making comprehensible alternative ways of life, ethnographies have the potential to be subversive. As Marcus and Fischer have convincingly demonstrated in their seminal work of the 1980s, *Anthropology as Cultural Critique*, many anthropologists have historically used the analysis of other cultures to highlight problems in their own society:

> As they have written detailed descriptions and analyses of other cultures, ethnographers have simultaneously had a marginal or hidden agenda of critique of their own culture, namely, the bourgeois, middle-class life of mass liberal societies, which industrial capitalism has produced. (1986:111)

However, due in large part to the pressures of the academy noted above, anthropologists have historically kept such critiques "hidden" or "marginal."

For instance, those early anthropologists deeply disturbed by the decimation of Native American societies and cultures as a result of U.S. military, legal, and economic policies often focused their concern on the loss of Native American cultures. They sought to understand and document Native American religions, languages, technologies, histories, and cosmologies before they were completely transformed or eradicated. In preserving material from the past, these committed anthropologists have been helpful to Native Americans, and they have implicitly critiqued the massive destruction of Native American ways of life. However, many recent critics—including Native Americans and social scientists—have pointed out that these early anthropologists were well placed to overtly protest the American governmental policies that were effectively destroying the ways of life they were depicting. Had they been more explicit in explaining the daily struggles of native groups to survive the adverse effects of U.S. policy, they might have influenced the outcomes of those struggles.

As notable exceptions, early dynamic leaders in anthropology such as Franz Boas[9] and Margaret Mead did attempt to influence and participate in public debate over social issues through research and writing about their own society as well as through comparison with places elsewhere.[10] Mead even wrote a column in the popular woman's magazine *Redbook* from 1961 to 1978. In a similar vein, Sol Tax created "Action Anthropology" in the 1950s. Tax envisioned anthropology as a clinical science, like psychology, in which anthropologists would work with the communities they study to diagnose problems and propose solutions to them while also building theory (Foley 1999). Unfortunately, such efforts remained relegated to the sidelines; as anthropology grew and ethnographers multiplied, usefulness and problem solving were not incorporated into the discipline as a legitimate aim (Eddy and Partridge 1978).

Indeed, as anthropology departments grew almost exponentially in the post–World War II era, anthropologists increasingly geared their writing to speak to other anthropologists rather than to a general public. Eventually, the discipline itself divided: "academic" anthropologists concentrated on developing theory, teaching in universities, and supervising doctoral students; those who wanted to apply their research to problems in health care, education, ecology, and other fields joined a subdiscipline known as "applied anthropology." Because they received much of their research funding from governmental and quasi-governmental organizations (to which they are then accountable), applied anthropologists have been accorded less prestige within the academy.

In the last twenty years major changes across academic disciplines have collapsed the scientific paradigm, paving the way for our collection of ethnographies about cultural activism in America. Multiple critiques of colonialism, gender relations, and various academic canons have shaken up academia. Such critiques have also challenged anthropology's historic separation of science from contemporary political and economic systems.[11] These works and the research that ensued began to examine the colonial relationships and histories that enabled ethnographic researchers to travel and study all over the world, making it clear that, historically, the societies labeled "modern" and "primitive" were never isolated.[12] An ever globalizing world brought Western and non-Western societies even closer, particularly in terms of higher education and media access. As a result, native peoples were able to increase their monitoring, assessment, and control of anthropological work about them. For instance, works such as those by Obeyeskere (1992) and Said (1979) argued against the very notion of "native." These authors, who hailed from the so-called exotic societies that anthropologists traditionally study, addressed their writing to academics as well to the people in the texts themselves.[13]

The launching of these critiques inspired a number of attempts to define a different model for research and theory that accounts for the motivation of researchers, the specific conditions of their research, and the ethical issues at stake. During this postmodern period most anthropologists began to conceive of their projects differently. Instead of seeking to discover the consistent, objective rules and norms that govern societies, they began to study the ways in which individuals explain those rules and act upon them.[14] In addition, many anthropologists began to challenge the image of the detached scientist by including descriptions of their personal involvements and ethical challenges in the field. Perhaps most productively, the radical questioning of distinctions between native and scientist and primitive and modern has meant that that many scholars became eager to better understand modern Western societies. Taking inspiration from the work of Michel Foucault, they spawned a growing body of literature that investigated the institutions, ways of thinking, and power of the West (see Bourdieu 1984; Comaroff and Comaroff 1991; Foucault 1979, 1973, 1978; Haraway 1989; Mitchell 1988).

As part of that trend, more and more academic anthropologists have been turning to the study of American life. In the past ten years American anthropologists have studied such topics as class formation and socialization, right-wing fundamentalism, factory workers, and the construction of popular ideas about culture, natives, and the exotic (see Harding 1984, 2000; Lamphere 1987; Lutz and Collins 1993; Nash 1989; Newman 1988; Ortner 1991).[15] Most concretely, American feminists of the 1980s were among the first academics to fully part with the ideal of detached research, offering a model of academic work that was both authoritative and engaged. Influenced by the global feminist movement and its consciousness-raising groups, feminist anthropologists had highly personal reasons for taking on their particular subjects of study. For example, in the collection *Uncertain Terms: Negotiating Gender in American Culture* the contributors make it clear that they write

> from an unapologetically engaged position. We are studying issues and conflicts that involve us as both analysts and actors. We are conscious of

> the political significance of research on both publicly debated topics . . .
> and on ongoing, local tensions. (Ginsburg and Tsing 1990:3)

Because they have a personal stake in the outcome of struggles over the gendered cultural discourses, resources, and rights that they describe, the work of feminist anthropologists exemplifies ethnography that strives to equalize power relations by providing the otherwise undescribed, on-the-ground perspectives that should inform public policy and decision making.[16]

Building on such examples, we offer this volume as a window into possibilities for future research that address issues of public interest in ways that advance social science *and* are accessible and useful to various audiences. Thus we gear this book not just to academics but to activists who may use it as a tool for reflection and to see their work in a broader context. We also invite general audiences to read these chapters and discover alternative points of view on taken-for-granted notions about American life.

In addition, by collecting samples of new work into one volume, and by presenting that work in clear, accessible language, we intend to illuminate some of the many possible ways in which anthropologists can enter public discourse. In reading these papers, the reader can imagine the various ways in which the material could be communicated, or the many venues in which it could be published, with different audiences in mind. In so doing, *Local Actions: Cultural Activism, Power, and Public Life* also elucidates how ethnography, through the personal ties and mutual understanding forged during long-term fieldwork, can serve as one example for breaking down the boundaries that divide academics from those they research. As they develop critiques of American society, the contributors question the power relationships between researcher and subject and offer ways that an activist-oriented approach to research can bring balance to those relationships. For example, some of the contributors to this volume chose to repay activists for allowing themselves to be studied by assisting with grant writing, tutoring, or organizing local protests. Others took positions in governmental or quasi-governmental agencies in order to assist activists' efforts to influence the institutions that affect their lives. Thus, we present a wide range of strategies and definitions of engagement, from writing jargon-free texts that address multiple audiences to directly joining the groups under study.

While the contributors engage in straightforward observation and analysis of ethnographic data, we have also encouraged each to make clear his or her stance on the issues at hand. Whether or not we share the specific goals of the people we present, the intimacy and in-depth knowledge derived from long-term fieldwork gives us firmer ground from which to speak about our own attitudes and commitments toward those goals. Thus, as we examine the various strategies and cultural resources upon which activists draw in their efforts to reconstruct an America that resonates with their own experiences, we also make explicit the strategies and cultural resources that inform our own efforts to reconcile our dual roles as academics and as engaged citizens.

Recognizing our multiple connections to what we research raises several new challenges. First, we must ask, in a society where "they read what we write"(Brettell 1993), how do we write ethnographies that are responsible to both our subjects and to our readership? Such questions are central not just to anthropological inquiry but to any form of academic study. As the reader will see, throughout the volume we provide answers to this question by example. Second, while many academic anthropologists (following more general academic trends) have begun to promote a focus on "public anthropology" to increase the impact of anthropology on public discourse, questions remain about the degree to which such projects can be integrated into the academic mainstream.[17] As anthropologists from senior faculty to graduate students have pointed out in numerous academic forums, academic administrations must also incorporate this paradigm shift into the foundations of their institutions. For example, engaged anthropology will not gain academic value until the current bases for tenure in universities attribute more prestige to nonacademic activities and publishing venues.[18] Moreover, a call for a more "public anthropology" has underscored divisions between academic and applied researchers, with the latter claiming that this discourse ignores the work they have been doing for years.[19]

That being said, it is our aim that in presenting new ethnographic work and considering its multiple uses and potential this volume will further open the door for conversations across the divide between academic and applied researchers. First, we contend that, although intellectually stimulating, arguments over labels such as *applied, public, engaged,* or *activist* anthropology distract our attention from the larger issues at hand—such as finding different ways to make our work accessible and useful to a public both within and without the academy and promoting the use of ethno-graphic research to address real-world problems. Second, we propose a perspective that recognizes knowledge is *always* produced under institutional and cultural constraints. Researchers, then, might envision negotiating their positions along a continuum. On one end academic institutions and ideologies tend to push scholars towards erudite, overly nuanced distinctions, or "theory for theory's sake," which are publicly inaccessible. On the other end, applied researchers face institutional sponsors and timetables that push them toward the overly utilitarian and context-bound production of data.

In this volume we aim to demonstrate why and how Americans form various kinds of collectivities and gather together to improve their lives. We argue that these groups are not separating themselves but are struggling to join their voices to the mainstream and organizing to change public discourse. Furthermore, we view ourselves as cultural activists who seek to make public engagement part of mainstream academic practice and describe America to itself. It is our hope that through these essays we can reconstruct dominant American concepts, theories, and strategies such as "culture," "the arts," "the digital divide," "ethnicity," "transgender," and "academia" itself.

It is also our goal to show how ethnography, our particular mode of inquiry, can uniquely contribute to social problem solving. Our historic role of describing groups outside the mainstream in order to "make the strange familiar and the familiar strange" is only one part of our task as ethnographers. We additionally strive to take important public issues out of the realm of ideology, theory, and rhetoric and examine them in the context of how they are produced in daily life and how they play out in lived experience. The close relationships that we develop with those we study require us to take a stand and position us to make a contribution. We encourage readers to view the ethnographic essays in this volume as presenting one step on the road toward engaged academic practice.

We begin with a chapter that investigates how groups from very different racial and economic backgrounds work toward building productive activist coalitions. Melissa Checker focuses on a group of African Americans in Augusta, Georgia who are trying to save their neighborhood from toxic contamination. Over the years these grassroots activists developed ex-

tensive networks with professional environmentalists. Checker's fieldwork methodology emphasized reciprocity, and she volunteered as a full-
time staff member for the group she studied. She found that her own
identity as a white, middle class activist together with her growing knowledge of the community in which she conducted fieldwork positioned her
to understand the substantial differences in perspectives that the two
groups brought to environmental organizing. Paying particular attention
to the different ways computers and religion figured in their social movement organizing, Checker finds that race and class differences shaped activists' notions of "good" social movement organizing and, ultimately, access to power in American society.

In the following chapter we explore the less formally organized side of
cultural activism and present artist-activists who are using art to promote
social change. Here Maggie Fishman examines the struggles of artists to
alter the direction of education in New York City public schools. Critical of the product-oriented commercialism of professional art worlds,
many artists have turned to schools as a place to realize their ideal of democratic and transformative art making. Fishman describes how artists
taught children and teachers to create an opera based on their own experience and to interpret paintings based on their own observations and interpretations. She argues that their work challenges both the current national educational agenda and dominant roles and values associated with
artistic careers in fine art worlds. Finally, Fishman, who became an educational evaluator after her fieldwork, points out the affinities between
the artists' efforts to develop an artistic practice that moves beyond specialized professional art worlds and those academics who wish to expand
the role for academics in public life.

Next, we move back up the spectrum of organized activism as Kate
Spilde examines how American Indian nations are challenging popular
ideas about them by investing gaming revenues into cultural production,
preservation, and media messages about their history and identity. Spilde
finds that Indian nations are not just using gaming revenue to help themselves but are also working on multiple projects to develop much needed services and infrastructures in the communities surrounding their
reservations. She argues that Indian nation governmental gaming provides an opportunity for American Indian communities to define their
cultural, economic, and political future for themselves. However, as Indian nations have increasingly garnered political clout as a result of these

good works, they have also experienced a backlash against their gaming work that threatens their achievements. Notably, Spilde spent several years working for the Bureau of Indian Gaming where she used her ethnographic research to redirect gaming policy: her work demonstrates that ethnographic research can bring the much needed voices of communities into public policy decision making—an area often dominated by rhetoric.

Moving back east, we now take a closer look at the complex issues at stake in conducting engaged research. We begin with David Valentine's chapter, which addresses head-on problematic issues in both group formation and in activist anthropology. Valentine looks at how transgender-identified activists are coming together to demand that state institutions provide them with better protection from violence. Although the choice of "transgender" as an organizing category allows these activists to gain power in legal terms, it is also problematic because it erases the experiences of many of those represented under this category, especially poor, young people of color. Valentine also brings his research to bear on recent debates about the relationship between ethnographic research and the ethics of activism. He responds in particular to some recent calls for "barefoot anthropology" that argue that, in certain cases, anthropologists should abandon their pursuit of nuanced analyses for the sake of immediate ethical action. Through a critical reading of the category transgender, and based on his work as a cofounder of NYAGRA, a transgender rights organization, Valentine concludes that detailed long-term analysis is essential to anthropologists' abilities to make the best ethical choices.

At this point in the volume we counteract the assumption that engaged ethnographers always identify with the politics of the groups they study. As a progressive activist who wanted to better understand what was motivating the Christian Right, Tanya Erzen chose to research an ex-gay ministry, where Christian homosexuals come to renounce their gay identities in order to conform to their conservative religious beliefs. Through ethnography Erzen gained a deeper understanding of conflicts between ex-gay activists and right-wing discourse. For example, in their efforts to halt the progress of gay rights, some Christian Right political organizations have promoted ex-gay ministries as proof that homosexuality is not a biological or permanent state. However, Erzen finds that ex-gays disagree with this agenda and are disturbed to find their stories used for such a cause. Erzen's ethnography thus reveals the diversity of political views within conservative Christianity.

In another study that works to complicate our view of the Christian Right, and of the ways that cultural activists reach beyond the boundaries that might enclose them, Omri Elisha looks at suburban evangelical Christians in East Tennessee. He explores social ministries where church activists struggle to convince the mainly middle class members of megachurches to do outreach work in economically disadvantaged places. Elisha finds that these efforts reflect a deep ambivalence about activists' own middle-class identities—churchgoers realize that the middle-class lifestyles they enjoy take them further and further away from the Christian values that are central to their lives. Not only are these Christians resolving such ambivalence by reaching out to work with groups that are very different from them, they are also establishing a complex critique of American materialism and consumerism. Like Erzen, Elisha concludes that, contrary to common stereotypes, fundamentalist Christianity is not homogenous and has its progressive voices. Moreover, he demonstrates that evangelical preaching is not merely accusation directed at the sinful, unchurched world "outside" but is rather a medium of moral instruction often directed squarely at the people in the pews.

In order to illustrate the degree to which cross-class, cross-race, and multiethnic organizing is a complicated matter in America, we now present two case studies demonstrating the ways that some cultural activists are challenging dominant, superficial conceptions of multiculturalism. First, Henry Goldschmidt writes about relationships between African Americans and white Hasidic Jews in the Crown Heights neighborhood of Brooklyn, New York. Following the 1991 riots in Crown Heights, state agencies and other organizations asked blacks and Jews to participate in various forums for dialogue and exchange across the racial divide, including symbolically charged meals of customary foods. Some neighborhood residents, both black and Jewish, welcomed the opportunity to learn about the "cultures" of their neighbors, but many Hasidic Jews questioned the relevance of such activities and refused to participate. Such Hasidic resistance is often viewed negatively as an insistence on insularity. However, as Goldschmidt argues, it may also be seen as a form of resistance to pressures from state institutions to conform to dominant models of multiculturalism. Goldschmidt concludes by describing a more successful model of coalition building that focuses on the concrete problems and concerns these groups share as New York residents.

On the opposite coast Shalini Shankar furthers our understanding of the promise and failures of multiculturalism. As she describes the efforts of Northern California students to participate in their high schools' multicultural day, Shankar demonstrates how multiculturalism's charge of creating more inclusive and egalitarian environments gets sabotaged through its implementation in particular projects. These annual events, which were the only occasions for students to represent their ethnic identities in a public forum, were limited and competitive and ultimately perpetuated existing race and class hierarchies. At the same time, Shankar finds that the South Asian participants viewed these multicultural performances as an important venue in which to express their specific experiences as second-generation immigrants to their school. Thus, by creating a hybrid, fashionable dance, these teens contradicted audiences' expectations for "traditional" and "authentic" performance. In so doing, they reworked popular ideas about what it means to be South Asian in America.

Keeping our focus on the creative side of cultural activism, we next present a group of Korean American adoptees who are also struggling to reconstruct dominant ideas about who they are and their experiences in America. Kim highlights the ways in which a recent spate of cultural expressions of Korean adoptee identity—including web sites, literary work, film, and visual art—register a growing presence and self-conscious building of "community" among Korean-born adoptees in the West. Often seen as "model" minorities and adoption "success" stories, these venues provide important sites where adoptees can share stories of alienation, pain, and loss. Kim concludes that the narratives of Korean adoptees not only articulate an untold collective history but also have the potential to affect the course of transnational adoption in the U.S. and elsewhere.

In the final chapter Rabab Abdulhadi takes up the timely (and ever evolving) subject of the construction of Palestinian American activist identities. Given their ambiguous status in the world, Palestinian Americans have had a particularly difficult time creating an identity for themselves as "hyphenated Americans." Abdulhadi finds that over the years these activists have reconstructed their identities in relation to world events and to other activist movements. For instance, Palestinian Americans have at times allied and identified themselves with African American,

Native American, feminist, and particular Jewish American activists. Thus Abdulhadi demonstrates that, rather than developing an isolated activist identity and focusing on single-issue organizing, Palestinian Americans are continually reaching out to other groups and forming various alliances and coalitions for change.

NOTES

1. Unless, in many unfortunate cases, you looked Middle Eastern or South Asian.

2. See for example, Harvey 1990.

3. The absence of Latino/a or feminist activist groups from the roster of chapters attests to this fact.

4. For some reasons that the recent mobilization of interest groups is linked to an increased reliance on the arts and media to convey political positions and make cultural critiques, see Abu-Lughod 1993; Ginsburg 1991,1997; Mahon 1997; Ross 1989; Wallis 1990.

5. West defines organic intellectuals as "participants in the life of the mind who revel in ideas and relate ideas to action by means of creating, constituting, or consolidating constituencies for moral aims and political purposes"(1989:6).

6. West traces his genealogy of American scholarship from Ralph Waldo Emerson and John Dewey through the twentieth century, including historian W. E. B. Du Bois; theologian Reinhold Niebuhr; sociologist C. Wright Mills, and literary critic Calvin Trilling.

7. West has since tried such projects working in partnership with other scholars. See West and Hewlett, *The War Against Parents* (1999), and West and Lerner, *Jews and Blacks* (1996).

8. For Thomas Kuhn, paradigms are "accepted examples of actual scientific practice—which includes law, theory, application and instrumentation together—which provide models from which spring coherent traditions of scientific research." Cited in Turner 1974:29.

9. For example, Boas, often referred to as "the father of American anthropology," at times had a very explicit activist agenda to his research and his publications (e.g., 1940, 1932). In some, such as the well-known study in which he measured the heads of immigrants, he directly disproved the arguments of popular eugenicists about the brain size and intelligence of Jewish and other eastern European immigrants (1898).

10. Henry Schoolcraft, James Mooney, and Hortense Powdermaker also provide notable historic examples of anthropologists who engaged in public issues. For details on their activities see Eddy and Partridge 1978:11–13.

11. See for example: Clifford 1988; Fabian 1983; Marcus and Myers 1995; Martin 1989; Rosaldo 1989; Wolf 1982.

12. See, for example, Mullin 1992, 1993; Stoler 1995.

13. Obeyesekere, for example, draws on his own Sri Lankan background to refute the well-known anthropological trope about the beginning of imperialism in Hawaii, which portrays eighteenth-century Hawaiian natives as deifying the first white European man they had ever encountered. He argues that these anthropological accounts derive less from actual Hawaiian/native culture and far more from European cultural desires and ideas about colonialism.

14. Here, we especially refer to work that followed Clifford Geertz's groundbreaking essay "Thick Description" (1973) in which he calls for actor-oriented ethnography.

15. For examples and more extensive reviews of this exciting literature, see Harrison 1995; Peirano 1998; Rhodes 2001; Stewart and Harding 1999; Susser 1996; Traube 1996.

16. These feminists could build on a two-decade-long history of feminist revisionist scholarship across disciplines.

17. This interest in public anthropology was manifest in the theme of the 2000 American Anthropological Association's Annual Meeting, "The Public Face of Anthropology." In addition, the American Anthropological Association's "Anthropology Newsletter" recently announced that its 2003–2004 theme will be "Mapping an Engaged Anthropology."

18. There is exciting progress being made toward this end. In recent years a number of academic institutions, particularly urban institutions, have made explicit commitment to valuing engaged scholarship within their universities. These institutions are beginning to revamp tenure requirements to include "outreach" as a tenure requirement. While this term is defined in various ways across different institutions, it includes valuing new kinds of academic publications and establishing methods to evaluate the quality and impact of outreach work that may not translate directly or immediately into traditional academic products.

19. This comes from a series of articles by Eric Lassiter in *American Anthropology* on "theorizing the local." His most recent essay (2003) specifically addresses public anthropology and what it means. For additional examples of debates on this issue, see Singer 2000; Young 2001.

WORKS CITED

Abu-Lughod, Lila. 1993. "Finding a Place for Islam: Egyptian Television Serials and the National Interest." *Public Culture* 5(3): 493–513.

Bender, Thomas.1993. *Intellect and Public Life: Essays on the Social History of Academic Intellectuals in the United States.* Baltimore and London: Johns Hopkins University Press.

Boas, Franz. 1940. *Race, Language, and Culture.* New York: Macmillan.

—— 1932. *Anthropology and Modern Life*. New York: Norton.

—— 1898. *The Growth of Toronto Children*. Washington, D.C.: Government Printing Office.

Bourdieu, Pierre. 1984. *Distinction: A Social Critique of the Judgment of Taste*. Cambridge: Harvard University Press.

Brettell, Caroline B., ed. 1993. *When They Read What We Write: The Politics of Ethnography*. Westport, Conn.: Bergin and Garvey.

Clifford, James. 1988. *The Predicament of Culture: Twentieth-Century Ethnography, Literature, and Art*. Cambridge: Harvard University Press.

Comaroff, Jean and John Comaroff. 1991. *Of Revelation and Revolution*. Chicago: University of Chicago Press.

Eddy, Elizabeth M. and William L. Partridge. 1978. "The Development of Applied Anthropology in America" In Elizabeth M. Eddy and William L. Partridge, eds., *Applied Anthropology in America*. New York: Columbia University Press.

Escobar, Arturo and Sonia Alvarez. 1992. *The Making of Social Movements in Latin America: Identity, Strategy, and Democracy*. Boulder, Colo.: Westview.

Fabian, Johannes. 1983. *Time and the Other: How Anthropology Makes Its Object*. New York: Columbia University Press.

Foley, Douglas E. 1999. "The Fox Project: A Reappraisal." *Current Anthropology* 40(2): 171–191.

Foucault, Michel. 1979. *Discipline and Punish: The Birth of the Prison*. New York: Vintage.

—— 1978. *The History of Sexuality*. New York: Vintage.

—— 1973. *Madness and Civilization: A History of Insanity in the Age of Reason*. New York: Vintage.

Fraser, Nancy. 1992. "Rethinking the Public Sphere: A Contribution to the Critique of Actually Existing Democracy." In C. Calhoun, ed., *Habermas and the Public Sphere*, pp. 109–142. Cambridge: MIT Press.

Geertz, Clifford. 1973. "Thick Description." In *The Interpretation of Cultures*. New York: Basic.

Giddens, Anthony. 1990. *Central Problems in Social Theory: Action, Structure, and Contradiction in Social Analysis*. Berkeley: University of California Press.

Ginsburg, Faye.1997. "From Little Things Big Things Grow: Cultural Activism and Indigenous Media." In Richard Fox and Orin Starn, eds., *Between Resistance and Revolution: Cultural Politics and Social Protest*, pp. 118–144. New Brunswick, N.J.: Rutgers University Press.

—— 1991. "Indigenous Media: Faustian Contract or Global Village." *Cultural Anthropology* 6(1): 92–112.

—— 1989. *Contested Lives: The Abortion Debate in an American Community*. Berkeley: University of California Press.

Ginsburg, Faye and Anna Lowenhaupt Tsing, eds.1990. *Uncertain Terms: Negotiating Gender in American Culture*. Boston: Beacon.

Gregory, Steven. 1998. *Black Corona: Race and the Politics of Place in an Urban Community*. Princeton: Princeton University Press.

Habermas, Jurgen. 1981. "New Social Movements." *Telos* 49:33–37.

Haraway, Donna. 1989. *Primate Visions: Gender, Race, and Nature in the World of Modern Science*. New York: Routledge.

Harding, Susan Friend. 2000. *The Book of Jerry Falwell: Fundamentalist Language and Politics*. Princeton: Princeton University Press.

—— 1984. *Statemaking and Social Movements: Essays in History and Theory*. Ann Arbor: University of Michigan Press.

Harrison, Faye V. 1995."The Persistent Power of 'Race' in the Cultural and Political Economy of Racism." *Annual Review of Anthropology* 24:47–74.

Harvey, David.1990. *The Condition of Postmodernity*. Cambridge: Blackwell.

Lamphere, Louise. 1987. *From Working Daughters to Working Mothers: Immigrant Women in a New England Industrial Community*. Ithaca: Cornell University Press.

Lassiter, Luke Eric. 2003. "'Theorizing the Local' Anthropology News." *American Anthropology* 44(5): 13.

Lorde, Audre. 1984. *Sister Outsider: Essays and Speeches*. Trumansburg, N.Y.: Crossing.

Lutz, Catherine A. and Jane L. Collins. 1993. *Reading National Geographic*. Chicago: University of Chicago Press.

Mahon, Maureen. 1997. "The Black Rock Coalition and the Cultural Politics of Race in the United States." Ph.D. diss., Department of Anthropology, New York University.

Marcus, George E. and Michael M. J. Fischer. 1986. *Anthropology as Cultural Critique:An Experimental Moment in the Human Sciences*. Chicago: University of Chicago Press.

Marcus, George E. and Fred Myers. 1995. *The Traffic in Culture: Refiguring Art and Anthropology*. Berkeley: University of California Press.

Martin, Emily. 1989. *The Woman in the Body: A Cultural Analysis of Reproduction*. Boston: Beacon.

Melucci, Alberto. 1988. "Social Movements and the Democratization of Everyday Life." In John Deane, ed., *Civil Society and the State: New European Perspectives*. London: Verso.

Mitchell, Timothy. 1988. *Colonising Egypt*. New York: Cambridge University Press.

Mullin, Molly. 1993. "Consuming the American Southwest: Culture, Art, and Difference." Ph.D. diss., Department of Cultural Anthropology, Duke University.

—— 1992. "The Patronage of Difference: Making Indian Art 'Art,' Not Ethnology." *Cultural Anthropology* 7(4): 395–424.

Nash, June. 1989. *From Tank Town to High Tech: The Clash of Community and Industrial Cycles*. New York: State University of New York Press.

Newman, Katherine. 1988. "Falling from Grace: The Experience of Downward Mobility in the American Middle Class." London: Collier Macmillan.

Obeyesekere, Ganath. 1992. *The Apotheosis of Captain Cook: European Mythmaking in the Pacific.* Princeton: Princeton University Press.

Ong, Aihwa. 1987. *Spirits of Resistance and Capitalist Discipline: Factory Women in Malaysia.* Albany: State University of New York Press.

Ortner, Sherry. 1991. "Reading America: Preliminary Notes on Class and Culture." In Richard Fox, ed., *Recapturing Anthropology,* pp. 105–189. Santa Fe: SAR.

Peirano, Mariza G. S. 1998. "When Anthropology Is at Home: The Different Contexts of a Single Discipline." *Annual Review of Anthropology* 27:105–128.

Putnam, Robert. 2000. *Bowling Alone: The Collapse and Revival of American Community.* New York: Simon and Schuster.

Rhodes, Lorna A. 2001. *Toward an Anthropology of Prisons Annual Review of Anthropology* 30:65–83.

Rosaldo, Renato. 1989. *Culture and Truth: The Remaking of Social Analysis.* Boston: Beacon.

Ross, Andrew. 1989. *No Respect: Intellectuals and Popular Culture.* New York: Routledge.

Said, Edward. 1979. *Orientalism.* New York: Vintage.

Scott, James. 1985. *Weapons of the Weak: Everyday Forms of Peasant Resistance.* New Haven: Yale University Press.

Singer, Merril. 2000. "Why I Am Not a Public Anthropologist." *Anthropology News,* September 2000, pp. 6–7.

Stewart, Kathleen and Susan Harding. 1999. *Bad Endings: American Apocalypsis. Annual Review of Anthropology* 28:285–310.

Stoler, Ann. 1995. *Race and the Education of Desire: Foucault's History of Sexuality and the Colonial Order of Things.* Durham: Duke University Press.

Susser, Ida. 1996. *The Construction of Poverty and Homelessness in U.S. Cities. Annual Review of Anthropology* 25:411–435.

Taussig, Michael T. 1980. *The Devil and Commodity Fetishism in South America.* Chapel Hill: University of North Carolina Press.

Tocqueville, Alexis de. 1988 [1842]. *Democracy in America.* New York: Harper and Row.

Traube, Elizabeth G. 1996. *"The Popular" in American Culture. Annual Review of Anthropology* 25:127–151.

Turner, Victor. 1974. *Dramas, Fields, and Metaphors: Symbolic Action in Human Society.* Ithaca: Cornell University Press.

Wallis, Brian. 1990. "Democracy and Cultural Activism." In Brian Wallis, ed., *Democracy: A Project by Group Material,* pp. 4–11. Seattle: Bay.

Warren, Roland. 1963. *The Community in America.* Chicago: Rand McNally.

West, Cornel. 1989. *The American Evasion of Philosophy: A Genealogy of Pragmatism.* Madison: University of Wisconsin Press.

West, Cornel and Michael Lerner. 1996. *Jews and Blacks: A Dialogue on Race, Religion, and Culture in America.* New York: Plume.

West, Cornel and Sylvia Ann Hewlett. 1999. *The War Against Parents: What We Can Do for America's Beleaguered Moms and Dads.* Boston: Houghton Mifflin.

Wolf, Eric. 1982. *Europe and the People Without a History.* Berkeley: University of California Press.

Young, John A. 2001. "Assessing Cooperation and Change: The SfAA and the EPA." *Practicing Anthropology* 23(3): 47–49.

1

Treading Murky Waters: Day-To-Day Dilemmas in the Construction of a Pluralistic U.S. Environmental Movement

MELISSA CHECKER

On an unseasonably hot Saturday afternoon in early April, I bowed my head along with approximately forty other people in the main room of Hyde Park's Mary Utley Community Center. In his resonant baritone Reverend Charles Utley, Hyde and Aragon Park Improvement Committee (HAPIC), president led a prayer over lunch. Utley stood with his back to an LCD computer image projector and a wide screen and faced the unusually large crowd of Hyde Park residents who filled the community room that day. We had gathered at the community center for a free workshop entitled "Environmental Justice and Public Participation Through Electronic Access."[1] The Urban Environment Institute (UEI), a DC–based nonprofit, had organized the workshop and intended for it to be the first step in developing a community technology center. Their idea was to set up such centers in environmental justice communities around the country where people could use computers to research local environmental issues. Once people obtained the knowledge they needed, they could participate in environmental decision making.

As Hyde Park residents piled paper plates with fried chicken, salad, and cookies, I heard them muttering that the workshop had not turned out the way they had hoped. They told me that the morning had consisted of two presentations by Department of Energy staff members explaining how to calculate chemical doses and identify chemical risks. Residents were disappointed that the presentations were overly technical and hard to follow. After lunch things did not seem to get much better. A UEI staff person used the computer projector and the screen to demonstrate how to use Geographic Information System software to compare one neighborhood's environmental and health conditions with those of others. As she spoke, many Hyde Park residents quietly began rising from their chairs and filing out of the room. By 1:30 P.M., attendance had declined to a handful of people.

Hyde Park, a small neighborhood on the edge of downtown Augusta, is home to approximately two hundred African American families. In the early 1990s residents discovered that a nearby factory had leaked toxic chemicals into its surrounding environs. Since that time, HAPIC, a neighborhood organization, had been struggling to find a way either to relocate residents or to remediate environmental contaminants. I came to Hyde Park in 1998 and spent fourteen months there, working as both an anthropologist and an activist. As an anthropologist, I wanted to get to know Hyde Park residents and work with them over a long period of time in order to explore how their experiences as southern African Americans reflected their understandings of their environmental problems and their organizing efforts. As an activist, I intended to participate in HAPIC's daily organizing activities and assist them in their fight for environmental justice.

I too believed in the potential of computers for grassroots empowerment. To try and make up for the workshop's failure, I decided to organize a free weekly computer-training course. I especially encouraged the neighborhood's activists to attend, adhering to the belief that computer access was the key to public participation in environmental decision making. However, over the five months that I offered the course a total of only five residents ever showed up, and none of them were activists. Why did I so often hear people say that they really needed and wanted to start learning computers? Why were they actually so reluctant to do so? What was the significance of computers both for professional and grassroots activists, and how did those significances diverge? In this essay I explore the ways in which HAPIC activists' perspectives on the environment, technology, and the meaning of social movement organizing differed from those of professional activists. I argue that these differences are connected to and embedded in long histories of racial inequality. While I argue that such histories form initial obstacles to interracial organizing, I also demonstrate ways that recognizing and appreciating them might provide the means for strong and lasting intergroup connections.

The underlying premise of the workshop was that technology is an important part of organizing for professional activists. In the last several years connecting minority communities to computers, or bridging "the digital divide," has become a national priority. In 1999 the U.S. Department of Commerce devoted a Web site to it, and later that year AT&T, AOL, GTE, Compaq, and Microsoft all promised donations ranging from $500,000 to $1.2 million to nonprofits who would bring computer access and training to economically disadvantaged Americans (*Philanthropy News Digest* 1999).[2] Many activists that I met also seemed to embrace ideas about the importance of computer training. However, as I said, I found that a significant number of people resisted using and learning about computers. I also found that this resistance crossed occupational and income levels, and, contrary to popular assumptions, it did not seem to be based on computer access. While some of the reasons for such resistance were practical, close inspection reveals that reluctance to use computers also operated from fundamental, culturally constituted ideas and values. These observations suggest that computer technology has different meanings for different social groups and that, ultimately, capital investments alone will not suffice to bridge "the digital divide."

In a similar vein, I also found that Hyde Park activists' cultural beliefs and experiences shaped their understandings of the environment as well as of environmental justice. For example, in the winter of 1999 I attended a Sierra Club meeting with Arthur Smith, one of HAPIC's leaders. Although HAPIC rarely worked with the local Sierra Club, Smith and I went to their meeting to hear Augusta's recently elected mayor speak about his environmental agenda. During the question and answer period, Smith, who was the only African American in attendance, asked the mayor what he intended to do about violence in the inner cities. For Smith it was perfectly appropriate to address inner-city violence at a Sierra Club meeting because violence *was* an environmental concern for his neighborhood. In contrast, the Sierra Club members' questions were directed at recycling, cleaning trash off of roadways, and creating bicycle lanes. When HAPIC activists say that they are working to clean up their environment, they mean that they are not just working to remediate the damage left by toxic contamination, but the damage left by a larger legacy of institutional racism. I found that through environmental justice activism HAPIC activists inserted their own environmental meanings into mainstream environmental discourse. In part, activists built extensive networks with mainstream environmental groups, and in so doing they ensured that conceptualizations of contemporary environmentalism included minority and urban concerns. What I also found, however, was that this was not a simple task. While on an abstract level professional and grassroots activists shared a vague vision of "environmental justice," the day-to-day steps they took toward achieving that vision varied widely. Whereas computers and the Internet offered an obvious route to inclusion in democratic processes for professionals, the meaning of computers and technology for HAPIC activists was laden with connotations of exclusions and racism. Moreover, they valued other, more culturally salient roads to empowerment, such as religion.

Importantly, UEI's founder John Rosenthall was an African American man who hired mainly African Americans to work with him. UEI, however, is a rare case—mainly middle-class whites staffed most of the professional environmental organizations with which HAPIC worked. Nonetheless, I begin with UEI for several reasons. First, reactions to the environmental justice workshop provide a clear example of HAPIC members' general ambivalence about technology during the time that I worked with them. Second, I wish to emphasize that the "disconnects" and negotiations I am describing cannot be mapped in any simple way onto race or class differences. Rather, HAPIC activists' approach to organizing a social movement stemmed from the complex ways in which race and class experiences intertwine, especially in places where opportunities for poor African Americans are particularly limited. Finally, I do not wish to suggest that HAPIC activists' reluctance to use technology indicates that they were incapable of learning about computers. On the contrary, some of the people in this chapter who were not very computer savvy in 1999 are now quite up to speed and facile with computers. Rather, I wish to point out here some of both the practical and more deep-seated reasons for an *initial reluctance* to use such technology on a day-to-day basis. I argue that this reluctance reveals some of the fundamental values upon which activists based their organizing.

By asserting these values the environmental justice activists described here questioned certain contemporary liberal assumptions about the seemingly transparent meaning of public participation and how best to achieve it in the twenty-first century. Indeed, I find that their assertions echoed those of certain academics who argue that computer technology, particularly the Internet, is not necessarily the panacea for enacting dem-

ocratic and libertarian ideals that it is sometimes purported to be (see
Ribeiro 1998).

HYDE PARK: LIFE IN A TOXIC DONUT HOLE

To enter Hyde Park you must cross one of two sets of railroad
tracks. You must also pass a former junkyard, a power plant, and a ce-
ramic factory's smoke stack. In this almost 100 percent African American
neighborhood, seven polluting facilities surround approximately two
hundred homes. It is no wonder that Hyde Park residents refer to their
neighborhood as a "toxic donut."

Hyde Park's development began in the 1940s. Because the land was
swampy and had extremely low value, it was affordable for African American sharecroppers from nearby rural areas. Lots were relatively large, and
families could continue to raise enough vegetables to sustain them while
working in the surrounding factories or as domestics in the wealthier
neighborhoods. As people settled in, they invited relatives from the country to join them, and many households in Hyde Park remain "kin" to one
another. Until 1970 Hyde Park did not have running water, paved streets,
streetlights, or sewer lines. Residents pumped their own water and used
outhouses. This lack of infrastructure, however, paled in comparison to
the fact that the neighborhood would flood with each heavy rain. Floods
were so bad that residents could not get in or out of the neighborhood
and children could not attend school until the waters receded. In 1968
one resident initiated the formation of a neighborhood association called
the Hyde and Aragon Park Improvement Committee (HAPIC) to lobby
for improved living conditions. Within two years HAPIC had made itself
known to county commissioners and other local lawmakers and successfully secured running water, paved streets, street lights, sewer lines, and
drainage ditches.

In 1998, when I came to do fieldwork in the neighborhood, its racial
makeup (99 percent African American) was much the same as it had been
throughout its history (Sociology Research Methods Students 1998). In
1998, however, its population was also aging. Over half of its residents
were over the age of fifty (ibid). As neighborhood elders died, their houses were often left vacant. Rising unemployment rates in the 1980s and
1990s had also left many residents in poverty, and many of their homes
had fallen into disrepair as a result. In 1998 approximately 61 percent of

Hyde Park's two hundred families owned their homes; yet 77 percent of them earned less than $20,000 per year (ibid). Making matters worse, after toxic chemicals were found in Hyde Park's soil, selling homes in the neighborhood became almost impossible.

In 1983 routine tests at Southern Wood Piedmont (SWP), a wood preservant factory bordering Hyde Park, detected groundwater contamination on the site, after which SWP began a major cleanup of the factory area. Some time around 1990 HAPIC leaders discovered that the mostly white residents of Virginia Subdivision, another neighborhood bordering SWP, had filed a lawsuit charging SWP with contaminating their properties. The plaintiffs in this lawsuit received a small settlement in the early part of 1990. Recognizing that ditches from SWP's property ran directly into Hyde Park, HAPIC leaders began alerting their neighbors to possible contamination and alleging corporate racism. Soon after, two local attorneys approached them and started to organize a class action lawsuit. Subsequent tests on Hyde Park's soil, groundwater, and air revealed elevated levels of PCBs and lead.[2] Since 1990 neighborhood activists have dedicated themselves to finding some kind of relief from environmental contamination.

It was this ongoing struggle that I joined in 1998, when I came to Hyde Park. For me fieldwork with a grassroots environmental justice group was not only an opportunity to understand better how categories such as "environment" and "justice" are culturally constructed, it was also an opportunity to exercise my own commitments to environmental justice activism. To do so, I promised the HAPIC board of directors that I would join the organization as an unpaid staff member, performing whatever duties they requested. As the fourteen months I spent in Augusta progressed, these duties included the following: writing grant proposals for HAPIC, creating a Web site, organizing after-school and summer programs for youth, and helping plan community cleanup days as well as community meetings. My work as a HAPIC staff member also provided me with access to the organization's files, meetings, records, and budgets (all with prearranged permission from board members). As a white, middle-class northeasterner and a liberal activist, I was culturally aligned more with professional environmentalists than with HAPIC activists. I found that coupling my own cultural perspective with my emerging friendships with HAPIC activists enabled me to see and critique the sometimes subtle "disconnects" that I describe in this chapter and to develop an understanding of the cultural biases from which they stem.

While it is beyond the scope of this essay to detail all the advantages and pitfalls that my dual position as researcher and activist entailed, I have several points to make here. First, as I see it, the power imbalances between anthropologists and their subjects are a two-way street. While I have the power to represent these people to the public, they also have the power to restrict and control the information I receive from them. By making my commitments to their cause clear, I strove to level both these imbalances. In addition, by pitching in with their daily duties I could "repay" activists for assisting me with my research. Going through some of the same ups and downs that activists did—as we did or did not receive grants, encountered trouble from local officials, or worked with reluctant community members—enabled us to quickly build and cement the necessary trust between ethnographer and informants that provides the foundation of fruitful fieldwork. At the same time, including a historic perspective in this essay enables me to look critically at the cultural framings that have shaped my own ideas about social movement organizing in the U.S. In the next section I present a historic overview of the relationship between environmentalism and civil rights. In particular, I focus on the ways in which the discourses and ideologies associated with mainstream environmental movements in the U.S. have excluded minority issues.

AN UNLIKELY CONVERGENCE: ENVIRONMENTALISM AND CIVIL RIGHTS

In 1970 Douglas Moore of the Washington Black United Front called environmentalist Ralph Nader "the biggest damn racist in the U.S. . . . More responsible than any man for perverting the war on poverty to the war on pollution" (quoted in Scheffer 1991:19). Activists in minority communities have often complained that environmentalism's draw as a contemporary issue has actually diverted political attention away from matters such as housing and unemployment (Darnovsky 1992; Scheffer 1991:19; Tarlock 1994:483). Indeed civil rights and environmentalism emerged in U.S. history as two distinct and even adversarial social movements.

Historically, the ideals and goals of the environmental movement (recreation, aesthetic landscape, and natural resource preservation) have been tied to middle-class ideology (Darnovsky 1996; Taylor 1992:35; see also Austin and Schill 1994:58; Ross 1993). The launching of the Progressive era in the 1890s catalyzed reactions against Enlightenment-era progress. During this time "the environment," or "nature," began to be defined in opposition to the "the urban." It is no coincidence that an influx of immigrants was pouring into U.S. cities at this time, adding to their congestion and confusion. Middle- and upper-middle-class urban residents thus sought refuge from urban overcrowding and the decadence of urban life in natural settings.

As urbanization continued to accelerate, conservationists became absorbed with finding a "cure" for the weaknesses that came from city life (and that threatened the virility of men) (Darnovsky 1992:24). Theodore Roosevelt especially concerned himself with this issue. It was during the Roosevelt era that John Muir spearheaded the conservation movement and began the Sierra Club in order to expand the number of areas where people could enjoy nature in its pristine state. Yet, throughout the 1950s, the Sierra Club remained a "WASP enclave," or a mechanism for retreating from the mainly eastern European immigrants who inhabited the nation's urban areas (Darnovsky 1992). Such exclusionary practices have continued, and the national parks and preservation areas that the conservation movement installed are still inaccessible to most minorities because of the high costs of admission and travel to them (Bullard 1990; Taylor 1989).

In the postwar period changes in production and consumption produced unanticipated environmental hazards such as wastes and emissions, and air pollution started to capture the public imagination. Environmental concerns thus began to include pollution in urban centers. However, as this period wore on the middle-class continued to dominate environmental arguments. As geographer David Harvey states, in the sixties "a whole range of aesthetic, health and environmental quality questions were being placed upon the political agenda by the middle-class" (1996:395). Thus environmental agendas often left out the needs of people most affected by poor environmental quality—minority and low-income communities. As environmental movements gained momentum in the 1960s, a core sector, known as "the Big 10," emerged and came to define contemporary "mainstream" environmentalism (Gottlieb 1993; Pulido 1996; Schwab 1994; see also Moberg 2001). That core (including groups such as the Sierra Club, the National Wildlife Federation, and the Nature

Conservancy) had surpassed others in membership size and access to funding sources as well as in receiving policy makers' recognition as representatives of the "environmental point of view" (Gottlieb and Ingram 1988:22). Although today environmental groups in the U.S. represent a broad spectrum of interests, goals, and memberships, in this essay I define mainstream or professional environmentalists in opposition to localized grassroots environmental justice groups like HAPIC. Whereas mainstream groups have professional staffs, localized grassroots groups tend to be run by volunteers (most of whom hold other full-time jobs). Whereas mainstream groups also often have multiple and sophisticated ways of generating funding and accessing people with political clout, localized grassroots groups have limited funding resources and far less direct political access.

During the 1970s and into the 1980s pro-environmental groups continued to sidestep connections between race and poor environmental quality and, in fact, some say they exacerbated discriminatory siting practices (Bullard 1993:21; Gottlieb 1993:259; Rothman 1988). For example, since the 1970s tougher environmental regulations and increased public opposition to toxic waste have made the siting of new hazardous waste facilities more difficult. Affluent white neighborhoods have successfully harnessed stiffer environmental regulations to oppose hazardous waste generating facilities. Often these sites are then placed in minority neighborhoods because hazardous waste producers consider communities of color to be the least likely to organize against the placement of toxic waste sites. Minority communities have thus become the prime targets to solve "facility siting gridlock" (Bullard 1993:12). Moreover, minority groups receive a "double whammy" with regard to environmental hazards: they are exposed to greater risk while having less access to health and medical facilities (ibid. 11).

In 1982 an incident in Warren County, North Carolina instigated another shift in the course of U.S. environmentalism. In response to their being selected for a PCB landfill, a rural, poor, and mostly African American community launched an enormously successful public protest. Joined by such African American political luminaries as Jesse Jackson, Benjamin Chavis (former director of the NAACP), and Reverend Joseph Lowery (then head of the Southern Christian Leadership Conference), the Warren County protests led to the highly publicized arrests of over five hundred persons (Lee 1993). The Warren County incident also led the United

Church of Christ Commission for Racial Justice to commission a study on environmental racism. The study estimates that three out of five African Americans and Hispanic Americans live in communities with uncontrolled toxic waste sites and that 40 percent of hazardous waste landfills in the U.S. are in predominantly black or Hispanic communities, both low and middle income (Commission for Racial Justice 1987). These kinds of statistics led to the study's conclusion that race (not income) is the most significant variable associated with the location of waste facilities. In his foreword to the United Church of Christ report, Benjamin Chavis coined the term *environmental racism* (Lee 1993). Along with environmental justice, environmental racism became the rallying cry for minority activists across the country as they began to learn about the disproportionate amount of pollution from which they suffered. While certain scholars have disputed the statistics cited here (see, for example, Anderton et al. 1994), minority activists widely accept them as an accurate representation of the environmental hazards facing their communities.

Not only did environmental justice activists initially struggle to publicize their plight, they also successfully protested their lack of representation in mainstream environmental groups (Rothman 1988). As a result, mainstream environmentalists began to diversify their staffs and add urban and minority concerns to their agendas. By the end of the 1990s a significant number of mainstream environmental leaders were thus eager to change their reputations as exclusive, middle-class organizations by setting environmental justice priorities. Mainstream groups therefore needed the credibility that came from working with grassroots, minority groups. In turn, grassroots groups began to count on the financial and in-kind support as well as the access to government agencies that they received from mainstream organizations. Thus alliances between mainstream environmental and grassroots environmental justice groups transformed into symbiotic relationships.

However, for grassroots activists a history of being excluded from (and in some cases indirectly harmed by) the environmental movement generated a certain amount of mistrust and resistance to establishing those relations. Moreover, as I mentioned, the ways in which African Americans defined the environment differed significantly from the ways in which it was defined in mainstream American discourse. In the next section I describe in more detail how Hyde Park residents defined the environment according to their experiences as southern African Americans.

LASTING IMPRESSIONS:
ENVIRONMENTAL UNDERSTANDINGS

Although many people I interviewed in Hyde Park disagreed about exactly when or how HAPIC got into environmental organizing, all of them did agree on one thing: none had been concerned about the environment before learning that their water was contaminated. A few residents said that they had heard some things about the environment on TV, especially regarding events at Love Canal, but most agreed that they were "too busy trying to live" to care about it very much. The president of HAPIC, Charles Utley, said, "[We] didn't even think about it." Even as late as 1990, the Army Corps of Engineers halted a drainage project in the Hyde Park area because it endangered wetlands, but HAPIC activists took no part in the corps' efforts (Hewell 1989:A1).

Once word got around about Southern Wood Piedmont, however, Hyde Park residents began to suspect that toxic chemicals could be linked to some of the health problems they shared. Some people had inexplicable rashes that broke out and then went away. Many children were born with asthma, and many local deaths resulted from respiratory and circulatory diseases as well as from rare forms of cancer. Hyde Park residents thus began to categorize the environment as something dangerous and even deadly. For HAPIC activists, organizing to improve their environment became (as a poster in one major protest stated) a "matter of life and death." Further, residents interpreted the fact that a white neighborhood had received compensation from SWP while they had not as a clear case of racism. When I questioned activists and residents about why they received no compensation from SWP, or why, in all these years, they had received so little help from governmental agencies, they all answered that the primary reason was because "the people here are black." Residents also agreed that corporate racism was the reason that factories and plants surrounded their neighborhood in the first place. Utley explained, "It's a form of genocide. It's not by accident. And there's no one to tell people they shouldn't be there." As Utley suggests, other forms of institutional racism perpetuated the problem. As activists began and continued their struggle, they found little help from local, state, or national government agencies.[3] In 1994, after they discovered that an EPA contractor hired to conduct tests on Hyde Park soil also had a number of contracts with SWP's parent company, ITT, HAPIC activists even filed a civil rights claim against the EPA.[4]

For many residents their introduction to environmental awareness was linked to toxicity and racism. For example, I asked one of HAPIC's leaders to define the environment. His response was to explain what most people in Hyde Park thought of it, "I don't think it's just chemicals, but a lot of people just think that. Racism is not just chemicals." Although he personally maintained a broader view of the environment, this activist's immediate association of the words *chemicals* and *racism* with *environment* revealed the way it had come to be defined in the larger Hyde Park community. Framing environment as a racial issue enabled HAPIC members to incorporate it into their organizing activities and to make it a priority.

At first HAPIC approached environmental organizing in the same way it would have approached a traditional civil rights protest. Rather than researching the problem or pursuing policy reform, activists contacted local churches, staged a demonstration, called a boycott, and filed a class action lawsuit. These actions led various governmental agencies to conduct the assortment of tests mentioned earlier, which yielded varying and inconclusive results.[5] At the same time, HAPIC activists continued to work on other neighborhood problems. For example, HAPIC activities included after-school tutoring programs, teen pregnancy programs, and applications for environmental cleanup grants. Thus, HAPIC sustained its original mission to advocate for the civil and social rights of its constituents. Although contamination had become their main focus, it did not preclude their engagement in more traditional organizing activities.

HAPIC activists are not unique. Across the country, minority activists have gone through similar processes of recategorizing the environment as something that includes "where we live, work and play" (Novotnoy 1995). As I mentioned earlier, environmental justice activists have made significant progress in expanding environmental discourse on a national level. In addition to national environmental justice policy enacted by President Clinton in 1994, almost all mainstream environmental groups now include some aspect of environmental justice on their agendas.[6] Still, while environmental justice activists may be slowly challenging mainstream notions of the environment—from something natural and pristine to something that includes a host of urban dangers—their ways of conceptualizing other aspects of activism remain very different. The next section addresses one persistent and problematic area of disconnection—technology.

Intermovement (Dis)Connections

As environmental discourse has expanded and mainstream environmental groups have increasingly sought to expand their constituencies, HAPIC activists have made contacts with a variety of environmental nonprofits. When I came to do fieldwork in Augusta, HAPIC had
already worked with groups such as Greenpeace, the Georgia Air Keep-
ers Campaign, and Nuclear Information and Resource Service, an antinuclear organization. Many of the professional activists with whom
HAPIC worked were either white or middle class, and most were both.
Yet as HAPIC and professional activists worked to build coalitions they
encountered differences in their approaches to social movement organizing that threatened to undermine their collaborative efforts.

In 1998, for instance, learning about computers was becoming more
and more pressing for HAPIC leaders. Their funders especially urged
HAPIC leaders to start keeping track of organization finances on computers, to report on their activities via email, and to initiate computer training programs. Yet I found that, although leaders tended to have easier access to computers and in a couple of cases had them in their homes, they
showed reluctance to incorporate them into their daily lives. For example,
activist Arthur Smith took a position on the board of Waste Not Georgia,
a statewide recycling organization. Because they were statewide, Waste
Not conducted almost all their business via email. At first Smith promised
to learn how to use email (he had several places where he had access to
free training and computers) and to stay current with board business elec-
tronically. But, after several months, he said he was too busy and asked
board members to telephone and air mail him all the information he needed. While HAPIC activists generally used faxes to transmit printed materials such as flyers announcing meetings and conferences, their preferred
mode of personal communications was almost always the telephone or
face-to-face communication. Having easy access to a personal computer,
or some basic knowledge about how to use it, made little difference in
whether grassroots activists' used it as a medium of communication

Professionals efforts to bring HAPIC activists up to speed on computers was obviously well intentioned and reflected some of their basic organizing goals. Professional activists who were concerned about minority
communities believed that computer use was crucial to "capacity building" or "empowerment." For example, John Rosenthall argued that the

success of environmental justice struggles depended on computer technology. In *Environmental Justice and Public Participation Through Electronic Access*, a booklet written for the workshop I described at the beginning of this paper, he wrote, "Access to, and the ability to use computers and the information on the Internet will, to a great degree, define those who will have access to economic opportunities and power in shaping public policies, and those who will not." According to Rosenthall's statement, the Internet is a conduit of the kinds of knowledge necessary for citizen participation in policy decisions. Thus, for professionals, in their ability to "build capacity for public participation," computers, and the Internet in particular, presented a thoroughfare for accessing power in the U.S. Yet those liberal free-market ideologies that present the Internet as a great equalizer ignore the fact that various hierarchies of connections,[7] many of which are generated by U.S. elites, control its content (Ribeiro 1998).[8] Similarly, people's experiences with computers differed according to class and race backgrounds. Moreover, for HAPIC activists a vague idea of shaping public policy in the future did not solve their immediate problems of toxic poisoning.

Cross-cultural approaches to computers are a relatively new and small area of anthropological research. Some of those who have studied the issue have found that responses to technology are culturally informed and occur within "the context of deeply-held culturally supplied narratives" (Pfaffenberger 1995:78; see also Ingold 1997; Miller 2000; Strathern 1997). However, many of these studies bifurcate Western and non-Western ideas about technology and assume a totalizing Western culture. My research shows that Western, and especially U.S., culture cannot be totalized but should be examined in specific regional and race and class contexts.

Upon noticing a pattern of reluctance toward computers, I questioned activists about it. In answer they pointed to a variety of practical factors: some said that older folks tend to be afraid that they will mistakenly erase files. Others pointed to the fact that many neighborhood residents could not type very well or their spelling was poor. Communicating via email, then, could be laborious and expose poor composition skills. It is important here to reiterate that I am not arguing that race and class are barriers to learning about computers or technology. On the contrary, the mostly black UEI staff members held the same beliefs about the benefits of computers to environmental justice organizing that white professionals did. In addition, many HAPIC activists regularly used mobile phones, pagers, and faxes. Rather, I am arguing here that the practical reasons for HAPIC members' reluctance to use computers were tied to much more fundamental ideas about technology in general.

The issue of technospeak reveals some of the connections that activists made between computers, specifically, and the more general problems they saw in a technocratic approach to environmental organizing. At some point environmental issues, particularly those dealing with contamination, become scientific; and HAPIC activists found that discussions about their ecological problems often involved details about specific chemicals, parts per million, and scientific facts about ozone layers, groundwater, and point source pollution. Although many HAPIC activists had become rather fluent in scientific discourse by the time I began fieldwork in 1998, technospeak continued to be a major source of community member's feelings of alienation from the professionals that entered the community.

A favorite tale in HAPIC's organizational lore related a community meeting held at the Clara E. Jenkins Elementary School in 1993. The EPA called the meeting to present the results of a $1.2 million investigation of Hyde Park and Virginia Subdivisions' air, water, and soil conditions. After thirty minutes of listening to EPA officials discuss concentrations, key contaminants, and sample data, residents still had no idea whether and to what degree their environment was contaminated. At this point HAPIC President Charles Utley stood up and addressed EPA officials:

> You need to know one thing. All of your data says, primarily, something we can't even comprehend. Secondly, what is happening to the people? Why is this going on? Why are there respiratory problems like we have? Why are people dying of circulatory [diseases]? That is what they want to know. They don't want to know how much arsenic per million, per billion, per trillion. (Quoted in Cooper 1993.)

As the meeting wore on and residents' frustrations escalated, EPA officials grew increasingly defensive. Tensions in the room finally exploded when one resident got so angry that he threw a chair onto the elementary school stage.

HAPIC activist Robert Striggles explained some of the reasons for the extreme frustration that he and other community members felt at the time:

RS: I was over at the school and [laughs] they wasted, I believe two million dollars—what the study cost them—which should have been used in the area to relocate the people. When you started coming in dealing with numbers they was talking about, so many millions, I forget what they was talking about. Something that we can't relate to. The peoples couldn't relate to it. All they wanted to know at the meeting was there's contamination or there's no contamination. . . . But even if you was up on all [the lingo] you still couldn't understand what they was talking about, so they did not, in my opinion, give us the information we really needed in layman's terms.

MC: Why do you think people got so angry?

RS: I think [the EPA officials] looked down at the area. That's exactly what it was in my opinion. And the reason was, if you come into this area and you're giving them statistics that they don't understand, that they had never been dealing with, then what are you doing? You're looking down on them.

Striggles describes how the community characterized technical talk as an aggressive act designed to exclude, belittle, and disempower them. When I further questioned him about why the EPA looked down on Hyde Park, Striggles responded simply, "This is a minority area." Due to their history of exclusion from decision making, Hyde Park residents already harbored substantial mistrust of government officials. For them EPA officials speaking in incomprehensible language only confirmed and revealed their latent racism.

As a result of the 1993 community meeting, relations with the EPA remained mistrustful and somewhat adversarial. Even after President Clinton issued an executive order in 1994 making environmental justice an official government priority, technical talk continued to create problems between governmental agencies and Hyde Park residents. For instance, in 1998 Department of Energy (DOE) officials working at the Savannah River Site (SRS) visited Hyde Park. At the time SRS was lobbying for a grant to process plutonium, and part of that process required them to solicit community approval of their intended operations. Arthur Smith described SRS officials' failure to win over the community members. He said, "SRS came out to educate the people of Hyde Park about plutonium process. But, they put it over the people's heads."

The problem of technical talk was not limited to government officials. As the workshop described at the beginning of this chapter illustrates, many of the professional activists who came to work with HAPIC also spoke in an unfamiliar language that created barriers between themselves and HAPIC members. Technospeak, then, represented the race and class differences between professional and grassroots activists—differences that had led to their disparate in education and job opportunities. Because technical language also excluded them from accessing important information about their health and safety, HAPIC activists folded its use into their experiences of environmental racism. Thus, for them, technospeak was a mode of communication that both reflected and translated into racism. Like technical language, computers also symbolized the ways in which HAPIC activists had historically been excluded from education, particular types of employment, etc.

In Hyde Park technology did not represent the obvious road to empowerment that professionals assumed it did, because it was also circumscribed by complex social inequalities. In addition, Hyde Park activists did not necessarily assume, given their race and class experiences, that information access translated into democratic participation. Finally, computer use was at odds with HAPIC members' traditional mechanisms for establishing and seeking inclusion, participation, and power. In the following section I briefly discuss perhaps the most important of those traditional mechanisms—religion.

Jesus's People for Environmental Justice

As Hyde Park residents filed into folding chairs for a late October 1998 HAPIC community meeting, Arthur Smith lifted his raspy, tuneful baritone and began to sing the hymn "Nobody But You Lord." Immediately, meetinggoers picked up the tune and began singing along. Soon the hymn filled the room and was on everyone's lips. That is, everyone except the six of us white people in attendance. At the end of the hour-and-a-half meeting Reverend Utley gave a closing prayer as everyone bowed heads. We then joined hands and sang (or hummed) HAPIC's theme song, "Reach Out and Touch Somebody's Hand."

Every grassroots-led meeting that I attended during fourteen months of fieldwork unfailingly began and ended with a prayer, and if there was food at a meeting someone blessed it. Almost all HAPIC flyers have some reference to God or Jesus in them, and most prepared public speeches included a mention of God. Christianity, specifically black Baptist faith, was an integral part of grassroots environmental justice organizing across the South.[9] This section's title, for example, borrows the name of a long-standing and successful group in Alabama. I found that a number of southern environmental justice organizations were similarly founded out of church groups. Even those groups that were founded on a secular basis, such as neighborhood organizations, were built on strong religious roots that could not be separated from environmental activism.

This way of organizing bore a striking difference from professional environmentalists' secularism. On the surface professionals easily accommodated HAPIC activists' religious practices. When HAPIC activists bowed their heads over their food, professionals "Amen'd" along with them. When HAPIC members clasped their hands at the end of a meeting, closed their eyes, and swayed to a hymn, professionals swayed along in respectful silence. It was evident that professional activists recognized the need to show consideration for the cultural differences of grassroots activists and that grassroots activists appreciated their efforts. However, differences in religious practice could not be overcome by the simple sharing of prayers and hymns. Rather, religion was embedded in HAPIC activists' experiences as African Americans and, more important, in their experiences of fighting for their rights as citizens. Although hierarchical to a certain extent, black Baptist practices emphasize group participation, face-to-face interactions, and the power of the spoken word. Religion, then, has traditionally provided a type of spiritual empowerment. It is not surprising that it also provides a strong platform from which to organize social action.

Researchers on southern African American life have argued that religious spaces traditionally functioned as spaces of inclusion and self-determination (see, for example, DuBois 1905, 1967; Frazier 1963; Morris 1984; Myrdal 1944). Although whites historically monitored southern black churches, as long as black preachers were not too radical in their sermons African Americans could direct their religious institutions in relative freedom from white control (McAdam 1982).[10] In Hyde Park activists believed that the Church was a crucial element in civil rights struggles. For instance, when HAPIC members were staging a large-scale boycott, protest, or march, they immediately turned to local clergy members to rally the support of their parishioners. Along with providing a somewhat independent institutional setting, religion also provided a deeper kind of spiritual empowerment. For instance, labor historian Robin Kelley points out that a belief that God is by one's side has a significant effect on one's willingness to stand up to a foreman or participate in a strike (1994:43). The independence, self-determination, and power that religion and the church fostered thus easily translated into activism.

In many ways activists' faith thus underpinned their approaches to social movement organizing. For instance, religious beliefs shaped understandings of authority and legitimacy. I found that many black activists in Augusta (and elsewhere in the South) were ordained as ministers to legitimize them in the eyes of their communities. I asked Terrence Dicks, an African American community organizer, about the ties between local activists and ordination. Dicks explained, "Many of them feel that that's the only way you can be taken seriously. Now I'm going to be ordained eventually, but the point is that I was doing it [activism] before. I didn't need any special call from God to do that." Dicks's statement confirms that, despite the fact that he had been an activist for at least ten years, to be taken more "seriously" and achieve legitimacy as a community leader he felt the need to become Reverend Dicks. Ordination after years of activism was not uncommon: Reverends Utley, Oliver, Truitt, Lyde, and Cutter, for example, had also "heard the call" after many years of taking community leadership roles.

For HAPIC activists "good social movement organizing" adhered to religious values and deferred to God as an ultimate authority. For example, in February 1999 I attended a meeting organized jointly by HAPIC and some antinuclear activists. The meeting was held to discuss the potential dangers and ramifications of a new method for processing plutonium at SRS, the nearby nuclear weapons facility. Reverend Utley facilitated the meeting, which included national representatives from the antinuclear movement, some concerned Augustans, and a number of HAPIC activists. Utley concluded the meeting with a short speech that began, "I don't care if you're white, blue, pink, green, I could care less. Only thing I care about is those who fear God. If you don't fear God you'll do anything. Whoever your God may be." Ending his remarks, Utley went on to say, "And bless you as you go on your way and I pray that God will give you the energy to stand for what is right. Amen." According to Utley, deferring to this ambiguous higher power directed activists toward "right" actions and nourished their activism itself. Thus for Utley and other HAPIC members their power as activists is derived from a higher, spiritual power that gives them "the energy to stand for what is right."

Each time a group of mainstream environmentalists visited Hyde Park, activists drove them around the neighborhood on a "toxic tour." Not only could these environmentalists get a good view of each polluting site, but they also got a good look at Hyde Park's drug dealers and the disheveled houses whose residents could not afford repairs. Their alliances with professionals thus presented HAPIC activists with opportunities to make their situation known to outsiders and to publicize their neighborhood's social and ecological problems. In a larger sense working with professional environmentalists enabled Hyde Park activists to emphasize the ways that environmental justice broadened environmental discourses to include urban minority issues. In other words, through developing and maintaining cross-race and cross-class alliances, HAPIC activists sought to redefine environmental issues in ways that reflected their own environmental experiences.

At the same time, both grassroots and professional activists believed that, on a general level, environmental justice meant empowerment, participation, and inclusion. However, their understandings of how to achieve those goals diverged. While professionals viewed computers as a medium for democratization, for HAPIC activists computers represented the same hierarchical systems that had historically excluded them from mainstream society and that they had historically contested through their organizing practices. Moreover, professionals' attempts to impose computers on activists and to insist on using them to mediate communication threatened to destabilize traditional modes of organizing that emphasized inclusion and participation. These findings suggest that computers do not offer a universal, magical empowerment potion. As anthropologist Guştavo Lins Ribeiro aptly states,

> It is true that diffusion of information is positively correlated to democratization of access to power. However, if we take into consideration that books, publications, CDs, and the mass media have destroyed neither profound existing social inequalities, nor the abuse of power, we can predict that computer networks will come no closer to representing a true libertarian panacea. (1998:345)

For HAPIC activists accessing information meant assimilating it into culturally salient frameworks that reflected their own values and experiences.

Rather than completely altering their organizing practices to accommodate the ideas of professionals, HAPIC activists were able to maintain and in certain cases assert some of their organizing traditions and frameworks for environmental activism. In this subtle and indirect way they sought to reconstruct dominant ideas about what participation, inclusion, and empowerment mean in the post–civil rights United States. In other words, for them empowerment entailed not just relief from environmental contamination but also resisting being folded into white, middle-class ways of organizing and deciding for themselves how to define "right" actions.

NOTES

I would like to thank the activists and residents of Hyde Park, as well as those of the UEI Institute, for providing me with the information and material for this paper. A National Science Foundation Doctoral Dissertation Improvement Award funded my ethnographic research, and a Udall Foundation Dissertation Fellowship provided support for its completion. I would also like to thank Owen Lynch, Omri Elisha, Henry Goldschmidt and Maggie Fishman for their valuable insights and editorial comments on earlier versions of this paper

1. In brief, environmental justice groups oppose the disproportionate siting of hazardous waste facilities in minority neighborhoods.

2. It should be noted that these chemicals were determined to have come from the recycling plant that also bordered Hyde Park.

3. There are some exceptions to this. Cynthia McKinney, Hyde Park's U.S. congresswoman, tried to help in relocation efforts, and a few local elected and appointed officials were also sympathetic to Hyde Park's cause.

4. For more detailed information on these processes, see Checker 2002a, 2002b.

5. Approximately ten studies were conducted on Hyde Park and surrounding areas between 1988 and 1999. They included three major soil studies and five health studies, all of which tested for the same contaminants and environmentally related illnesses. All the soil studies found significant levels of lead and/or PCBs in Hyde Park's groundwater, soil, and air. Two of the health studies found substantial links between the health of residents and contamination, however three of them no links (Newell 1997:16; see also Pavey 1994:9A).

6. In short, Clinton's Executive Order No. 12898, entitled "Federal Actions to Address Environmental Justice in Minority Populations and Low-Income Populations,"

mandated that federal agencies develop environmental justice strategies and working groups to ensure that their operations did not negatively effect the environments of minority and low-income populations. While the order did raise awareness about environmental justice within government agencies, many environmental justice activists have criticized it for containing "no teeth," or no real means for enforcement.

7. For example, each individual Internet Service Provider (ISP) connects to a larger Internet routing point, which in turn connects to an even larger routing point that is owned by some large telecommunications company. In the end, Internet connections are controlled by a handful of telecommunications corporations. MCI Worldcom, for instance, owns approximately 60 percent of all Internet routing points.

8. At the same time, many other anthropologists studying international social movements have noted the ways in which Internet access is used by activists and facilitates their organizing. See Castells 1997; Miller 2000; Nash 1997.

9. See also Kelley who argues that, in the 1930s, black workers also brought religion into union organizing, "turn[ing] union gatherings into revival meetings" (1994:41).

10. The degree to which the church was instrumental in facilitating civil rights struggles is the subject of great debate among both scholars and activists. For more information on some of the issues at stake in this debate, see Checker 2002a.

WORKS CITED

Anderton, Douglas, Andy B. Anderson, John Michael Oakes, and Michael Fraser. 1994. "Environmental Equity: The Demographics of Dumping." *Demography* 31:229–248.

Austin, Regina, and Michael Schill. 1994. "Black, Brown, Red and Poisoned." In Robert Bullard, ed., *Unequal Protection,* pp. 53–76. San Francisco: Sierra Club.

Bullard, Robert. 1990. *Dumping in Dixie: Race, Class and Environment.* Boulder: Westview.

—— 1993. Confronting Environmental Racism: Voices from the Grassroots. Boston: South End.

Castells, Manuel. 1997. *The Power of Identity.* Malden, Mass.: Blackwell.

Checker, Melissa. 2002a. "'It's in the Air': Redefining the Environment as a New Metaphor for Old Social Justice Struggles." *Human Organization* 61(1): 94–105.

—— 2002b. "Troubling the Waters: Race, the Environment and Activism in the U.S. South. Ph.D. diss., Department of Anthropology, New York University.

Commission for Racial Justice. 1987. *Toxic Wastes and Race in the United States: A National Report on the Racial and Socio-Economic Characteristics of Communities with Hazardous Waste Sites.* New York: United Church of Christ.

Darnovsky, Marcy. 1992. "Stories Less Told: Histories of U.S. Environmentalism." *Socialist Review* 22(4): 11–54.

Frazier, E. Franklin. 1963. *The Negro Church in America*. New York: Schocken.

Gottlieb, Robert. 1993. *Forcing the Spring: The Transformation of the American Environmental Movement*. Washington, D.C.: Island.

Gottlieb, Robert and Hal Ingram. 1988. Which Way Environmentalism? Towards a New Movement." In C. Hartman and M. Raskin, eds., *Winning American Education*, pp. 114–130. Boston: South End.

Gregory, Steven. 1998. *Black Corona: Race and the Politics of Place in an Urban Community*. Princeton: Princeton University Press.

Harvey, David. 1996. *Justice, Nature, and the Geography of Difference*. Cambridge, Mass.: Blackwell.

Hewell, Hal. 1989. "Samples Collected at Park." *Augusta Herald,* June 24: 1A, 8A.

Ingold, Tim. 1997. "Eight Themes in the Anthropology of Technology." *Social Analysis* 41(1):106–138.

Kelley, Robin D. G. 1994. *Race Rebels: Culture, Politics, and the Black Working Class*. New York: Free.

Lee, Charles. 1993. "Beyond Toxic Wastes and Race." In Robert Bullard, ed., *Confronting Environmental Racism: Voices from the Grassroots*, pp. 5–17. Boston: South End.

McAdam, Doug. 1982. *Political Process and the Development of Black Insurgency*. Chicago: University of Chicago Press.

Miller, Daniel. 2000. *The Internet: An Ethnographic Approach*. New York: Berg.

Moberg, Mark. 2001. "Co-Opting Justice: Transformation of a Multiracial Environmental Coalition in Southern Alabama." *Human Organization* 60(2): 166–177.

Morris, Aldon. 1984. *The Origins of the Civil Rights Movement: Black Communities Organizing for Change*. New York: Free.

Nash, June. 1997. "The Fiesta of the World: The Zapatista Uprising and Radical Democracy in Mexico." *American Anthropologist* 99(2): 261–274.

Newell, Mark. 1997. "Augusta's Toxic Neighborhood." *Metropolitan Spirit*, April 24–30, pp. 1, 14–17.

Novotnoy, Patrick. 1995. "Where We Live, Work, and Play: Reframing the Cultural Landscape of Environmentalism in the Environmental Justice Movement." *New Political Science* 23(2):61–78.

Pavey, Robert. 1994. "Subdivision Study Offers Little Solace." *Augusta Chronicle*, March 20, p. 9A.

Pfaffenberger, Bryan. 1992. *Social Anthropology of Technology. Annual Review of Anthropology* 21:491–516.

Philanthropy News Digest. 1999. "Tech Firms Fund Academies to Help Bridge Digital Divide." *Philanthropy News Digest* vol. 5, no. 28.

Pulido, Laura. 1996. *Two Chicano Struggles in the Southwest*. Tucson: University of Arizona Press.

Ribeiro, Gustavo Lins. 1998. "Cybercultural Politics: Political Activism at a Distance in a Transnational World." In Sonia Alvarez, Evelina Dagnino, and Arturo Escobar, eds., *Cultures of Politics/Politics of Cultures: Re-Visioning Latin American Social Movements,* pp. 658–682. Boulder, Colo.: Westview.

Ross, Andrew. 1993. "The Chicago Gangster Theory of Life." *Social Text* 35:93–112.

Rothman, Hal. 1988. *The Greening of a Nation? Environmentalism in the U.S. Since 1945.* New York: Harcourt and Brace.

Scheffer, Victor. 1991. *The Shaping of Environmentalism in America.* Seattle: University of Washington.

Schill, Karin. 1998. "Study: SRS Downsizing Hurt Economies." *Augusta Chronicle,* January 23, p. 1B.

Schwab, James. 1994. *Deeper Shades of Green: The Rise of Blue-Collar and Minority Environmentalism in America.* San Francisco: Sierra Club.

Sociology Research Methods Students, Kim Davies, Robert Johnston, Ernestine Thompson, Robin Bengtson, Sarah Firman, Albert Jimenez, Karen Jones, and Regina Murray. 1998. *Hyde Park Neighborhood Survey Report.* Augusta: Department of Sociology, Augusta State University.

Strathern, Marilyn. 1997. "A Return to the Native." *Social Analysis* 41(1): 15–28.

Tarlock, Dan. 1994. "City Versus Countryside: Environmental Equity in Context." *Fordham Urban Law Journal* 21(3):461–491.

Taylor, Dorceta. 1992. "Can the Environmental Movement Attract and Maintain the Support of Minorities?" In Bryant Bunyan and Paul Mohai, eds., *Race and the Incidence of Environmental Hazards,* pp. 28–54. Boulder, Colo.: Westview.

—— 1989. "Blacks and the Environment: Towards an Explanation of the Concern and Action Gap Between Blacks and Whites." *Environment and Behavior* 21:175–205.

2

Creating Art, Creating Citizens: Arts Education as Cultural Activism

MAGGIE FISHMAN

In the spring of 1975, the year I graduated from a New York City public elementary school, we learned to sing "Dona Nobis Pacem" in the chorus. After the purple-inked rexographs with the song's words were handed out, Miss Geasland translated the title for us—"Give Us Peace"—and then we practiced the three complicated melodies until we knew them well enough to sing them in a round. We performed that musical feat in our end-of-the-year concert along with "Blowin' in the Wind," "The Cruel War Is Raging," and other songs from the antiwar, civil rights, and folk music revival movements. By offering us some of the music her generation had used to voice their critique of that time, Miss Geasland gave us an experience of connection between our musical education and the world outside the school walls and the sense that our singing was important—or so it felt to me.

The next time I was asked to sing "Dona Nobis Pacem" in chorus by a New York City music teacher, twenty years had gone by. This time I sang as an anthropologist doing ethnographic research, having set aside plans for an artistic career. The confidence that activities such as singing, painting, and staging plays are socially valuable that my seventies public school experience had nurtured in me was eroded over years spent preparing for a career as a painter. I returned to the New York City public schools in the nineties as a researcher with questions about the connection between the arts and social change that had been implicit in my experiences as a student.

Upon my return I found that the very conception of music teaching, along with the mission and organization of arts education in its entirety, had changed dramatically. As it turned out, the value of the arts to schools had come into question the year after I graduated from elementary school, when the absence of a broad consensus for the arts and the presence of a fiscal crisis had meant the deletion of arts education from New York City's public elementary school budget. At that time the arts became something to fight for, and activists emerged to do so. This essay will explore the new conceptions of art that activists had determined were worth fighting for, which developed through the crucible of their activism. But before I examine the current arts education movement, I will dwell for a moment on the anthropological and arts activist lineages this project draws from and on the anthropology of art itself as a critical and potentially activist endeavor. For, as the opening anecdote signals, this essay presents a research project of the kind mentioned in this volume's introduction—one in which personal and professional agendas overlap.

The anthropology of art offers a fine example of Marcus and Fischer's argument, cited in our introduction, that historically, anthropologists have often been cultural critics: dissatisfied with conditions in their own society, they have sought alternatives in others. Stephen Caton, for example, opens his ethnography of poetry in Yemen by juxtaposing his own love of poetry as a child with a moment remembered from his teenage years: at the inauguration of John F. Kennedy, the poet Robert Frost stood speechless after a strong gust of wind blew his poem out of his hands. For Caton this image fit with his own growing sense as a young adult of the powerlessness of poetry in his society. He writes that he went to Yemen to "find a place" where "the poet has power over men" (Caton 1990:4).[1] In another example, Nancy Munn eschews the term *art* completely to describe aboriginal women's sand drawings, the focus of her research. She wrote that to classify them as art would not convey to her readers the crucial role those drawings play in the lives of the Walbiri (1973:2).

In recent years, however, many anthropologists have begun to study this "art" that Munn repudiated as one of our own cultural categories, drawing on research by writers in many fields who develop an interdisciplinary critique of art and the institutions that support it in modern societies. They have studied the evolution of museums and the gallery system, the impact and workings of international art markets, and the social significance of aesthetic ideologies.[2] This work has underscored the many contradictions between our artistic ideals and the ways in which they have been institutionalized since the modern era, brilliantly accounting for the art world I experienced, with all its dissatisfactions.[3] However the literature did not encompass the critical perspectives of insiders like me and the efforts by activists who have chosen to bypass dominant ways of practicing and working in the arts. In addition, at present these social science critiques of art appear to lend support to politicians and others who would once again massively cut arts funding across the U.S. The documentation of democratic uses of the arts in more populist venues has become increasingly important.

A century-old legacy of criticism and activism exists by American writers, artists, and arts promoters of all kinds who have also felt that the modern institutions of art undermine its value to their communities and society. For example, John Dewey's ever popular classic of 1934, *Art as Experience,* contains a critique of art under modernity that is in sync with recent scholarship.[4] Dewey argues that the forces of modernity, capitalism, and nationalism have alienated the arts, placing them on a "remote pedestal" that belittles "the interests and occupations that absorb most of the community's time and energy" (Dewey 1980 [1934]:9). Consequently, the arts no longer serve to inspire most people in their daily lives or express their concerns.[5] Unlike most social science scholars, Dewey and other American arts activists have sought to move from critique to the reform of our modern conception of art. Dewey framed the problem as the need to recover the connection between art and the experiences of people in their daily lives. This has been a common theme in the work of a wide range of arts activists before and after Dewey.

To pursue contemporary exponents of this vision, I decided arts education would be the subject of my research. Since the turn of the last century, arts education practiced in schools, museums, performance spaces, and other cultural institutions has attracted arts activists of all stripes, including—especially in recent years—artists. Most American museums and performing arts centers created during the last century have included education "among their fundamental purposes" (Schubart 1972:4). These education departments, which legitimate the public funds spent on cultural institutions, have been charged with realizing democratic ideals, determining how the art they house could in some way serve the broader public. For example, museum educators in New York City commonly distinguish their concerns about art from other museum departments:

while museum curators work on developing specialized knowledge about how artworks are made, chains of influence among artists, and histories of patronage, many arts educators often view that information as of little interest or use in making artwork meaningful to visitors. They are more likely to focus on helping museum visitors articulate their own responses to artworks and to engage them in art projects on related themes.

Artists who choose to practice in education worlds sacrifice glamour, prestige, and potential fame and fortune in order to work in a milieu they perceive as a site for social change, citizenship building, and democratization. This attraction to education is common among American activists. In fact, historian Rush Welter has argued that "[Americans'] faith in education has been and remains our most characteristic political belief" (1964:6).[6] The body of this essay focuses on arts education as cultural activism. First, I look at the conditions that transformed the arts in the schools into a cause as well as at the testimony of artists who believe they can more effectively enact their artistic values as teachers. I then present several examples of the highly conscious specific vision and practice of art teaching I observed, the fruit of twenty five years in which arts education activists had to think through their own beliefs and practices carefully and convince others that the arts should be taught in public schools at all. In concluding, I will argue that artists' activism involves a critique of dominant educational practices and trends and a vision that artistic values can create better citizens, better schools, and a better society.

HISTORY: THE RISE OF TEACHING ARTISTS

History determined that teaching the arts in New York City public elementary schools should become the subject of activism. In 1976, the year after I sang my final song with Miss Geasland, the entire budget for arts education—teachers, materials, equipment—was eradicated from New York City's public elementary school budget. The one million children attending public elementary schools in New York were no longer to have art and music teachers, rooms, or supplies during the whole course of their elementary school career. From the city's point of view the arts were the most expendable item on the education budget in the midst of a devastating fiscal crisis.

Although the fact that New York City was the art capital of the U.S. had no significance in the context of budgetary debates about the value of art to school children, it ultimately shaped the outcome of this radical eradication in New York. For it was New York City's vast array of cultural organizations, institutions, and artists that began to fill in the breach; they created new and extended old arts education programs, drawing on the financial support of arts funders.

By the time I did fieldwork in the mid nineties, what had begun as a stopgap effort, a temporary solution, had become the way arts education was handled in most of New York City's elementary schools. Although New York's nationally acclaimed graduate programs in arts education, such as that of Teachers' College, Columbia University where I did research, each year produced thoughtfully trained and committed teachers in art, music, dance, and theater, the vast majority of graduates could find jobs only in private schools or in the suburbs, where much higher per capita budgets made fully wrought arts programs a part of the curriculum taken for granted. To have an influence on New York City's public schools, these institutions had to create short-term elective staff development programs for public school teachers and administrators and develop collaborations with arts organizations.

Instead of employing permanent arts teachers, a school whose administration had an interest in the arts would periodically contract with an arts organization for an artist to come to their school and work with students for a short period of time. More than one hundred of the city's arts organizations, from the major institutions down to the tiniest fragile dance ensembles had a roster of "teaching-artists" doing one- to thirteen-week gigs in school classrooms in a wide range of art forms that included collage, African drumming, Chinese calligraphy, modern dance, opera, flamenco, and puppetry, to name a few.

These artists and their organizations had diligently developed programs so that by the 1990s they were convincing teachers, principals, education reformers and funders that the arts were more than a frill. Not only were teachers around the city making time in their overloaded schedules for teaching artists to visit their classrooms but artists as well were increasingly training teachers and school staff.[7] The greatest boost to the prestige of these programs came when the Annenberg Foundation announced its third New York City education initiative, Education Reform Through the Arts. The grant created a Center for Arts Education and offered large grants for which partnerships between schools and arts organizations could compete on the basis of their plans to restructure, reorganize, change priorities, develop staff, or improve curriculum through a three-year phase-in of art programs.

The Annenberg initiative convinced the Board of Education and the city that arts education had broad uses and implications for the city's public schools. Mayor Giuliani announced the creation of PROJECT ARTS to begin the same year. To help in the restoration of arts in the city's schools, one million dollars a year would be divided up and distributed to all elementary schools in the city over three years. At the same time, the thirty-plus district arts coordinators positions would be restored to the city's school districts. Although the actual figures for arts education were a drop in the bucket compared with other items in the city's education budget (and their existence in schools was still quite precarious), for the arts community the change was great.[8] One long-time arts administrator, lately returned from retirement to ride the wave, told an audience of arts coordinators that she felt like she'd died and gone to heaven.

It was into this arts education scene that I arrived with my tape recorder, notepad, and questions both personal and professional about how art was ascribed meaning and value in communities and public arenas outside professional art circles. I became well acquainted with arts education practice during my eighteen months of fieldwork. I observed many artist' residencies around the city and conducted over thirty in-depth interviews with arts activists from different institutions, including twelve teaching artists. I attended classes and events at Teachers College. I also observed and participated in many public forums—monthly meetings, conferences, and training sessions for teachers such as the one I describe in the course of this essay—in which arts activists communicated their methods, mission, and ideas to each other, to teachers, principals, and students. While there is considerable diversity and independence in the institutions and artists across this movement, I found much coherence in artists' underlying assumptions about the value of art and the kinds of changes they hope to effect. Perhaps not surprisingly, many of these activists had had critical responses to their experiences in art schools and marketing their work that resonated with mine and with academic critiques of the institutions of art. Through this research I began to view artists, arts education teachers, administrators, and the people of this world as cultural activists. The rest of this essay will explore the nature of their activism and artistic practices.

"START WITH THE SMALLEST CITIZENS":
CHOOSING TO TEACH

Although for many artists teaching in schools begins as just a gig to make a little money, working as a teaching artist is highly demanding, time-consuming, and emotionally draining work that offers limited remuneration and no health benefits, paid vacations, or job security. For those who stay with it, including those who go on to develop particular programs, lead advocacy efforts, and work with teachers, arts education becomes an end in itself to which they are often passionately committed.

As Ilana Martinelli, an artist in her early forties, put it, it was not because she "loved children" and "liked the atmosphere" of the classroom that she had decided to enroll in an arts education program; rather, "for me it was from a social change perspective. It was: if you are going to change society you have to start with its smallest citizens." Most of the artists I interviewed echoed Martinelli's view that teaching in public schools was a way to enact their social and political values while working as artists. Beth Coldwell, whose work with children I describe below, directed feminist and political theater in college and later became a playwright. She began to teach as a way "to mix my interest in politics and the thought that there was a way the world could be saved and blah blah blah with theater. . . . It was . . . an optimistic way of thinking that theater could actually have—other than it being art—could have a positive impact."

The choice to teach expresses a critique of professional art worlds as the main place to "be an artist." Artists consistently voiced their dissatisfaction with professional art worlds as not being socially useful or democratic and thus in contradiction with the understanding of art they had developed through years of developing their artistic practice. For example, Wade Johnson described the ways in which during the seven years it took to get a BFA and MFA in theater he left behind his teenage desire to become a "movie star": "By the time that I played Peter in the Cherry Orchard—of course I was playing the young Russian Revolutionary—by that time I felt that theater needed to impact on people" and that "I had the creative power to make positive change in the world." However, when "we did our show on Broadway, and I got an agent very quickly, they were interested in marketing me, and me wearing red bathing suits and prancing about" and in "making a lot of money." After his agent told him it was good that "no one could tell" that he was gay, Johnson decided he could not practice his art in such a setting; he got a job working with kids. Two years later he started his own theater company in which actors teach in public schools as well as stage professional performances.

Wade's story exemplifies the experiences of many teaching artists and the administrators of the education programs who employ them, people who believe that "art" can play a subversive and critical role in society. These artists find they can better achieve both the artistic and democratic ideals instilled in them during the process of learning their art outside the institutions and art worlds through which artists typically build their careers. They have developed a vision of what arts education can contribute that depends on very particular kinds of teaching strategies—what one artist called "taking art off the walls." The two sections that follow illustrate their vision through examples of how teaching artists apply their ideas in the course of their day-to-day cultural activism working with teachers and students.

"TAKING ART OFF THE WALLS"

To begin the discussion of artists' practice I return to the moment when I encountered "Dona Nobis Pacem" after a twenty-year hiatus. It was "Arts Day 1995" at Teacher's College, Columbia University and the head of the music education program was presenting a workshop called "Musical Thinking: The Heart of the Process" to an audience of arts teachers, prospective students, and community members. This time, after handing out photocopies of the music, our teacher turned to us and asked, "What is happening in the world today that might drive people to sing 'Give us peace?'" The active audience produced a list: "racial tensions," "Bosnia," "terrorist bombing attacks," "domestic violence," "violence in the schools," and "violence against creativity." She went on: "Let's take one of humanity's afflictions. If you were in Bosnia on the wrong side, how would you sing this song? Not like heavenly angels, right?" We explored different possible emotions that might motivate one to sing that song, then tried them out—singing first with anger, then with longing, and finally with sadness. As the director led us through a discussion of the choices we could make as conductors and performers, we each had a chance to come up with our own version, demonstrate it, and then conduct the group.

This moment from my fieldwork underscores how arts education had changed in the course of twenty-five years of activism. In the seventies our task and achievement as young musicians had been to sing three-part harmony while keeping up with the piano accompanist. By the nineties that work—what this educator dismissed as "musical products and skills development"—wasn't enough. As the arts themselves became a cause, what arts educators had over time chosen to fight for was a place for what this director called *musical thinking*, and its kin in dance, drama, and visual art. As in this workshop, arts education activists consistently emphasized questioning, helping children and adults perceive connections between art works and life experiences, and encouraging them to believe that they had the power to make and interpret art. The arts were a means to develop children's own critical voices; in many cases this started with the teachers that worked with them, as in the next example.

Steve Bartlett, a leading teaching artist affiliated with the Museum of Modern Art and Lincoln Center, was demonstrating his approach to teaching to a group of elementary school classroom teachers by guiding them through a discussion of a painting by Frida Kahlo. Bartlett began with a comment about his teaching method: "I'm a collaborator. I'm not going to tell you what art is. I never tell you the lesson. I say, 'What do you see in this picture?'" Bartlett wanted them to see that interpreting a painting begins with the "visual evidence"—with looking, questioning, and thinking—and not by consulting museum signs or other forms of specialized knowledge.

Thus began a twenty-minute discussion in which the teachers collectively described, questioned, and hypothesized. He encouraged them to begin by looking closely at the painting and describing it. They reported: "I see a woman who cut her hair and is wearing men's clothes"; "She's holding a scissors in her hand"; "There's a lot of hair everywhere" and "There are musical notations of Spanish music." Next he asked them to interpret what they saw: "She seems determined, or angry." "It's as if she's looking at her reflection in a mirror." He rarely disputed their interpretations; instead he drew them out with questions. When a teacher said that the woman in the painting looked "frail" because her clothes were "too big," he asked, "Whose clothes are they, do you think?" When someone answered, "Her husband's," he asked, "How do you know?"

Bartlett saw his role with children as a facilitator rather than an expert on the art and suggested that the teachers, in their work with children, do the same. He wanted them to see how much they could understand without turning to art historians or other authoritative analyses. For instance, when one teacher began to describe what she knew about Frida Kahlo's marriage to the painter Diego Rivera, Bartlett gently intervened, saying, "I'm not going to dismiss information about the painting, but first let's work with our *intuition*." Later, when someone prefaced their statement with "Could it mean that . . . ?" he told her, "This is *your* time to find meaning."

Bartlett's workshop was one session in a three-week-long intensive summer session for public school teachers at the Lincoln Center Institute, one of the oldest, largest, and most influential arts-in-education organizations in New York City. Each year the institute commissions artists to create repertory—tango, political theater, storytelling, jazz, art installations—and sends other artists into public schools to work with children over several months on art activities to prepare them to see selections from the repertory. During the previous summer the hosting public school teachers spent three weeks at the institute working in groups of about twenty-five with a visual artist, a musician, an actor, and a dancer. These artists introduced them to arts education through immersion in arts interpretation activities—writing in journals, choreographing dances, improvising scenes, creating collages, forming percussion trios.

Teachers were taught to probe their own observations and reactions as a starting point for analyzing a work of art. In fact, as in the example above, all the workshops and discussions depended completely on the input and perceptions of the participants. The artists would provide us with a structure—questions to answer, activities to engage in—and we would produce drawings or duets, improvisations or journal entries. Rather than give participants knowledge about the artwork or art form, the teaching artists passed on a way of talking about art, the kinds of questions to ask, and a sense of what information could be brought to bear when one interpreted a work of art.

Bartlett referred to this process of interpretation as "using conversation to take art off the walls." To do so, the teachers are encouraged to think of each painting or performance not as a fait accompli but rather as the result of a series of decisions made by another person. In another workshop a dance artist led a group in interpreting the choreography a single dancer performed for them during the session. She had them observe and interpret the choices the choreographer had made, then try changing those choices—having the dancer move faster or slower, use jerkier movements, and cover more space in the room.

Artists don't believe that artworks can be completely understood without reference to context. Rather, they work with the conviction that to develop a critical perspective teachers and children must first acquire confidence in their own opinions and distance themselves from authoritative analyses. For these arts education activists, arts education gives children and their teachers a voice to talk about their own experiences, to ask questions, to learn that there is not one interpretation, that their opinions are legitimate, and that they have something to say. These artists felt this was something not offered by the dominant school system or other subjects in mainstream education.

In the next section I describe ways that teaching artists working for the Metropolitan Opera Guild carried out this democratic process of learning in their work with a group of children. Their Create Original Opera program did not teach children about opera as a genre. Rather, the artists used a working definition of opera, as a play where the action moves forward through songs, and taught the children to create such an original opera based on their own experience.

BEYOND THE ELVIS PHONE: CREATING AN OPERA FROM EXPERIENCE

Forty-eight nine and ten year olds, along with their backpacks and jackets, violins and Beanie Babies, colonized the first rows of the P.S. 366 auditorium. Facing them were two teaching artists, whose casual body positions as they lounged on the edge of the stage belied their intense gazes and serious demeanors. Beth Coldwell, a playwright, and Rodger Duncan, a composer and musician were introducing the children to Create Original Opera, a program they had helped to create and that involved them in public schools all year round.

The din of children saving seats, chanting, complaining, and searching wildly for permission slips subsided as Coldwell explained, "We have no idea what the opera will be about—that will come from you. The writers group will work together and come up with a script about something from your experience." Coldwell's description of the writer's job followed a more general introduction to the program. She had explained to them that their work over the next three months would be different from the typical elementary school play experience, where a teacher chooses an existing story or script, divvies up the parts, and conducts rehearsals. Although the opera program would end with a polished half-hour performance, the process that would bring that opera to the stage would be quite different. Instead, students would create and name their own P.S. 366 opera company. Only eight of the children would be performers. Others would compose the music, write the script, design costumes, do the lighting, electrical work, makeup, and publicity, build the sets and act as stage managers. "Everybody is equally important here," she had told them: the company would be a group effort, with no star writers, composers, or performers. In other words, as the children and I discovered over time, the focus of their work was not on getting the performance up but on all the behind-the-scenes, invisible work, and the work process involved in creating an opera and bringing it to the stage.

Polishing the performance would occupy a very minor role in the time and energy spent in the entire program. Only in the last few hours of the residency did the artists work with the performers on speaking loudly and clearly and practicing their lines. Indeed, much of their work with the performers focused on interpreting their roles and the script. For instance, after writing up a page-long biography of their characters, all the performers had to come up with an alternate for every one of their lines; the alternate line was to be the "subtext"—what the speaker really meant in saying the actual line. They then rehearsed the new subtext script as a group. Furthermore, rather than devote the bulk of the work sessions to rehearsals, the program typically devotes sixteen hours to composing the music and the first twenty-five to thirty hours to creating the script itself—the job of the writer's group.

Coldwell concluded her brief initiation to the writing process with deference to the children's knowledge and experiences and a summary of her role: "I don't know anything about growing up in New York City, but I will work with you writers to help figure out who the characters will be and what they'll sing about. Keep in mind, we're looking for people with ideas, not good penmanship." Following Coldwell's work with the writer's group, I examine here the specific ways "experience" is transformed into "art" through a rigorous artistic process. The four children in the writers group met with Coldwell for one to two hours twice a week for two months. The structure was informal—no hands were raised and the discussions were heated at times. Coldwell's aim was for the children to create a script together about issues and concerns in their own lives. To achieve this she had carefully developed a method for teaching the children an artistic process. The scriptwriters found that writing the thirty-page libretto would be the last stage in the writing process, the culmination of hours of work in developing the themes, characters, and psychological relationships among them. They were to begin by finding the right issues for the opera to focus on and then go on to develop its underlying structure. Creating the script required many hours of hard work, and often was not perceived by the children as "fun." However, developing a particular kind of content through a particular work process was Coldwell's mission.

For example, in one of the first sessions the goal was for the children to come up with a theme and thesis for the musical. As they brainstormed, the children repeatedly launched into storytelling, enthusiastically generating long and intricate plots of the kind they'd seen on TV—often about dating, murder, or the supernatural. Nevertheless, the children were told not to begin with the plot, but with what the play would be about overall—the theme—and a statement about the theme—the thesis. Furthermore, Coldwell advised them, "The theme needs to be something you really know something about": the characters in the show should be kids, and any adults should be seen from the kids' point of view.

They began work on the theme by consulting homework assignments each had completed in which they were asked to list four things they cared about and discuss why. They had written "books," "music," "family," and "friends"; they had named their pets both live and stuffed, along with a few possessions, such as an "Elvis phone." Coldwell asked questions such as "What do those things and people do for you?" "What makes a friend, and why are they important?" As the children offered answers such as "Friends cheer you up when you are sad" and "You can tell them things—it stinks to keep a secret to yourself" and "Music keeps me sane," they aired anxieties, fears, and grievances against their families. As the discussion went on, Coldwell had them focus on the obstacles, the things that get in their way. The children talked of not being good at a sport, of feeling unliked by friends or unloved by family, and about the pressures from their families to achieve, to get into good schools, and to practice an instrument.

The children were amazed and exhausted by how much work was involved in identifying a theme. At one point Jane insisted that her Elvis phone would make the best theme for a story, and she offered this:

> It's about a girl whose parents fight a lot. She can't bear it so she buys an Elvis phone so when the parents fight she turns it on to blast them out. When she tries it, though, they just talk louder. So then she buys a dog who can bark even louder, but then the neighbors start pounding on the walls.

After each child had offered up a potential Elvis phone plot, Coldwell brought them back to their task. After all, the Elvis phone was not a theme but a prop, and plot development was weeks away. Ultimately, they settled on the theme "overcoming family obstacles." After splitting into pairs, the children came up with "theses," such as " trying to be like your family so they'll like you. If your family hates you, trying to make them like you."

The next step was to have the children develop characters based on psychological characteristics—what Coldwell called "qualities that describe how they are on the inside." The children required a long discussion to understand the distinction between "jealous," an inside characteristic, and "likes to wear green" an outside one; then each child came up with a list of twenty such "inside" words for homework. When it was time to compose their protagonists from this long list of adjectives, Coldwell asked the children to remember as they selected qualities that *nobody* is wholly good or bad. In addition, she advised them to create genderless characters at this point in the process, named by letters, in order to avoid stereotypes. So they came up with eight characters, such as "F: nosy, jealous, greedy, blissful, and a quick thinker." Finally, she asked them to figure out "what each protagonist needs to display her character." "No, not to improve her character," she repeated after several attempts, "You are writers, not shrinks." Ultimately they got it: a nosy character needs a secret; a bossy character needs someone to control.

The children had learned that a plot is really the tip of the iceberg. The play's story expresses a set of relationships and actions that exist beyond its borders. When they did finally get to the plot, Coldwell asked them to consider the practical constraints of their lives, just as they had considered its psychological content. For instance, before they could agree on graffiti in school as a central component in the plot, the children had to figure out a plausible explanation for how two city children could actually get out of their apartments at night in order to do the graffiti. Even though the opera would open with graffiti already on the school wall, the "backstory" must still make sense. Finally, in the final few weeks the children wrote the scenarios and the song lyrics to "False Truth," a dark opera whose motifs included sibling rivalry, social hierarchies in school, lying, and the complexities of friendship.

Although nuances of method, philosophy, and technique vary among the more than one hundred arts programs run by New York City arts and cultural organizations, the opera program serves as a good example of common tenets, practices, and strategies of arts educators. As in the example that introduced this paper, the teaching artist put across the idea that "artistic thinking" was the "heart of the process." Important to this process was the teaching artist's role. Coldwell believed that hers was to provide a clear work structure and convey very specific information about what did, and what did not, count as artistic thinking. At the same time, she presented herself as a facilitator in order to transfer some power and authority to the children and to downplay hierarchies, particularly those based on expertise. For her it was crucial to give kids a voice and make them feel that "they could figure things out without being told" and "think for themselves and make choices." Especially significant was that in thinking for themselves the kids create a relationship between their own lives and their opera.

Indeed, *experience* is a key word here. In learning to make art, the emphasis is on observation, on articulating one's experience of the world, one's emotional reality, and learning a form of expression for it. Although teachers, parents, and administrators commonly praise kids' artistic work as "creative" or "imaginative," the artists rarely if ever used these terms. While the children do have to imagine scenes, characters, and plots, much more central to the artists' mission was showing the children how their own impressions of life and the world were substantial and suitable as the subject of art.

Although, on the face of it, experience is meant to be something we all have, it was not easy or natural for the children to create a story about growing up in New York City—it took a lot of work and prodding. Coldwell was not there to help them build on their existing story ideas; the children's experiences of television and film genres, especially, had not socialized them to think that telling a story would demand a critical observation of their world. In fact, Coldwell's work focused on a very particular aspect of their experience: their home and school lives, seen from a psychological and empirical perspective. Her mission was to focus them on their own struggles and emotions, to help them look at the politics of their social world, and to teach them a method for articulating their points of view as children, so they could be heard.

The work of the artists that I have described and the organizations they represent is cultural activism in two senses. First, artists are charting out a different way to be artists, and to think about art. In their work as teaching artists they often downplay the specialist knowledge of their art form, developed over many years, in favor of helping children and adults feel competent to make and interpret art regardless of their backgrounds. Rather than directly instruct, they model how to respond to art works or create art works without prior knowledge. Their interest, then, is in democratizing art—or taking art off its "pedestal." Rather than celebrating a few great artists, they teach adults and children that experiencing an artwork can be an occasion to articulate a point of view, to think about various ideas, and to think critically about their environments. This belief that individuals without specialist knowledge can play a role in public life is central to American thinking. Yet, while emotions and personal opinion are common currency on daytime TV and in middle-class child-rearing manuals, identifying issues in their own lives did not come easily to the students and speaking their impressions about art works was a revelation for many of the teachers. Thus, in the current highly charged public arena of public education, giving value to the opinions of teachers and students is a subversive move.

Which leads us to the second sense in which this work is cultural activism. As a number of artists and directors told me, what they were teaching was something broader than art. In teaching the rigorous thought process they call "artistic thinking," arts educators intend to socialize qualities of independence, self-confidence, observation, and questioning. For them enabling children to become active citizens is the ultimate goal of a democratic education—a goal, many argue, that the current educational system does not otherwise support. Their teaching methods thus directly challenge the dominant educational ethos and agenda in America, which focuses on the production of an educational product, judged through relentless testing (Sacks 2002). In these hierarchical and positivist approaches to education there are things that must be known, and children are measured by whether they can prove they know them on a test. The arts educators in my study focus on the artistic *process* rather than the *product*, on looking beyond the visible thing to the unseen thinking and work that went into its making. Furthermore, a very different model of personhood underlies arts education initiatives. Artists, in teaching art, present a view of education as a process of growth and development and remind teachers that there's more in children than what comes out in tests.

In the view of artists and program administrators the mental dispositions and work processes they are teaching are essential elements of creative, productive thinking in *any* field of work. However, in order to teach such things in public schools, they must be categorized as "artistic." As one artist put it, "'Art' is what the system seems to require." By segregating these teaching practices as part of learning about "art" (which is expected to be different and especially appealing to children), the artists' serious and radically democratic efforts have been slipped into public schools.

Finally, as I mentioned above, I left the art world for the same reasons given by the artists chronicled here. As artists left to teach the arts in schools, I chose to further my involvement with art through higher education. Yet I found that academia is subject to the same problems of specialization (as discussed in this volume's introduction) that dismayed me in the arts. The creation of *Local Actions* thus has affinities with these arts education projects. As editors we too believe that social science research need not only be shared among experts but can, and must, be shared with the broader public.[9]

NOTES

1. Caton elaborates further on the contrast between his own and Yemenite society: "If this book awakens the reader to another kind of world, one very different from his or her own, a world in which poetry is centralized, not marginalized, in the arena of social and political conflict, and if that reader can learn, as I did, to be in awe of the craft needed to make that spectacle possible, then I will count it a success" (Caton 1990:22).

2. For two valuable collections of critical literature on museums that include their early history, see Karp and Lavine 1991 and Karp, Kreamer, and Lavine 1992. For aesthetic ideologies see Eagleton 1990, Williams 1983 and Bourdieu 1977. For brilliant explorations of the cultural specificity of arts discourse and institutions as seen through their relationship to non-Western artists, see Myers 1994, 1991, 2002; and the essays in Marcus and Myers 1995. For the growth of the gallery system in Paris, see White and White 1963.

3. Some examples of those contradictions: Pierre Bourdieu has challenged the notion that the love of art transcends other tastes: he has argued that all aesthetic judgements communicate and help to perpetuate social and economic hierarchies (1977). Raymond Williams demonstrates how Romantic artists increasingly defined the inherent artistic value of their works in opposition to economic values and popularity just as they came to depend increasingly on markets to sell their work and make a living (1983). Daniel Miller finds our modern notion of art so rife with contradictions he states that it could be considered a "historical mistake."(1991). See also Leach 1993 on the relationship between the shared origins and development of museums and commercial culture in America and Burger (1984) on avant garde critiques of art as an institution.

4. For example, a number of contemporary theorists have documented the institutional transformations that helped bring about this situation in America. They have examined the way some art forms were relocated during the late nineteenth century from circus tents and festival circuits to the grand spaces of new museums and performance halls. No longer presented through entrepreneurial endeavors, exhibited or performed alongside fire eaters or bearded women, these songs, poems, paintings, operas, and symphonies were now presented in new nonprofit organizations managed by wealthy elites, thus acquiring a distinct collective identity as "art." Those forms of visual display and performance that continued to be supported through moneymaking alone, became increasingly known as "popular culture" (DiMaggio 1991; Levine 1988).

5. Dewey writes that the forces of capitalism and modernity that "have alienated so much in our modern life" have also alienated most people from art. Whereas, in earlier societies, artistic expression was integrated into the rituals of community life, in modern societies most people's involvement with art is limited to passive contemplation; "art" is created only by professional artists. Art is accessible to most people through a visit to a museum or opera house, which confers "superior cultural status." There it is found on a "remote pedestal" to be viewed with awe, formality, and a self-conscious sense of virtue that is for many mixed with insecurity. The experience of art is removed from the daily meaningful stuff of life as well as from daily aesthetic pleasures like poking a fire or planting a garden (1980:3–10).

6. As Welter points out, public schools in particular have been a focus of social change efforts since the early years of nationhood. For example, the common school movement of the 1850s, which established public education in America, was supported nearly unanimously by the workers' movement as a central reform effort. At the turn of the nineteenth century there was a nationwide social movement for educational innovation, criticism, and reform linked to social and political progressivism (Cremin 1961:22). See also Adler's discussion of the role of education in sixties counterculture (1979:25–28).

7. Since visiting artists are not "certified," teachers cannot leave their classrooms when artists visit.

8. The arts education leadership was also anxious about how to make the most of this peak of support and ensure that it wasn't the latest educational trend to be replaced in following years. For a detailed chronology of arts education history since the 1960s, see Remer 1990.

9. For an exploration of important dimensions of the shared histories and cultural position of art and anthropology, see the introduction to Marcus and Myers 1995 and Mullin 1992.

WORKS CITED

Adler, Judith E. 1979. *Artists in Offices: An Ethnography of an Academic Art Scene.* New Brunswick, N.J.: Transaction.

Benedict, Burton. 1983. *The Anthropology of World's Fairs: San Francisco's Panama-Pacific International Exposition of 1915.* London and Berkeley: Lowie Museum of Anthropology and Scholar Press.

Bourdieu, Pierre. 1977. *Distinction: A Social Critique of the Judgement of Taste.* Cambridge: Harvard University Press.

Burger, Peter. 1984. *Theory of the Avant-Garde.* Minneapolis: University of Minnesota Press.

Caton, Steven C. 1990. *Peaks of Yemen I Summon.* Berkeley: University of California Press.

Cremin, Lawrence A. 1961. *The Transformation of the School: Progressivism in American Education, 1876-1957.* New York: Vintage.

Dewey, John. 1980 [1934]. *Art As Experience.* New York: Perigree.

DiMaggio, Paul. 1991. "Cultural Entrepreneurship in Nineteenth Century Boston: The Creation of an Organizational Base for High Culture in America." In Chandra Mukerji and Michael Schudson, eds., *Rethinking Popular Culture,* pp. 374–395. Berkeley: University of California Press.

Eagleton, Terry. 1990. *The Ideology of the Aesthetic.* Cambridge: Basil Blackwell.

Karp, Ivan and Steven D. Lavine, eds. 1991. *Exhibiting Cultures: The Poetics and Politics of Museum Display.* Washington: Smithsonian Institution Press.

Karp, Ivan, Christine Mullen Kreamer, and Steven D. Lavine. 1992. *Museums and Communities: The Politics of Public Culture.* Washington, D.C.: Smithsonian Institution Press.

Leach, Bill. 1993. *Land of Desire: Merchants, Power, and the Rise of a New American Culture.* New York: Pantheon.

Levine, Lawrence. 1988. *Highbrow/Lowbrow: The Emergence of Cultural Hierarchy in America.* Cambridge: Harvard University Press.

Marcus, George and Fred Myers. 1995. *The Traffic in Art and Culture*. Berkeley: University of California Press.

Miller, Daniel. 1991. "Primitive Art and the Necessity of Primitivism to Art" In *The Myth of Primitivism: Perspectives on Art,* pp. 50–71. London and New York: Routledge.

Mullin, Molly H. 2001. *Culture in the Marketplace: Gender, Art, and Value in the American Southwest*. Durham: Duke University Press.

Munn, Nancy. 1973. *Walbiri Iconography*. Ithaca: Cornell University Press.

Myers, Fred. 2002. *Painting Culture: The Making of an Aboriginal High Art*. Durham: Duke University Press.

—— 1994. "Beyond the Intentional Fallacy: Art Criticism and the Ethnography of Aboriginal Acrylic Painting." *Visual Anthropology Review* 10(1): 10–43.

—— 1991. "Representing Culture: The Production of Discourse(s) for Aboriginal Acrylic Painting." *Cultural Anthropology* 6(1): 26–62.

Remer, Jane. 1990. *Changing Schools Through the Arts*. New York: American Council for the Arts.

Sacks, Peter. 2002. "A Nation at Risk." *Nation,* vol. 275, no. 17, November 18.

Schubart, Mark. 1972. *Performing Arts Institutions and Young People*. New York: Praeger.

Welter, Rush. 1964. *Popular Education and Democratic Thought in America*. New York: Columbia University Press.

White, Cynthia A. and Harrison C. White. 1963. *Canvases and Careers: Institutional Change in the French Painting World*. New York: Wiley.

Williams, Raymond. 1983. *Culture and Society, 1780–1950*. New York: Columbia University Press.

3

Creating a Political Space for American Indian Economic Development: Indian Gaming and American Indian Activism

KATHERINE A. SPILDE

The decade of the 1990s was a time of unprecedented economic and social change in Indian country. Yet, while many people have
written about the growth of Indian gaming in the United States,[1] little attention has been paid to the fact that America Indian political activism has
also grown at a rapid pace. In many ways Indian gaming has driven this
increased political engagement by Indian nations, since it has served as activism's primary economic engine. Additionally, Indian gaming has become a lightning rod in many political contexts, fueling the need for increased political involvement by Indian nations to protect their sovereign
rights in general and their gaming rights in particular. This chapter ana-
lyzes the relationship between the growth of Indian gaming and the
growth of American Indian political activism and argues that Indian gaming and political activism are mutually reinforcing.

Taking an anthropological approach to the analysis of the rise of what
I have come to understand as "Indian gaming activism" provides insights
into the ways that Indian nations have created a political space for economic development.[2] This chapter examines the creative and culturally
appropriate means tribal governments employ to seek political power,
primarily by investing gaming revenues into improving local Indian and
non-Indian communities. The goodwill generated by investment at the
community level translates directly into popular support, which tribal
governments can then leverage with state and federal policy makers. As
tribal governments have deliberately moved their political organizing to
the local community level in the gaming era, the model for activism de-

veloped by Indian nations has the potential to revolutionize the route to power in American politics. This local investment, ranging from infrastructure improvements to outright charity, provides a model for philanthropy as a conduit to political power by establishing that investment in human capital produces political capital.

INTRODUCTION

Since the late 1970s approximately two hundred American Indian nations have established some sort of gaming operation on their reservation or trust lands.[3] As Indian nations begin to wrest themselves from centuries of damaging federal policies and severe social conditions, they find themselves facing two related tasks: the first is to negotiate and then to protect successful economic development strategies through tribal and federal policy channels; the second is to educate the American public and policy makers about why they retain the sovereign right *as governments* to pursue economic development strategies in the first place. These interrelated projects have created a need for new political practices in Indian country.

American Indian tribal governments occupy a unique legal and historical position in American politics. The U.S. Constitution institutionalized the political or "government-to-government" relationship between the U.S. government and Indian nations and made that relationship distinct from that between the U.S. government and the states or foreign nations. Identical to the constitutional provisions dealing with international sovereigns, the U.S. Constitution granted Congress the power to "regulate commerce with the Indian Tribes,"[4] while the president was empowered to make treaties with the consent of the Senate.[5]

In 1987 the U.S. Supreme Court decided a landmark case, *California v. Cabazon Band of Mission Indians*,[6] which reaffirmed tribal regulatory authority over gambling on Indian reservations. In essence this decision also confirmed the inherent nature of tribal sovereignty.[7] As a result, many states were concerned about what they perceived to be a loss of jurisdiction with regard to gaming within state borders. Under pressure from state interests, Congress passed the Indian Gaming Regulatory Act (IGRA) in 1988. The IGRA addressed concerns expressed by the states and also recognized the inherent rights of tribal governments. The delicate jurisdictional balance struck in IGRA relies upon the classification of gambling activity: Class I to be wholly tribally controlled, Class II to be regulated by the tribal governments with oversight from the federal government through the National Indian Gaming Commission (NIGC), and Class III to be regulated through a compact between the tribes and states, thus allowing states to share regulatory jurisdiction with tribes over casino-style gambling within their borders.[8]

The provision of IGRA requiring state governments to negotiate Class III gaming compacts with tribal governments was not popular among state policy makers who were opposed to tribal sovereignty in general and Indian gaming in particular. From the outset numerous state governments have refused to negotiate gaming compacts with tribal governments in spite of a federal law requiring they do so. Some states simply do not understand tribal sovereign rights, others are outright hostile to them. What is common to all states is that IGRA's compacting requirement has heightened their level of engagement with tribal governments. In order to facilitate the compacting process, tribal governments that negotiate with state governments are often forced to both interpret and defend their gaming rights while also articulating the federal foundations upon which they rest.

Tribal governments are meeting the political challenge of encouraging state governments to abide by IGRA to negotiate Indian gaming compacts by investing in the welfare of the state's constituents. Through a combination of outreach projects ranging from education and charitable contributions to public relations and community investment, tribal governments are building a foundation of public support. By sharing their good fortune and making life better for their neighbors and employees, tribal governments are building political capital by investing locally. What is remarkable is that Indian nations have found a way to reconcile their history of generosity with their increasing need for political power.

Tribal testimony presented before the National Gambling Impact Study Commission (NGISC) in 1998–1999 documented the wide range of social investments made by tribal governments in the United States. For example, the Viejas Band of Kumeyaay Indians in Southern California has invested heavily in improving basic infrastructure on and near its reservation, improving property values in the region and resulting in a safer environment. According to Viejas's Chairman Anthony Pico:

> Our gaming revenues provide such government services as police, fire and
> ambulance to our reservation, neighbors and casino. Earnings from gaming

have paved roads, provided electricity, sewage lines, clean water storage
and recycling, trash disposal, natural habitat replacement and watershed and
other environmental improvements to our land.[9]

Through investment in basic infrastructure that most communities take
for granted, tribal governments are striving for what one tribal leader
calls "a level playing field as compared with the majority of society in
this country."[10]

For instance, nowhere are the disparities between Indian country and
the majority of Americans more pronounced than in access to health care.
In order to address the need for better healthcare facilities, the Choctaw
Nation of Oklahoma used gaming revenues to become the only Indian
tribe in the United States to build its own hospital.[11] The $28 million
Choctaw Nation Health Care Center, completed in June 1999, and located in Talihina, provides comprehensive health care services and features 37 hospital beds for inpatients and 52 exam rooms for outpatients.
The Choctaw Nation also operates four health centers in other towns in
the region.[12] Together these five health care facilities provide 3,734 services on a typical day.[13]

In addition to basic infrastructure investments that benefit local residents and visitors alike, tribal governments are also investing in social institutions such as community groups and schools. According to Harry
Cooper of the Nooksack Tribe of Washington, "We contribute to a variety of charities and are actively involved in promoting the local Boys
and Girls Club, Chamber of Commerce, local churches, and the Cancer
Society. We provide fund-raising venues for seniors, disadvantaged children, and support the local Head Start Program."[14]

Tribal governments are very aware of the rapid shift they have made
from a largely dependent economy to a state of self-sufficiency that allows
them to be generous with local communities and other tribes.[15] For example, in Arizona the Yavapai-Prescott Indian Tribe feels a sense of re-
payment when contributing to good causes in the local community of
Prescott. According to Tribal President Stan Rice Jr.:

> Once the recipient of charity and governmental support, we are now giv-
> ing back to our community and supporting many of those charitable
> groups which once helped us. . . . The surrounding Prescott area benefits
> from [our] economic development efforts. From cultural development to

support for charities and nonprofit groups, the Yavapai-Prescott Tribe has moved from being a recipient to a provider.[16]

The fact that some Indian nations have literally *created* an economy in the short span of a decade is unprecedented, as is their immediate generosity.

Tribes do not limit their investment to the local geographic region or even to the state in which they find themselves. Many tribal governments donate funds to other tribal governments in need. Recently the San Manuel Band of Mission Indians of California donated $1 million to the White Mountain Apache Tribe of Arizona in an effort to provide aid for the massive destruction caused by the Rodeo-Chedeski fire, the largest wildfire in Arizona history. In addition to donating money, the San Manuel Band used this opportunity to challenge other tribes with the means to also contribute to the Apache Nation. Tribal Chairman Deron Marquez stated, "We feel it is our responsibility as American Indians to help our fellow tribal nations in a time of need. . . . We can only hope that other tribes will follow suit to join us in the important mission of rebuilding the lives of the Apache people of Arizona."[17]

THE RISE AND PERSISTENCE OF THE "RICH INDIAN" IMAGE

At first blush these tribal governments' generous social investments would seem uncontroversial, even welcomed. After all, most cost/benefit analyses of Indian gaming find that many endemic social problems respond quickly to economic investment.[18] It seems reasonable to assume that lowering the unemployment rate and improving safety, health, and infrastructure would be universally embraced by tribal, state, and federal policy makers alike. However, the generosity of tribal governments has had unforeseen political consequences. The social investments made by tribal governments, which they translated into political clout in many regions of the country, have produced opponents who seek to defer or stop the growth of Indian gaming and thereby limit tribal governmental gaming revenues.[19] Attacks on Indian gaming take many forms; however, they all rely upon misrepresentations of Indian nations and tribal sovereign rights. The success of a handful of tribal government gaming enterprises across the United States feeds a misconception that all tribal governments are now multimillion dollar businesses. The "story" of Indian gaming, nationally and locally, is often reduced to the exceptional success of tribes who happen to have land near population centers.[20] Anti-Indian policy makers and other opponents make use of the idea that all Indians are now wealthy by mobilizing the image to serve their own political agendas. The simplistic images and stereotypes that now clutter the debate about Indian gaming and tribal sovereignty are strategic devices meant to distract from the grim reality that lingers in much of Indian country, where only one-third of tribal governments pursue Indian gaming.

I first encountered the "rich Indian" image after returning home to the White Earth Reservation in northern Minnesota to conduct anthropological fieldwork. During the 1970s and 1980s, when I was growing up there, the unemployment rate at White Earth was over 80 percent. Because of this bleak economic environment, many White Earth tribal members lived in more urban areas where it was easier to make a living. The White Earth Indian Nation started building a casino in my hometown of Mahnomen while I was away at college in the early 1990s. After the Shooting Star Casino was completed, I moved back home to study the impact of the casino as the basis for my Ph.D. dissertation. Most of my fieldwork entailed interviewing a wide range of people about the perceived impacts of the casino on the local community, on the Nation and on the region. Immediately, I was surprised at the consistency of people's opinions and remarks about the casino's impact at White Earth. In a nutshell, many non-Indians in the area thought all White Earth tribal members were now rich. Meanwhile, tribal members consistently talked about how good it felt to finally be working and to have the option of returning home to live. The striking thing about the perceptions of the non-Indians was that there was no evidence that tribal members were wealthy. For example, few people drove new cars or built new homes, which are typical signs of new wealth in that region. The idea that "Indians were rich" simply did not match the facts. I began to wonder what non-Indians were implying by insisting tribal members were rich in spite of evidence to the contrary. What was behind their remarks about new Indian wealth?

At the same time that I was doing ethnographic research at White Earth, I was immersed in the history of federal Indian policy. I was struck by the similarities between the ways federal policies were justified in popular opinion and the political scenario I was finding at White Earth. After nearly a year of research at White Earth I began to see that popular images of Indians consistently work in two ways. First, popular images of Indians silence contemporary Indian people. Second, popular images are used to justify harmful, anti-Indian federal policies. I found this pattern consistently documented in historical federal policies and was interested in the ways it persists today.

For example, in the 1820s, when Indians were portrayed as savages, Chief Justice Marshall ruled that American Indian people could not rightfully care for or own their land.[21] And in the 1830s, when American Indian people were stereotyped as childlike, that image justified the creation of a so-called ward/guardian relationship between Indian nations and the federal government.[22] When Indian nations were portrayed as uncivilized and lawless, the federal government imposed constitution-style governments onto Indian nations with the Indian Reorganization Act in 1934.

When I arrived in Washington, D.C. in 1998 and entered the contemporary political world, first as a staffer for the National Gambling Impact Study Commission (NGISC) and later as the director of research for the National Indian Gaming Association (NIGA), I realized I was witness to a contemporary piece of this long-running project of creating images of Indians for political purposes. In some ways both my jobs on Capitol Hill were simply an extension of the fieldwork I started in my hometown. At times I felt like I was doing anthropological research on Capitol Hill to strengthen the arguments already developed in my dissertation. In Congressional hearings, newspaper articles, and the many research and media calls I fielded at NIGA, I continued to hear people speak about the "rich Indians" in spite of the impoverished conditions that exist in many parts of Indian country and the incredible unmet need among tribal nations. In many ways the opinions of many policy makers and other Americans mirrored those of the non-Indians in my hometown. That is, they continued to embrace one idea (that Indians are rich) in spite of overwhelming evidence to the contrary.

It seems obvious now that those employing Rich Indian imagery are ultimately targeting the very foundation of tribal government: tribal sovereignty.[23] Indeed, I would argue that Rich Indian imagery works today to justify anti-Indian policies by calling into question both the economic need of tribal governments and their authenticity as "real" Indians. Furthermore, portraying any economic development success as a "surplus" provides a distraction from the federal government's miserable record on Indian affairs and justifies targeting tribal resources for state or federal ventures.[24]

The first way that "rich Indian" imagery can be used to undermine tribal sovereignty is by insisting that Indian nations do not *deserve* sovereign rights because they are not really Indian anymore. In this argument non-Indians equate authentic "Indianness" with poverty or suffering and create a distinction between so-called rich Indians and some romantic real Indians. By this logic, once a tribal nation acquires wealth they cannot be real Indians. This use of the rich Indian image supposes that economically thriving Indian nations are no longer sufficiently different from other Americans (i.e., not suffering enough) to deserve sovereign political rights. When confronted with this assumption, one tribal representative from California remarked, "It used to be that the only good Indian was a dead Indian. Now it seems that the only good Indian is a poor Indian."[25]

Second, the claim that Indians are rich has been used to argue that "Indian nations no longer need what they used to need." In the 1890s this notion of "surplus" was used during the land allotment period to alienate tribal land holdings. At that time the U.S. government decided to break up the communal land holdings on reservations and allot all Indians lands to individual Indians. The U.S. government decided how much land each individual Indian would receive within the reservation's border based on the number of land allotments. Given this system, of course, the number of individual Indian allottees and the number of land allotments were never equal. By design there were always more parcels of land than there were individual Indian allottees. After the small land parcels were allotted to individuals, these so-called surplus land allotments within the reservation were then sold to non-Indians.

In the 1990s Rich Indian imagery achieves the same ends by allowing non-Indians to decide what resources Indians needed, declaring that there was a surplus and then taking the rest. For example, the notion of surplus was a key argument against the Mille Lacs Band of Ojibwe (Minnesota) in a recent treaty rights case in the U.S. Supreme Court. Local Minnesota fishermen argued that having a casino job negated the rights of tribal members to take fish from the lake before the state fishing season opened. Rich Indian imagery was also employed in an effort to deny land-into-trust acquisition by the Shakopee Mdewakanton Sioux in Minnesota based on the notion that "they could afford to pay the taxes." The notion of surplus and need is also implied in proposed legislation that would have required so-called means testing, whereby tribes would have had to prove they still needed their federal moneys.

There is also a not so subtle corollary to the use of the Rich Indian image that defines the term relationally by contrasting it with some imagined "real" Indians. That is, Rich Indian imagery is often combined with quasi concern about the threat that gaming presents to "traditional tribal values"—the paternalistic argument that tribes should resist offering gaming "for their own good" because it somehow threatens traditional culture. Rick Hill, chairman emeritus of NIGA, pointed out the irony of this concern when he stated, "It is a fact that very few people were concerned about the impact of poverty, or diabetes, or unemployment on 'traditional tribal culture.' Now, it seems, money is a real threat. Does that make sense? No!"[26]

In addition to using Rich Indian imagery to challenge tribal sovereignty in the two ways I have just described, the Rich Indian image also provides a convenient distraction from the fact that two-thirds of America's Indian nations do not have gaming and that many native people continue to suffer inferior living conditions. Among tribes that do have gaming, profits are not evenly distributed but depend on access to markets. The fact is that thirty-one facilities account for 62 percent of the total Indian gaming revenue, and on some of the more rural, yet typical, reservations, gaming facilities act primarily as job centers, not revenue generators. In light of these facts, members of the National Gambling Impact Study Commission as well as many policy makers have suggested that the "rich" Indians should be doing more to help the "real" Indians that continue to suffer, again naturalizing that distinction and simultaneously distracting Americans from the federal government's miserable record on Indian affairs.

One tribal leader turned the debate on its head when he exposed the distraction provided by the "rich Indian" and proposed that policy makers instead focus on the unmet needs in Indian country. In testimony before the Senate Committee on Indian Affairs, Keller George, president of the United South and Eastern Tribes (USET), outlined the severe shortfall in federal appropriations for Indian country. During the questions period Senator Daniel Inouye (D-Hawaii) discussed with Mr. George the recurring interest by some members of Congress in proposing "means testing" for Indian nations, which would link federal funding to tribal governmental revenues. During this discussion Senator Inouye reminded the committee,

Many of the agreements between Indian country and the government of the United States are based upon treaties—solemn promises made by both parties. If the U.S. government promised you, then the U.S. government should honor that promise, even if you become multimillionaires. Means testing is one way of breaking treaties. . . . We are opposed to means testing because it violates provisions of the treaties.

President George replied that the USET Tribes "oppose means testing, and we propose to turn it around. . . . We propose 'needs testing.'"[27] President George's comments are meant to underscore that while many policy makers seem to focus on what Indian nations appear to have (wealth) they should be focusing on the fact that there is still a desperate need for basic services in much of Indian country.

Senator Inouye and President George understand that the legal and policy stakes are high in Washington, D.C. because the false stereotype of the Rich Indian can be codifed in federal policies that both affect all American Indians and have nothing whatsoever to do with gaming policy or tribal sovereignty. The federal government has an enormous amount of power over Indian affairs and each year more anti-Indian legislation is proposed and justified by the idea that Indian nations are now rich. Indeed, some federal policies are being revisited based on the popular notion that Indian nations are "rich." A striking example is the call for changes to (or even a moratorium on) the Federal Acknowledgment Process (FAP), a petitioning process whereby Indian nations that are not federally recognized seek a government-to-government relationship with the federal government. The FAP is widely and publicly portrayed by some policy makers and the media as a mechanism through which Indian nations are pursuing gaming. Of course, this accusation overlooks the many historical reasons why a tribal government would lack federal recognition and what federal recognition means in terms of access to basic governmental services. What these attacks accomplish is the linking in people's minds of Indian identity and Indian gaming, implying that the latter creates a demand for the former.

Some policy makers have also attempted to drive a political wedge between already recognized tribes and those seeking recognition by implying that "more tribes" or "new tribes" would create competition for the existing gaming market. (Of course, this threat relies on the assumption that any tribe to receive recognition will pursue gaming.) In 2002 Congressman Chris Shays (R-Conn.) addressed the members of the National Indian Gaming Association (NIGA) with the intention of gathering support for his investigation into the FAP. His offer to delay federal recognition decisions or alter the process on behalf of federally recognized tribes was unanimously rebuked by the NIGA membership. As one tribal leader from California reminded him, "There are no new tribes, Congressman. They may be new to you, but they are not new to us."[28]

THE TRIBAL RESPONSE

Legitimate information about American Indian issues, particularly Indian gaming, is scarce. In this vacuum much of the information about contemporary American Indian tribal governments and nearly all data about Indian gaming is produced in the mainstream media. Many influential Hill staffers believe that the media plays a disproportionate role in shaping the opinion of policy makers. According to one person,

> In general, and from my experience, media *is* public policy, and drives it, and the decisions of a few well-placed media elites in our information-overloaded society have an impact well out of proportion to what it should be. Look at how [media] define the debate on virtually every political issue and how the general populace is so uninformed that they do not realize it.[29]

Given the inordinate amount of influence that various media hold for shaping the perceptions of the public and policy makers alike with regard to Indian issues, many Indian nations in the United States have begun investing in public education and public relations campaigns.

For example, tribal governments in California chose to supplement their community investment strategy with an extensive media campaign when they had to fight for a legitimate political space for Indian gaming in California. Perhaps the most dramatic example of the collective exercise of tribal sovereignty and self-definition in recent history was the Proposition 5 campaign in California in 1998.[30] Unifying around a common theme (and, some would argue, against a common enemy),[31] tribal governments in California undertook a massive referendum campaign that included investment in local communities, public education, coalition building, and savvy media relations. I argue that in this case Indian nations in California leveraged tribal sovereignty to a degree and purpose that has never been seen before, when they changed the landscape of California law for good. Just as important, however, is the way the tribes achieved their victory: by investing locally in community development and cultivating popular support close to home.

California's Indian nations began to offer some forms of gaming in the early 1980s. At that time tribes who were looking to create a few jobs and generate badly needed revenues to pay for tribal government services offered bingo halls and some card games. As gaming began to grow and spread throughout the state, local governments began to oppose these enterprises. In the late 1980s Riverside County attempted to enforce state gambling laws on lands held in trust by the Cabazon and Morongo Bands. These actions eventually went to the Supreme Court, ultimately resulting in IGRA. Meanwhile, as the courts spent the decade of the 1980s debating the statutory framework for Indian gaming, tribes in California continued to expand their operations, building economies and investing in community development.

After the passage of IGRA, California's then-Governor Pete Wilson refused to negotiate Class III compacts with the California tribes in spite of a federal mandate to do so. To create political leverage with the governor, Indian nations in California decided to rally the support of the California voters by placing the gaming issue on the ballot in 1998 as Proposition 5. The ensuing political campaign is a case study in the ways that community investing can lead directly to political power. It also illustrates the powerful backlash against American Indian activism and the persistence of the Rich Indian image.

In addition to Governor Wilson, the primary opponents to Indian gaming and Proposition 5 in California were Nevada casino interests, who created front groups such as the Coalition Against Unregulated Gambling to oppose Indian gaming.[32] Casino owners and other industry representatives viewed Indian gaming in California as a threat to Nevada gaming markets and invested heavily in misinformation campaigns about tribal sovereignty, Indian identity, and the law, complex issues that can easily be reduced to false sound bites.[33] The most popular themes employed by the opposition were that Indian gaming was unregulated and that it would have negative social consequences for California communities. Later in the campaign the opposition employed the Rich Indian image when it launched a television advertisement shot from a helicopter flying over the San Manuel Band's reservation in Highland, California. The image was of large homes on a hillside, and the ad's narrative implied that individual tribal members did not need Indian gaming because they already lived in nice homes. With its focus on "the mansions of San Manuel," the ad became the emblem of Propositions 5's anti-Indian advertising.

Rather than respond to these images or to attacks on their identity and their growing industry, Indian nations in California continued to invest heavily in law enforcement, infrastructure, and community development in their local communities. This investment benefited both Indian and non-Indian residents who came to see their communities as an integrated a voting bloc. In addition, tribal governments organized politically and invested heavily in media campaigns of their own.

Proposition 5 was also known as the Indian Self-Reliance Initiative. Instead of countering the Rich Indian image with stories about centuries of Indian poverty or the ways that California's Indian nations continue to suffer from inadequate federal funding, California's Indian nations reframed the Proposition 5 debate from one about Indian gaming to one about human rights. Thus Indian nations simply changed the terms of the discussion and ultimately reshaped the debate about Indian gaming as one founded on tribal self-reliance rather than on gaming rights.

Mark Macarro, chairman of the Pechanga Band of Luiseno Indians, was chosen as the tribal spokesman for the Proposition 5 campaign. He was charged with carrying a simple message to the California voters: "Because of Indian gaming, tribes have begun the long march back from poverty and hopelessness to prosperity and hope for a better future." Chairman Macarro notably invited California voters to "join with us," and, according to one account, "Macarro's invitation . . . captured the imaginations of all but the most ardent anti-Indian bigots."[34] In addition to the clear message of community building delivered by Chairman Macarro, the Yes on 5 campaign, organized by the Californians for Indian Self-Reliance, provided multiple resources regarding the answers to common questions about the proposition. Yes on 5 materials included brochures, initiative summaries, impact studies, fact sheets, presentation folders, proposed laws, and other background information.

On voting day 64 percent of California voters supported Proposition 5. This public support ultimately measured more than just approval of Indian gaming: it documented the ways that tribal giving has positively affected the majority of Californians who have witnessed its impacts and participated in its myriad rewards. Proposition 5 was a visible legitimation of Indian nation investment, both human and financial.[35] It was also a testament to the power of political organizing, as more than eighty tribes worked together to educate California voters about the initiative.

The Proposition 5 campaign is a perhaps the most dramatic example of

Indian nations collectively reconstructing dominant ideologies and discourses to create social change, but it is not the only one. Indian nations across the country are realizing a range of social and political payoffs for their community investments. Most tribal governments find that the most immediate reward is a renewed sense of optimism at the community level. For example, Jacob Lonetree, president of the Ho-Chunk Nation, testified before the NGISC that

> gaming has provided a new sense of hope for the future, among a Nation that previously felt too much despair and powerlessness as a result of our long term poverty. Opportunities from gaming have provided our people with a greater sense of optimism for the future and a renewed interest in our past. The economic development generated by gaming has raised our spirits and drawn us closer together.[36]

Other tribal leaders echoed the sentiment above when they stated that "pride in our Indian entrepreneurship is the most valuable commodity of all"[37] or "Gaming represents renewed hope for a brighter future."[38] Taken together, these testimonies capture how in Indian country self-definition, both at the individual and tribal level, translates into social change. Indian gaming activism has had an impact on many other Indian nations in the same way, by reconfiguring tribal members' self image from that of receiver to that of giver, and their environment from one of scarcity to abundance. The result is a generation of tribal members who are changing both the ways they think about themselves and portray themselves to the larger society.

GENEROSITY AS A NEW ROUTE TO POWER

Indian governmental gaming is a tribally initiated strategy for many American Indian tribal governments to define their cultural, economic, and political future for themselves, in some cases for the first time. Thus, I argue that Indian gaming acts as more than a self-determination policy: it could rightly be considered a *self-definition* policy.[39] By defining the particular ways they want to develop economically, investing revenues as they see fit, developing messages about the impacts of their economic development strategy, and resisting imposed and antiquated images of "Indianness," Indian nations are currently engaged in a process of self definition on a scale that could not have been contemplated two decades ago.

Tribal governments with gaming invest in schools, roads, emergency services, health care facilities, nursing homes, and local charities. They are major employers, often providing jobs in areas of historically high unemployment. Being a good neighbor and a good employer is not an overtly political act for tribal governments. But a consequence of tribal generosity is that both Indian and non-Indian communities near tribally owned gaming facilities know firsthand the benefits of Indian gaming and become powerful allies. Because tribal neighbors benefit from tribal casinos, a vote for Indian gaming becomes a vote for their own livelihood.

By focusing on local communities, tribal governments are creating a new political model and a new economic space in which investing in people pays off politically. This type of political participation creates a truly win-win situation. Tribal government political participation is a significant departure from the "old way" of gaining power in American politics. By emphasizing human capital rather than the old-fashioned kind, they are forever altering both the route to power and the political use of money.

Changing the system that once excluded them has not been popular among some anti-Indian groups. Opponents who seek to limit or deny tribal political engagement have tried to undermine the overwhelming popular support for tribal governments through misinformation and attacks on the integrity of Indian governments and their gaming businesses. Accordingly, the political backlash against Indian gaming has shifted from one focused strictly on the bottom line to a battle over public perception and public sentiment. For now, tribal governments continue to believe that generosity is the best political strategy yet—as well as the most culturally appropriate.

In spite of the backlash against Indian gaming, Indian nations continue to push the borders of political participation in American political and public life. The newfound political clout of tribal governments has forever altered the landscape of American politics. Tribal governments are not simply participating in the American political process but providing models for changing it. They are forging new routes to power by investing in local communities and being generous to their neighbors and employees as a way of strengthening their position as both governments and corporate citizens. This investment then has a ripple effect of reshaping the public perception of tribal governments and reframing the debate surrounding Indian gaming. This chapter only begins to explore the various strategies employed by Indian nations and identify the space that Indian

nations have opened for themselves in America's political and social milieu. The project begun in the 1990s is far from over. As Indian nations
continue to empower themselves and their surrounding communities, I
suspect these relationships and alliances will reshape the American political landscape even more dramatically.

Notes

Some of this material has appeared in other, unpublished manuscripts
and/or been presented at conferences. One California tribal leader who graciously
agreed to read a draft of this chapter suggested I use the term *pro-activism* rather than
activism throughout the chapter. For the purposes of this publication I have maintained
the latter term in order to be consistent with the other book chapters. However, I
think his point is well made, that "activism connotes the 1960s and it did not work for
us. This phenomenon is something new and different and should be named as such."

1. I use the term *Indian gaming* throughout as a gloss for the more cumbersome but
more descriptive term *Indian nation governmental gaming*. For the purposes of this chapter *Indian gaming* is used to refer to both class II and class III gaming. Indian gaming
is also known as *tribal gaming, tribal governmental gaming, American Indian tribal gaming*,
and various other combinations.

2. Moving through the chapter it will become clear that I have been involved in
Indian gaming political activities while also observing and documenting their scope
and influence. While not a focus unto itself, the chapter inherently deals with the subject of activism in anthropology through my own subject position as a researcher, witness, participant, and advocate.

3. As of July 2002, 200 tribal governments operate 290 gaming facilities across the
United States (National Indian Gaming Commission). This number changes periodically as the result of factors ranging from tribal-state compacting to market forces.

4. U.S. Const. art. 1, § 8, cl. 3.

5. U.S. Const. art. 2, § 2, cl. 2.

6. 480 U.S. 202 (1987).

7. Tribal sovereignty guarantees tribes the right to establish their own forms of
government, determine membership, police, adjudicate individual conduct, charter
businesses, and regulate certain activities, among other things. Because Indian governmental powers originate with tribal governments, a comprehensive list of powers
cannot be made by reference to a Congressional or Constitutional delegation of powers. Comprehensive treatments of tribal governmental powers can be found in
William C. Canby, *American Indian Law in a Nutshell* (St. Paul, Minn.: West, 1988);
and Rennard Strickland and Felix S. Cohen's *Handbook of American Indian Law* (Char-
lottesville, Va.: Bobbs-Merrill, 1982).

8. Some tribes claimed that the compacting provision of IGRA was unconstitutional. See *Red Lake Band v. Swimmer*, 740 F. Supp. 9; *Red Lake Band v. Brown*, 928 F. 2d 467.

9. Testimony of Anthony R. Pico, chairman, Viejas Band of Kumeyaay Indians, November 9, 1998.

10. Testimony of Apesanahkwat, chairman, Menominee Indian Tribe of Wisconsin, November 10, 1998.

11. For more information, see www.choctawnation.com/programs/new.

12. The other locations are Broken Bow, Huge, McAlester, and Poteau.

13. See "Social and Economic Analysis of Tribal Government Gaming in Oklahoma." Katherine A. Spilde, et al., www.ksg.harvard.edu/hpaied.

14. Testimony of Harry Cooper, Nooksack River Casino, January 7, 1999.

15. A recent study by the National Indian Gaming Association (NIGA) found that Indian nations give at least $68 million a year in charitable donations. See Charitable Gaming Survey, May 2001.

16. Testimony of Stan Rice Jr., president of the Board of Directors, Yavapai-Prescott Indian Tribe, July 31, 1998.

17. Press Release, San Manuel Band of Mission Indians, Highland, California, July 10, 2002.

18. Jonathan Taylor, Matthew Krepps, and Patrick Wang, "The National Evidence on the Socioeconomic Impacts of American Indian Gaming," (Cambridge: Lexecon, April 2000); Spilde et al. "Social and Economic Analysis."

19. For example, local governments often resent the exercise of tribal sovereignty and a perceived loss of jurisdiction over such issues as zoning or environmental regulations. Other gaming industries (riverboats, horse and dog tracks, state lotteries, commercial casinos) consider the growth and expansion of Indian gaming to be an economic threat to their businesses. Some policy makers simply do not approve of any form of gambling and find Indian gaming a convenient target. Finally, there are non-Indians who resent what they perceive to be "special rights" for tribal governments and actively attack Indian gaming as a symbol of tribal sovereignty.

20. Of course, this pattern of generalizing from one tribe's circumstances (in this case economic success) to all "Indians" is well documented.

21. *Johnson v. M'Intosh,* 21 U.S. (8 Wheat.) 543 (1823).

22. *Cherokee Nation v. Georgia*, 30 U.S. (5 Pet.) 1 (1831).

23. See "Acts of Sovereignty, Acts of Identity: Negotiating Interdependence Through Indian Governmental Gaming on the White Earth Reservation." Ph. D. diss., University of California, Santa Cruz, 1998.

24. To strengthen this point, Indian gaming revenues were targeted when the industry was just getting started. For example, within weeks of the passage of the Indian Gaming Regulatory Act in 1988, federal legislation to tax Indian casino revenues was presented in Congress as a way to balance the federal budget while state govern-

ments began to consistently pressure tribal governments into so-called revenue sharing agreements during their compact negotiations in order to benefit from Indian casinos that are technically not under state jurisdiction.

25. Jacob Coin, executive director of the California Nations Indian Gaming Association (CNIGA), personal communication, December 15, 2000.

26. Rick Hill, personal communication, March 27, 2002.

27. Keller George, testimony before the Senate Committee on Indian Affairs, April 5, 2001.

28. Chairman Deron Marquez of the San Manuel Band of Serrano Mission Indians, March 31, 2002.

29. Personal communication with a staff member from Speaker of the House Dennis Hastert's office regarding the link between public policy and public opinion. March 29, 2001.

30. Proposition 5 is shorthand for "The Tribal Government Gaming and Economic Self-Sufficiency Act of 1998," which initiated a statute change allowing tribal governments in California to offer slot machines, arguably the most lucrative form of gaming, in their gaming facilities.

31. According to one tribal account, Governor Pete Wilson's attempt to block Indian gaming in California "gave birth to a tribal unification that became the most powerful political coalition in California." Michael Lombardi, "Long Road Traveled," unpublished MS, p. 4.

32. See Californians for Indian Self-Reliance, "Nevada Casino Interests Create Another Front Group to Oppose Indian Gaming." June 23, 1998.

33. Media accounts estimate that Nevada interests spent $30 million fighting Proposition 5.

34. Lombardi, "Long Road Traveled," p. 6.

35. Proposition 5 was the first of two major referenda passed by Indian nations in California. The second, Proposition 1A, passed in March 2000.

36. Testimony before the National Gambling Impact Study Commission, November 9, 1998.

37. Steve Cadue, vice chairman of the Kickapoo Tribe of Kansas, testimony before the National Gambling Impact Study Commission, November 9, 1998.

38. Testimony of Clinton Pattea, president, Fort McDowell Mohave-Apache Indian Community, July 31, 1998.

39. This claim also allows for the fact that the majority of Indian nations in the United States chose not to engage in gaming as an economic development strategy. Of course, to opt out of gaming is an exercise of tribal sovereignty.

4

"The Calculus of Pain": Violence, Anthropological Ethics, and the Category Transgender

DAVID VALENTINE

The last time I saw Vianna-Faye alive was on a Saturday night in November 1997. We cruised the cool, dangerous streets of the so-called Meat Market on the far west side of Manhattan in her car, talking as she kept one eye on the cars crawling past, alert for the possibility of a date—code word on these streets for someone who will pay for sex. This car was paid for by sex work, and the money she had saved by working these streets would pay for her sex reassignment surgery (SRS). Like most of the African American and Latina fem queens (an "indigenous" category to which I will return) who work the Meat Market, Vianna-Faye was what many Americans have come to recognize as a "transgender person."

Since the early 1990s "transgender" has emerged rapidly in the United States in a variety of contexts—from legislative and academic settings, to social service provision, popular representations, and journalism—to describe someone assigned to one gender who, in one respect or another, does not perform or identify as that gender and has taken some steps—temporary or permanent—to present in another gender. My eighteen months of ethnographic research focused on the emergence of this category in a variety of contexts, from the streets of the Meat Market to the U.S. Congress. In these settings *transgender* is variously defined, but is most

This chapter originally appeared in a longer version as " 'The Calculus of Pain': Violence, Anthropological Ethics, and the Category Transgender" in *Ethnos* 66(1): 27–48 in 2003. Please also see http://www.tandf.co.uk. Readers are directed to that version for a more in-depth discussion of some of the theoretical issues raised by this essay.

frequently used as a *collective* term to incorporate a variety of social and medical identities—including, but not limited to transexual,[1] transvestite, cross-dresser, drag queen, drag king, and even intersex people[2]—that had previously been seen as separate. Like many other grassroots movements in the 1990s, the explosion of internet technologies facilitated the establishment of something called a transgender community. However, the activism around transgender in particular has most recently been mobilized around violence experienced by transgender-identified[3] people. My argument here is that violence—both its visceral experience and the stories people tell about it—has been increasingly central to the establishment of the category transgender, especially since the late 1990s.

Despite the fact that Vianna-Faye fit the above description as a transgender person, she did not use the term *transgender* to talk about herself. If I pushed her she would say she was a woman or, sometimes, a fem queen. But she certainly fit the definition: that evening Vianna-Faye told me she had a date—not a trick but an appointment for SRS instead—on January 14, 1998, in Montreal. She planned to kick sex work and get a job. Despite her skills (both as a bank teller and as a trained phlebotomist), she had been unable to find legitimate work, a common story in the Meat Market and among other transgender-identified people. After transition she said she would be able to move on, get a real job, and stop being "Felicia" (her "street" name) forever.

But she never made that appointment. On Christmas she was murdered in her apartment in Jersey City, apparently by a twelve-year-old boy who was a neighbor. She was found in her nightgown, with multiple stab wounds to her back, neck, and chest. I found out about her death almost by accident. A few weeks later, on my way to a bar on 13th Street in the Meat Market, I bumped into Alexis, one of the working girls:

"Did you hear Felicia was killed?" she asked, lighting a cigarette. It took me several seconds to register.

"Vianna-Faye?" I asked in disbelief. Yeah, said Alexis, and proceeded to give me the details. And, she continued, she used to be Felicia's roommate and she still had a key, and the cops said she could have her stuff, and wasn't that cool?

I didn't know whether to cry, to yell at her, or to dispute the ludicrous idea that the police would give her such carte blanche with a murder victim's belongings. Instead, I said goodbye and walked on in a daze. It was while I was clutching my beer in the bar that I realized with a dual sense of horror and certainty that I had an ethnographic story to tell about violence against transgender people.

THE USES OF VIOLENCE

What is an anthropologist to do with such an experience? In a 1995 article in *Current Anthropology* Nancy Scheper Hughes argues for the "primacy of the ethical" in anthropological practice, that is, the moral imperative for anthropologists to act on the suffering and violence they witness in the course of their research. She describes how she intervened in the community-led rough justice meted out against three young men accused of theft in a South African squatter camp near Cape Town. Flouting the wishes of some community leaders, she arranged medical attention for the youngest offender whose flogging had brought him close to death. Scheper-Hughes argues that her ethical responsibilities—as an anthropologist and as a human being—meant ignoring the demands that she not intervene. She writes:

> To speak of the "primacy of the ethical" is to suggest certain transcendent, transparent and essential, if not "precultural" first principles. . . . I will tentatively and hesitantly suggest that responsibility, accountability, answerability to "the other"—the ethical as I would define it—is precultural to the extent that our human existence as social beings presupposes the presence of the other. (1995:419)

In Scheper-Hughes's account, postmodernist trends in anthropology—a focus on the diffuse nature of power, the ambiguity of social practices, the flows of discourse and symbolic capital—have distracted anthropologists from the local and specific, and the evidence of profound suffering. As an alternative, Scheper-Hughes calls for a "new cadre of 'barefoot anthropologists'" who

> must become alarmists and shock troopers—the producers of politically complicated and morally demanding texts and images capable of sinking through the layers of acceptance, complicity, and bad faith that allow the suffering and the deaths to continue. (417)

In many ways I find Scheper-Hughes's call for an ethically oriented anthropology to be galvanizing. Since Vianna-Faye's death several more of my study participants have been murdered; more have been subject to verbal and physical harassment. These stories are not uncommon: a recent survey by the advocacy and lobbying group Gender Public Advocacy Coalition (GenderPAC) found that almost 60 percent of transgender-identified people surveyed had experienced some form of harassment or abuse, directed at them because of their non-normative expression of gender (GenderPAC 1997). In recent years transgender-identified activists and advocates have begun to use these stories to appeal to state bodies, demanding legislative action to address such violence (a process I have participated in, as I discuss below).

Yet at the same time I want to take issue with Scheper-Hughes's call for "precultural" ethical stances on violence. As scholars such as Arthur and Joan Kleinman (1996) and Allen Feldman (1991) have shown, violence and suffering are neither simple nor self-evident categories. These and other scholars argue that violence must be understood as a complex cultural category, drawing in both the visceral reality of murder but also a set of representations, discourses, and stories *about* such social realities (Feldman 1991; Kleinman and Kleinman 1996; see also Axel 2001, Daniel 1996, Krohn-Hansen 1994, Riches 1986). Daniel writes:

> The point is this. Violence is an event in which there is a certain excess: an excess of passion, an excess of evil. The very attempt to label this excess (as indeed I have done) is condemned to fail. . . . Everything can be narrated, but what is narrated is no longer what happened. (208)

Yet, for violence to be comprehensible, for such acts to be conceived of as constituting a social problem, the production of a discourse about violence—and what is evil—*is* required. Writing of how paramilitaries in Belfast speak of interrogation, Feldman (1991) argues that violence is not simply an event or practice but is also necessarily about how the event becomes narrated and represented (see also Axel 2001; Knox 1998). He writes: "The oral history of interrogation recounted by paramilitaries is a cultural tool kit, an empowering apparatus that paramilitaries take into the theater of interrogation in order to mediate, and possibly invert, the interrogator's scenario of violence" (14).

However, while these scholars point to the centrality of narration, sense making, and representation in considering violence, they tend to focus on moments of violence that seem to resist analysis or that seem to be—surely must be—understandable cross-culturally as quite evidently violent: beatings, murders, massacres, torture. I have started this paper with a similar kind of horrifying story. But I want to consider how "violence" is capable of drawing a range of practices and experiences into its purview.

The category of violence is complicated by the ways in which all and any practices by others may come to be understood as violent in and of themselves, in the context of lives where simply walking down the street can be a terrifying experience. Indeed violence can come to incorporate not only physical abuse and murder but all practices that may be perceived as impacting negatively upon a life as well, including the practices of anthropology itself. The violence of representation and of physical harm, of emotional and physical scarring are hard to consider apart precisely because they can be experienced and narrated simultaneously.

Moreover, this conjuncture—of practices and representations, social realties and their narration—produces for transgender-identified activists a way of presenting stories of lives constantly in danger of harm, a possibility all too readily supported by statistics, personal experiences, and others' narratives. In this way, in activist and personal narratives, transgender becomes a repository not only of non-normative gender and bravery in the face of adversity but of adversity itself.

These violences, large and small, have been increasingly part of the process whereby the idea of transgender has been constituted in the U.S. This is not to say that transgender identities are formed, or transgender activism conducted, exclusively in relation to violence. However, as Moran and Sharpe (2002) write, in discussing community-based surveys of violence against transgender-identified people, "The sites and techniques of mapping violence, the methods of reportage deployed by activists and the police practices of recording violence are . . . all process [sic] through which transgender identities and politics take shape" (270).

My use of *violence* in this paper is thus uncomfortably situated: I am using it in its most evident, least theorized sense, to refer to the mind-numbing, monthly reports I receive of another decomposed body unearthed, another informant or friend dead, another story of a thrown bottle or a catcall—the sense that Scheper-Hughes and others implicitly invoke. I am also using it to refer to the ways that transgender-identified people recognize certain discourses and representations to be linked to practices of physical violence and again, by including catcalls and murder in the category of violence, I am also doing some of this work. I also think about violence as a series of discourses that are being used, precisely, to help constitute the category of transgender, to make it something that people should care about, write books about, legislate about. But finally, to return to Vianna-Faye's story, I want to look at how transgender as the vehicle for activist practices posits coherent and readily identifiable experiences and states of identity to the exclusion of other social identities and other ways of conceptualizing gender and sexual identity. As such, these activist practices and discourses perform *another* set of exclusions—a form of unintended representational violence

Like Scheper-Hughes, I am impassioned by the evidence of violence to write about it, and my analysis here does not aim to draw attention away from the facts of murdered friends, abused bodies, and shattered lives—indeed, quite the opposite. Yet, ethical action on the facts of violence is often enmeshed in different claims about what is moral and what is not, about what does or does not constitute violence and harm. I will argue that only an investigation of these complexities can enable effective and politically engaged work by anthropologists.

VIOLENCE AS DISCOURSE: GENDER LOBBY DAY

To introduce the increasing role that hate crimes have played in transgender advocacy, I begin with an early experience from fieldwork. On a morning in early May 1997, I was in front of the Capitol Building in Washington, D.C. with about sixty mostly white activists. The occasion was the Second National Gender Lobbying Day, an event sponsored by the Gender Public Advocacy Coalition (GenderPAC), a group devoted to "gender, affectional, and racial equality," to highlight issues of gender variance for Congress members. Those present included transexual men and women, cross-dressers, and others who refuse gendered identities, intending to bring their issues to their representatives. With us were a couple of staffers from the Human Rights Campaign (HRC), the largest national political and lobbying group for lesbian and gay rights, who were there to offer their expertise and advice about lobbying.

The task before us this morning was to get Congress members to sign onto a letter requesting that the Department of Justice hold a meeting with GenderPAC representatives. Our strategy was to use *The First National Study on Transviolence* (GenderPAC 1997) recently produced by GenderPAC, the largest research project to date (with 402 respondents) on violence against transgender-identified and gender variant people (see also

Moran and Sharpe 2002). At the prelobby conference the night before, Riki Anne Wilchins, GenderPAC's executive director, told the assembled group: "Violence is a perfect issue, like motherhood. No one can be against motherhood and no one can be for violence."

In the months prior to this Lobby Day GenderPAC and its members had wanted to focus their lobbying efforts on amending the Employment Non-Discrimination Act (ENDA) to include transgender people as a protected class. ENDA, if passed, would criminalize employment discrimination based on sexual orientation, but would not include a provision for discrimination on the basis of gender identity or expression. However, HRC had persuaded officers in GenderPAC that a more productive way of introducing transgender issues on the Hill would be to lobby for the inclusion of "transgender" in the Hate Crimes Statistics Act (see Valentine 2002). This had been an initial strategy of gay and lesbian lobbyists, and it had opened the way for work on more complex legislative concerns around gay/lesbian issues. More to the point, HRC feared that ENDA would be derailed by language protecting transgender-identified people. While HRC's position still angered many of the activists gathered in front of the Capitol this morning, GenderPAC officers had recognized the political realities at hand, and most of those present had agreed that a focus on hate crimes would be the official theme of Lobby Day.

Nervously, we split up into small groups and set off to call on the offices of our Congressional representatives. Riki, Rosalyne Blumenstein, the director of the Gender Identity Project in New York, and I went off by ourselves to visit New York representatives. Some time later that morning we were seated in the offices of Jerold Nadler, a House of Representatives Democrat and vocal supporter of the gay and lesbian community. As his legislative assistant flipped through the GenderPAC report, we described transgendered friends' and informants' murders that we knew all too well and whose stories—in short paragraph form—were included at the end of the report: Deborah Forte ("Ms. Forte suffered three stab wounds to the chest—each half a foot deep, and in addition a number of slash wounds across her chest, a smashed nose, multiple severe blows to her head and face, and signs on her throat of partial strangulation"), Chanell Pickett ("strangled to death in Watertown, MA early on the morning of November 20, 1995"), Brandon Teena ("On Christmas day 1993, Brandon Teena was raped and assaulted at a Christmas party by two men"), and a host of others.

"Now this is something we can work with," the assistant said, nodding. Indeed, he had personally suggested that some sort of statistical study be conducted in order for GenderPAC activists to have an impact on the Hill. By the end of the day, sitting in the cafeteria in the Rayburn Office Building, we were all somewhat dazed: twelve Congress members had signed the letter. None of us had anticipated this level of success.

"We're two years ahead of schedule," Riki kept saying, shaking hir head in wonder.[4]

GenderPAC got its meeting with the D.O.J. (a very productive one); in short order it was also invited to join the Hate Crimes Coalition, a group made up of black, Jewish, gay and lesbian, and other groups. Through the work of the coalition, the Hate Crimes Prevention Act was introduced in 1999, defining as a crime the willful bodily injury of any person "because of the actual or perceived religion, gender, sexual orientation, or disability" (106th Congress 1999) of that person.[5] This means that the provisions of the bill could potentially cover transgender-identified people.

I want to back up from this progress narrative for a moment, though, to note some of the complexities of these politics. The comments of Nadler's assistant, and the willingness of the twelve members to sign on to the letter speaks to the ways that in a representative liberal democracy the path to *being* represented is to form oneself as a constituency. There is nothing new about this kind of politics and, as Fraser (1997) points out, such a "politics of recognition" has become central to social movements in the United States (and elsewhere in the West). The common critique of such politics is that the lives of people such as Brandon or Vianna-Faye become evened out, represented as "transgender people" without attention to the complexity of their lives, their social identifications, their capacity for agency, or the circumstances of their murder. Indeed, it is not clear that the twelve-year-old boy accused of Vianna-Faye's murder was motivated by her gender identity, but her death is, nonetheless, narrated as a hate crime against a transgender-identified person.

This critique of identity politics, though, requires a complication in this case. While GenderPAC was founded primarily by transgender-identified people, its policy (directed by Riki Anne Wilchins) has been to attempt to straddle the divide between a "politics of recognition" and a broader politics of gender. GenderPAC resists being labeled a *transgender* organization precisely because its executive director, staffers, and members argue that *all* people are potentially subject to violence and discrimination because of variant expressions of gender. This position attempts to recognize the multiple nature of social identity and that "transgender" may obscure that complexity. Indeed, during our visits to the offices of Congress members that morning we took care to speak of "gender variant people" rather than "transgender people," attempting to include within that framework anyone who is attacked on the basis of a perceived non-normative gender presentation.

However, GenderPAC's national predominance, and the way it has come to be the de facto voice for transgender politics, is infuriating for many other transgender-identified activists because of GenderPAC's unwillingness to focus specifically on transgender-identified people. Critics of GenderPAC range from those who propound the theory that GenderPAC has been "bought off" by HRC to protect ENDA's chances of passage to more sophisticated analyses that recognize that, while a broad vision of gender-based violence is necessary, political realities require a simultaneous engagement with identity categories (Cartwright 2001). Other critics make a direct link between GenderPAC's politics, its use of murder narratives such as those discussed above, and what these critics see as the implicit violation of transgender-identified people by GenderPAC. As one activist put it:

> Is it morally right for GenderPAC to use [the stories of] Transgender and Intersex victims to raise the bulk of their funds, yet only use a tiny portion of those funds to work for issues that affects those same individuals? Would this not make our dead brothers and sisters victims a second time? (Helms 2000)

In other words, the very terms in which people understand their politics—even the primary organizing categories used in activism and advocacy—complicates an easy ethical stance. The very use of an alternative form of political organizing and theorization of gender can *itself* be seen as an exercise in representational violence.

In short, engaging in carefully positioned and effective advocacy is intimately connected to a range of complex understandings of violence and suffering—and what that violence constitutes. Is legislative advocacy that reproduces sufferers as simply victims ethical? How does one "take sides" in disputes between different groups with divergent analyses of what action is required? What does it mean to reduce the complexity of lived ex-

periences into narratives and statistics, or to represent people as "transgender" when they do not identify as such? Or is this simply postmodernist theorizing? Shouldn't an anthropologist simply act? However, as I
will discuss in the following section, anthropological practices, even those
motivated by good intentions, can themselves be seen as violent.

DISCOURSE AS VIOLENCE I: WORKING FOR THE FBI

December 1996: There were already about twenty-five mem-
bers of the Gender Identity Project (GIP) transgender support group in the
overheated room when I came in, regrettably late. I was initially invited
by Melissa, a group facilitator, in October to give a presentation about my
work. In that group it was immediately apparent to me that, while Melissa had vouched for me, my presence was not altogether welcome. As a
support group this venue was supposed to be a safe space for transgender-
identified people, and as I am not transgender-identified I did not strictly
have the rights to be there. After some discussion the group agreed that I
was welcome to take notes but could not tape record the session.

Tonight was the final meeting of the group before the Christmas
break, and everyone was taking turns saying what they had found ben-
eficial about being in the group. There were several people present
whom I had not met in the October meeting but, as the group had already started, I simply sat down next to Nick, the other group facilitator, and—in retrospect without consideration of the ethical issues—
pulled out my notebook. When my turn came I identified myself as a
nontransgender gay man and as an anthropologist working with the
GIP. I thanked the group for the opportunity to listen and learn from
their experiences. I finished, and the next person began to talk, but, as I
dutifully wrote down her reactions, Jillian—one of the people I hadn't
met previously—suddenly burst out, "Would you mind not taking notes
in a confidential meeting!"

All hell broke loose, in a kind of controlled way. Nick asked her to re-
phrase the request in a more polite manner. Melissa jumped to my defense. I apologized, explaining that I had received permission from the
group on a prior occasion to take notes, that everything was confidential,
that she could see my notes, and that I would stop writing. Jillian was not
mollified, however. She said that she would rather pay "my two dollars"

than have me in the room, drawing a connection between the free services of the group and "government funding" that, she argued, made my
presence possible.[6] Later, after the group had ended, she told me that
"people from the FBI" wanted to take notes on groups such as this, and
I was suspected as part of this process. She was tired, she told me, of having notes taken down about what she says and who she is. After some fifteen minutes of explaining my project and convincing her I was not an
FBI agent, we parted, if not friends at least not enemies.

Jillian's was not the only negative reaction I encountered during my
fieldwork. The perception of anthropology as simply another arm of the
social sciences that has sought to pathologize, exoticize, and objectify gender variance is understandable in a field of discursive relations and practices
that has always placed gender variance as the thing to be explained. Jillian's
reaction speaks to the fact that practices of ethnography, and more broadly of representation, can be seen as harmful in and of themselves.

Transgender-identified people's experience of social scientific investigation of their lives puts Jillian's reaction into perspective. The origin of
transsexuality as a medical term, and its current incarnation as "Gender
Identity Disorder" in the *Diagnostic and Statistical Manual of Mental Disorders* (DSM) (APA 1994) indicates the extent to which discourses about
gender variance have been located in psychiatric models of pathology.[7]
Writing of such academic and clinical investigations, Wilchins argues,

> Academics, shrinks, and feminist theorists have traveled through our lives
> and problems like tourists on a junket. Picnicking on our identities like flies
> at a free lunch, they have selected the tastiest tidbits with which to illus-
> trate a theory or push a book. The fact that we are a community under fire,
> a people at risk, is irrelevant to them. They pursue Science and Theory,
> and what they produce by mining our lives is neither addressed to us nor
> recycled within our community. . . . Our performance of gender is invari-
> ably a site of contest, a problem which—if we could but bring enough hi-
> octane academic power to bear—might be "solved." (1997:22)

Here Wilchins targets the way that scholarly discussions of transpeople
implicitly mark the writer as gender normative and, as s/he argues, the
way such analyses ignore the very facts of violence that I invoke here.[8]
Indeed, s/he posits a link between these two dynamics, the same link Jillian implicitly makes between my practices of note taking and the power

of the state in the person of an FBI agent: that representations are or can be inherently violent.

The linkage of representations and violence is even more complex, though when one considers the work of some feminist theorists who see the mere existence of transexual women or cross-dressers (though less often transexual men) *themselves* as a form of violence against a self-evident, essentialized category of women (Raymond 1994[1979]; Orobio de Castro 1993; Woodhouse 1989; Jeffreys 1996; McNeill 1982). In this view, propounded most famously by Janice Raymond, a patriarchally enforced gender binary, which locates femininity in female embodiment, dupes transexuals into undergoing SRS.

These discourses are in turn the very ones that Wilchins and others see as intrinsically harmful. In a heated, unplanned debate between Raymond and Wilchins at a book signing for Raymond's new book on reproductive technologies in New York in 1994, each implicitly accused the other of violence. Raymond saw Wilchins as evidence of patriarchy's attempts to "rape women's space." For Wilchins, Raymond's insistence on an essentialized category of "woman" violated hir own attempts to construct meanings about hir body (see Wilchins 1997:59–62). Like Jillian's perception of me as an agent of that state, representation is linked here to social power and the certainty of power's effects in the form of violence.

Wilchins's, Raymond's, and Jillian's competing claims as to what constitutes violence—be it sex reassignment surgery, taking notes in a meeting, or writing a book—all draw on a similar set of beliefs: that representations or ideologies have effects in and of themselves, that representations are linked in a causal way to institutions of power beyond the control of the individual, that individuals are willing automatons, bound to enact the demands of hegemonic representations, and that those who are acted on are victims.

What complicates this relationship between representation and violence, however, are the ways that such analyses can work against one other. For if Wilchins sees hirself as constrained by identity labels, hir solution is not always seen as liberatory by others. As I have noted above, GenderPAC's shift away from an identity-based politics under Wilchins's leadership has resulted in denunciations. But even Wilchins's analyses of hir personal embodiment and identity are sometimes seen as personally threatening to the very people s/he argues for in hir activism.

DISCOURSE AS VIOLENCE II:
FOUCAULT FROM A FAUCET

Cindy, along with Riki, is one of the people I am most indebted to in my fieldwork. We first met in the support group of October 1996 and quickly became firm friends and email buddies. At the time I met her Cindy was just beginning to transition, was still married (with two children), and was deeply depressed by her situation even as claiming her identity as a woman was liberating for her. Her history—of child abuse, rape, drug addiction, alcoholism, suppression of feelings—is one that is all too common. Her personal narratives abound with images of life held on to against enormous odds. I was immediately impressed by Cindy's courage and conviction, sometimes exhausted by the intensity of her experiences filtered through emails and conversations, and always ready to learn something new from her.

Shortly after the support group meeting I describe above, I promised to email Cindy a paper I coauthored with Riki, a version of which was published in the journal *Social Text* a year later (Valentine and Wilchins 1997).[9] Part of the motive for sending this paper to her was because she had asked to see it; another part was because, as I had said to her, her courage and drive reminded me of Riki's and I wanted the two of them to be friends.

The title of this paper, *One Percent on the Burn Chart*, refers to the percentage of the body's surface area represented by the genitals in assessing burns in a trauma unit, and is intended to draw attention to the fact that, for such a small piece of the body, it carries an enormous amount of cultural weight. In this paper Riki and I argued that the theoretical focus on gender or sexual variance in much academic writing obscures Butler's (1990) famous observation that *all* gender identities and performances are enactments of unrealizable, hyperbolic gender. In discussing a workshop that Riki does called "Our Cunts Are Not the Same: Transexual Sexuality and Sex-Change Surgery," we wrote,

> During a practical session in this workshop, s/he [Riki] invites the people present to don latex gloves and examine hir vagina. Despite requesting participants to think of hir genitals as they are, and not as they are in relation to something else, the comment s/he gets most often is: "it's just like mine!" Riki remarks that this comment illustrates, above all, the need these participants have to integrate that "one percent on the burn chart" into a

coherent idea about sexed and gendered bodies. The alternative, which forms the backbone of hir gender activism, is to seek an entirely different ordering of sex, gender, and genitals, for instance,"just your average, straight white guy with a cunt who really digs lezzie chicks like me," as s/he signs hir email. (Valentine and Wilchins 1997:218)

I emailed this to Cindy on Christmas Eve—a year to the day before Vianna-Faye would be murdered. Later that evening I got an email from Cindy, from which I quote the following with her permission:

> To me, my life has been a horror show. It maybe cute for a middle class punk like Riki Anne Wilchins to fuck with a speculum in front of geeks and gawkers. She can always go back to making a wonderful living with her computer talents if she doesn't sell enough tickets. My emotional reaction is that I'm deeply offended if I'm at all considered to be like Riki. Maybe I could have done more to help others but things were never quite as cushy for me. I haven't existed for twenty years. I don't earn very much money. I couldn't tell Foucault from a faucet. But now I am back and this is supposed to be the best that people who are supposed to be like me have to offer? . . . It makes me cry. . . . I feel so disappointed, so angry. . . . I don't know David, but I've been attacked by someone who calls themself a male lesbian. . . . I've been attacked by someone who ultimately says, through public discourse and self-definition, I, Cindy Schuster, am a man. This occurs because of her position in "the community." If she defines the terms of the debate, then I want no part in the arguments.
>
> In that way, Riki's words, Riki's definitions rape me because they undermine the credibility of my take on myself and Wilchins has "power over" me. (Wilchins has obtained a higher level of credibility by virtue of curriculum vitae, past actions. Wilchins words count more than mine because Riki has a standing. Anything I do or say as an unknown individual would be measured against Wilchins ideas plus credibility. Wilchins will be quoted, I will never be.) And if Wilchins can rape me by having power over me, then Wilchins is indeed, very much a man. Assertions can be violent and debilitating in that they always make one size fit all.[10]

Needless to say, a flurry of email correspondence followed this. I assured Cindy that my intention—and, I assured her, Riki's—was not to deny her her rights to identify as a woman, to undergo surgery, and to claim the gender and the life she desired (as she subsequently has). Cindy perceived our analysis as an attack on her desire to live as a woman—and believed that such a transition would be reread, rerepresented, as nothing more than a falsity. In this way Cindy's analysis mirrors those critics of deconstructive methods and theory that see the outcome of deconstruction as a world without meaning or distinction.

Cindy was angered by this essay precisely because she saw it as part of a broader discourse about the invalidity of transexual desires. She sees Riki's interrogation of the meanings attached to particular body parts (that is, genitals) as an implicit statement that she can never become a woman. Riki's point (I believe) is that *all* gender and *all* genitals are equally produced through discourses about gender and sexuality. Yet Cindy points out the complex political and personal effects of such an argument—and how even well-intentioned, ethically and morally carefully considered positions can be read as exercises in violence, even rape.

But most important for my purposes here is that both Riki and I (implicitly) are implicated as rapists and attackers. Our representations, Riki's perceived power in shaping the politics of transgender activism, and my position as an anthropologist are all perceived by Cindy as evidence of violence against her desire to transition, to claim the identity of woman, and to live a full life. As in the previous anecdotes, Cindy's interpretation of our paper posits a direct relationship between ideology and representation on the one hand and violence and power on the other. That this interpretation was made of a paper that, at its heart, aims to critique the ways systems of gender variance are implicated in all kinds of violence is all the more ironic.

The density of these fundamental disagreements among people identified as transgender highlights the central point that I am trying to draw out here: in making claims about how gender variant people experience violence, "violence" is neither an easy nor a self-evident category, and the ability of the anthropologist to counter such violence is deeply complicated by the interpretation of what counts *as* violence.

Narrating the Self to the State

Like Jillian's reaction to my presence in the support group, Cindy's reaction to this article does not exist in a vacuum. A vast range of experiences—the violence done against oneself in the past, being subject to the constraints of a binary gender system, having to jump through the hoops set up by medical professionals, social scientific representations, antithetical political positions—all these have potential to become part of a "tool kit" to make claims *against* those practices, positions, and representations. Violence, then, is not only a fact of life but can also be used to narrate one's past in order to explain the present, to characterize the actions of others who should be your allies as no better than the rapists, muggers, doctors, and hecklers who have made your life a horror. That is, in the constitution of transgender as a category of identity and political action, the experience of violence becomes available as a theory of the self, where it is assumed that one's attempts to claim a nonascribed gender are met, almost perforce, by violent opposition. In this way all harm or potential harm—whatever its origin or manifestation—can be reread through a framework of violence.

I am not suggesting that violence is the sole or even the central feature of all lives encapsulated by the category transgender. It must be noted, after all, that the GenderPAC study cited above shows, conversely, that 40 percent of transgender-identified people report *not* experiencing harassment, violence, or abuse. The point I am making here, rather, is that, whatever the statistics, in contemporary political activism violence has become a central tool kit in drawing the attention of the state to the lives of gender variant people. Even when political activism is focused on other issues, violence is rhetorically and narratively brought into play. For example, in early 2002 the New York Association for Gender Rights Advocacy (NYAGRA), of which I was a board member at the time, successfully led a campaign to introduce and pass a bill in the New York City Council that would include "gender identity and expression" (and therefore transgender-identified people) as a protected category in the city's Human Rights Ordinance. While much of the focus of the campaign was on discrimination in housing, employment, and public accommodations, these concerns were linked to practices of violence both in NYAGRA's own data collection (through our survey, which gathered information on "discrimination and violence") and the narratives of transgender-identified people who gave testimony at the two public hearings preceding the bill's passage. Indeed the context of this bill's passage gave individuals—sex workers, activists, homeless people, professionals—the ability to draw on that tool kit, which brings together transgender experience with the experience of violence, representations with practices, and agencies of the state with individual histories. The point here is not to reduce transgender identity to violence but rather to show how, through all these stories, transgender is institutionally, narratively, and biographically linked to the experience of violence with complicated, often painful, results. To use one of Cindy's phrases, this is the calculus of pain.

THE BAREFOOT ANTHROPOLOGIST

As such, then, the desire to act ethically is not as simple as Scheper-Hughes suggests it might be. While she recognizes the ambiguity of competing claims, what ethical "first principles" could be established that would enable the anthropologist (or anyone else) to act in a responsible, ethically grounded, and morally defensible way? I have argued here that violence, pain, and suffering are neither simple nor precultural facts—they are produced through and drawn into the complex calculus of daily experience, given meaning, talked about, mounted as claims, and deeply felt.

In discussing "violence as discourse" and "discourse as violence," I have attempted to show how the meaning of violence lies as much in narration and representation as it does in the brutal moment of a murder. For violence to be understood *as* violence, a story must be told about it, the horror relived with each telling. Conversely, other discourses—be they gossip, psychiatric diagnoses, books, or ethnographic fieldnotes—can be seen equally as stories to be retold and contested. And as they are told and retold, they enter a social field where the shadow of violence can be felt and new claims of violence can be made. Consequently, the possibilities for ethical and effective action are deeply fraught: it is a complex calculus indeed.

As an anthropologist who continues to work on issues of violence and discrimination in the community in which I conducted fieldwork, I am, moreover, conflicted by the ways in which my own data and conclusions put me in a difficult relationship to the advocacy work I engage in. Here I must return to Vianna-Faye and the Meat Market fem queens who introduced this paper. As I noted, most of the Meat Market girls do not consider themselves transgender—indeed, it is a category that many of them have never heard of. The idea of a transgender community—in which fem queens, cross-dressers, and transexuals are understood as full members by activists and social service providers—has arisen out of the contexts of activism and social service provision that I have described above in order to create a coherent polity as the basis for political recognition and the achievement of social justice. But the collective mode of transgender is only intelligible as a "community" in terms of these activists' conceptions of a shared identity and community based on gender-variance to the exclusion of other intersecting social differences: race, class, age, etc.

Those putative members of a New York transgender community—including the Meat Market sex workers such as Vianna-Faye—who have few links to formalized contexts of community such as community centers or social service agencies, derive identities from organizations of gender and sexuality at odds with academic and activist understandings. In brief, it is often young people of color, with few links to activist and academic institutions, and who identify as "gay" or as "fem queens" rather than as "transgender," who are excluded from the discourses of transgender identity and community. Transgender is formed on an implicitly white, implicitly middle-class model of identity-based claims that conceptually—and therefore effectively—excludes the people most at risk for violence (see Valentine 2002).

As Moran and Sharpe (2002) point out, the implication of the surveys they study is that transgender-identified people experience violence in structurally equivalent ways, without attention to other factors that can produce moments of violence—poverty, ethnicity, racial identification, age—and thereby elide the complexity of the lives represented by them. I would add that the use of transgender in this activism, then, itself produces and magnifies those elisions. Moreover, the fem queens who are driven to sex work to survive—and whose lives and identities are organized in quite different ways from the activists who represent them—are the ones most likely to find their way into the list of murdered "transgender" victims, their lives narrativized and evened out through stories told about them *as* transgender people in the halls of Congress.

Ironically, then, this analysis of transgender enables me as an anthropologist to make my own claim about violence: that the unquestioned inclusion of people like Vianna-Faye or even Brandon Teena (whose personal identification is not known) into the encompassing category of transgender produces a representational colonization of those lives. Given the above analysis, the ways that representation can be seen as violent, I could even write *representational violence*, but, again, the slipperiness of violence—and the implications for my own and my colleagues' advocacy work—makes this hard to write; indeed, I anticipate that this argument itself may be seen as a form of representational violence, another anthropological mischaracterization of transgender experience.

I agree with Scheper-Hughes—and indeed, who wouldn't?—that anthropologists are ethically responsible to the people with whom they are privileged to work. But such an ethical responsibility is undercut by attempting to find simple answers. I would argue, contra Scheper-Hughes, that to be an effective advocate and activist, as well as an anthropologist, one must engage in precisely the kinds of deconstructive methodologies she is dismissive of. That is, in order to understand and act upon local manifestations of violence, all those features of contemporary social analysis she disdains under the umbrella of postmodernism—the focus on multiple, shifting identities; the borderless nature of political discourses and practices; the investigation of what power is—are vital to committed, careful, and effective advocacy. Indeed, for the anthropologist who maintains a long-term commitment to a group with whom she or he works, an engagement with such complexity, rather than a denial of it in the face of brutality and horror, must underpin action if that action is to be effective. Violence, pain, and suffering, like all other arenas of social life, are messy, cut through with ambiguity and contradiction. Violence is not only murder or beatings; it can be identified in a text or a political position. To truly be a barefoot anthropologist requires of one to attend to such complexities and to try and sort them out—in context, sometimes thinking very fast on bare feet—in order to act in a way that you can live with. I would like to think that I would have the courage to stop a murder or deflect a thrown bottle. But "violence" is often less easily identified and more nebulous than such terrible acts.

In response to critiques of anthropological representation, Scheper-Hughes suggests that "'good enough' ethnography" is a compromise, a necessary one to allow anthropologists to act even as they recognize the complexities of their roles and work. I would argue just the opposite: we want excellent, reflexive, and critical ethnography but will probably have to settle for "good enough" ethics. In complex social worlds a final, primary, ethical stance is always complicated by good ethnography—and not just its critique, as Scheper-Hughes implies. In order to be ethical—and to try and act consciously, effectively, and with passion—we need to pay attention to the differences, complexities, and contradictions exposed by critically informed ethnography, our most powerful tool as anthropologists concerned with violence and suffering.

Notes

This paper is dedicated to the memory of Vianna-Faye Williams and to the courage of Cindy who also provided the title of this paper. They stand in for all those who have been murdered and those who survive against all odds. I would like to thank Bambi Schieffelin, Ben Chesluk, Henry Goldschmidt, and Heather Levi, and four anonymous reviewers of the original version of this paper, for their help and suggestions. My thanks also to Maggie Fishman and Melissa Checker for their hard work in helping me reshape this essay for this collection. The research upon which this paper is based was assisted by a fellowship from the Sexuality Research Fellowship Program from the Social Science Research Council with funds provided by the Ford Foundation.

1. This spelling is the choice of many activists in this study. For a discussion of language choices within activist communities see Valentine 2000.

2. *Intersex* is the term increasingly favored by those individuals previously labeled *hermaphrodites* in the medical literature.

3. I use the construction "transgender-identified" to mark the ways in which people both take on the category transgender as something meaningful about themselves; as well as the sense of being identified by others to fall into a category. This is a useful way of dealing with the conceptual mismatches I will be talking about in this essay, but it also speaks to the ways that self-identity and identification by others of the self are not separate but complexly related phenomena.

4. Wilchins prefers this nongendered pronoun, which is not uncommon among gender variant or transgender-identified activists and scholars. Likewise, Wilchins prefers *s/he* to *she* or *he* in both writing and speech.

5. The bill was reintroduced in March 2001 as the Local Law Enforcement Enhancement Act.

6. I assume that Jillian was referring to the (minimal) funding that the GIP receives from various state and local health agencies, primarily from HIV/AIDS funds.

7. For activists even the process by which transexual identities originated as medical criteria can be perceived as a violent act: "Transsexualism is rather like a country that has been colonized . . . and the flag is the caduceus, the medical staff. Physicians claimed the land of transsexualism about forty years ago, and have owned it ever since. . . . Transsexual is a slave name, and we conspired in it (Denny 1999).

8. Some contemporary ethnography of groups identified as transgender or as gender variant has shown much more sensitivity to these issues; see Johnson 1997; Klein 1998; and Kulick 1998.

9. The coauthorship of this paper was itself intended to respond to Wilchins's critiques in the quotation cited earlier.

10. I have made editorial changes to spelling and punctuation. The ellipses in square brackets are mine; those in the text are Cindy's.

WORKS CITED

American Psychiatric Association (APA). 1994. *Diagnostic and Statistical Manual of Mental Disorders.* 4th ed Washington, D.C.: American Psychiatric Association.

Axel, Brian Keith. 2001. *The Nation's Tortured Body: Violence, Representation, and the Formation of a Sikh "Diaspora."* Durham: Duke University Press.

Butler, Judith. 1990. *Gender Trouble: Feminism and the Subversion of Identity.* New York: Routledge.

Cartwright, Donna. 2001. "Whither GPAC? Reflections at My Time of Resignation." *Transgender Tapestry* 93:56–58.

Daniel, E. Valentine. 1996. *Charred Lullabies: Chapters in an Anthropology of Violence.* Princeton: Princeton University Press.

Denny, Dallas. 1999. "Beyond Our Slave Names." Keynote address delivered at the Southern Comfort Conference, Atlanta, Georgia, September 24, 1999.

Feldman, Allen. 1991. *Formations of Violence: The Narrative of the Body and Political Terror in Northern Ireland.* Chicago: University of Chicago Press.

Fraser, Nancy. 1997. *Justice Interruptus: Critical Reflections on the "Postsocialist" Condition.* New York: Routledge.

Gender Public Advocacy Coalition (GenderPAC). 1997. *The First National Study on Transviolence.* Waltham, Mass.: GenderPAC.

Helms, Monica. 2000. "The Death of GenderPAC: A Personal Opinion." *http://www.ntac.org/news/01/01/02gpac.html* (accessed August 11, 2002).

Jeffreys, Sheila. 1996. "Heterosexuality and the Desire for Gender." In Diane Richardson, ed., *Theorizing Heterosexuality: Telling It Straight*, pp.75–90. Oxford: Oxford University Press.

Johnson, Mark. 1997. *Beauty and Power: Transgendering and Cultural Transformation in the Southern Philippines.* New York: Berg.

Klein, Charles H.. 1998. "From One 'Battle' to Another: The Making of a *Travesti* Political Movement in a Brazilian City. *Sexualities* 1(3): 327–342.

Kleinman, Arthur and Joan Kleinman. 1996. "The Appeal of Experience; the Dismay of Images: Cultural Appropriations of Suffering in Our Times. In Arthur Kleinman, Veena Das, and Margaret Lock, eds., *Social Suffering*, pp. 1–23. Berkeley: University of California Press.

Knox, Sara Louise. 1998. *Murder: A Tale of Modern American Life.* Durham: Duke University Press.

Krohn-Hansen, Christian. 1994. "The Anthropology of Violent Interaction." *Journal of Anthropological Research* 50:367–381.

Kulick, Don. 1998. *Travesti: Sex, Gender, and Culture Among Brazilian Transgendered Prostitutes.* Chicago: University of Chicago Press.

McNeill, S. 1982. "Transsexualism . . . Can Men Turn Men Into Women?" In S. Friedman and E. Sarah, eds., *On the Problem of Men*, pp. 83–87. London: Women's.

Moran, Leslie J. and Andrew N. Sharpe. 2002. "Policing the Transgender/Violence Relation. *Current Issues in Criminal Justice* 13(3): 269–285.

106th Congress of the United States of America. 1999. "The Hate Crimes Prevention Act of 1999." Washington: Government Printing Office.

Orobio de Castro, Ines. 1993. *Made to Order: Sex/Gender in a Transsexual Perspective.* Amsterdam: Het Spinhuis.

Raymond, Janice. 1994[1979]. *The Transsexual Empire: The Making of the She-Male.* Boston: Beacon.

Riches, David. 1986. "The Phenomenon of Violence." In David Riches, ed., *The Anthropology of Violence*, pp. 1–27. New York: Blackwell.

Scheper-Hughes, Nancy. 1995. "The Primacy of the Ethical: Propositions for a Militant Anthropology." *Current Anthropology* 36(3):409-440.

Valentine, David. 2002. "We're Not About Gender": The Uses of "Transgender." In Ellen Lewin and William Leap, eds., *Out in Theory: The Emergence of Lesbian and Gay Anthropology,* pp. 222-245. Urbana: University of Illinois Press.

—— 2000. "I Know What I Am": The Category "Transgender" in the Construction of Contemporary U.S. American Conceptions of Gender and Sexuality. Ph.D. diss., Department of Anthropology, New York University.

Valentine, David and Riki Anne Wilchins. 1997. "One Percent on the Burn Chart: Gender, Genitals, and Hermaphrodites with Attitude." *Social Text* 52/53:215-222.

Wilchins, Riki Anne. 1997. *Read My Lips: Sexual Subversion and the End of Gender.* Ithaca: Firebrand.

Woodhouse, Annie. 1989. *Fantastic Women: Sex, Gender, and Transvestitism.* New Brunswick, N.J.: Rutgers University Press.

5

We Shall Overcome?
Changing Politics and Changing Sexuality
in the Ex-Gay Movement

TANYA ERZEN

In the summer of 1998 full-page advertisements appeared simultaneously in the *New York Times,* the *Washington Post,* and other national newspapers.[1] One version featured a woman named Anne Paulk,[2] her gleaming diamond wedding ring clearly visible. Underneath her picture the caption read, "wife, mother, former lesbian." The ad was conceived and paid for by a coalition of Christian Right groups coordinated by the Center for Reclaiming America (CRA) as part of a larger media offensive against gay rights on the state and national levels.[3] Anne's testimony, as well as pictures of other men and women who had changed, was designed to illustrate that homosexuality is a choice and that people can become married heterosexuals through a combination of Christian faith, therapeutic principles, and community living.

John Paulk, Anne's husband, was also visible in these ads. Formerly a drag queen named Candi, John met Anne in the early 1990s at New Hope Ministry, a residential ex-gay program in California where both spent several years trying to change from homosexual to heterosexual. John describes his transition from Candi to a married man with a wife and children as a physical and spiritual process: "Tons of makeup, jewelry and a blonde wig couldn't hide the pain. There was a beautiful woman staring back at me in the mirror. But that woman was me—John Paulk, a man."[4] In a pamphlet entitled "Time to Take off the Tiara" he continues:

> I opened my up my closet and I looked at all the dresses, wigs, high heels,
> makeup and jewelry I had accumulated over the past three years. It suddenly

hit me. Somehow I knew I didn't need Candi anymore. I realized that "crown of jewels" I wore left me feeling empty and alone. So I said good-bye to her, put everything in a cardboard box and threw it in a dumpster.

John Paulk is now a homosexuality and gender specialist working in the public policy division at Focus on the Family and a member of the board of directors for Exodus, the umbrella organization for the Christian ex-gay movement.[5] He and Anne have two children, and another on the way. With the help of Mike Haley, another New Hope Ministry gradu-ate, Paulk organizes "Love Won Out" conferences throughout the coun-try to reach conservative Christians with the message that homosexuals can change. Although the ad campaign couched the stories of John and Anne in the terms *Love Won Out* or *Truth in Love,* their message was clear: being gay is not a valid social or cultural identity and gay people do not merit political or civil rights.

Sensational and widely publicized as they are, the Paulks' stories are not necessarily unique. Hundreds of men and women have passed through ex-gay ministries since 1973 with the aim of curing their homo-sexuality. Many come to resolve a longstanding conflict between their Christian beliefs that the Bible condemns homosexuality and the reality of being attracted to members of the same sex. Some, like Anne and John Paulk, have become public activists, collaborating with organizations of the Christian Right to promote an antigay message that people can and should change their sexuality. Others occupy a more ambiguous position: trying to change and finding that it is a long and arduous process. Even more accept that they are gay and leave.

Since the early 1990s organizations of the Christian Right have taken their cue from people like Anne and John Paulk and utilized their stories of sexual conversion to move from a politics of condemnation of homosexu-ality to one of compassion. Christian Right activism now directly relies upon the personal testimonies of ex-gays. Antigay legislation is no longer supported simply by antigay rhetoric but through the message that there is hope for healing. Based on the grassroots struggles of ex-gay men and wo-men to change their sexuality, the Christian Right promotes wider antigay activism cloaked in the rhetoric of choice, change, and compassion.

At the same time, public activists like John and Anne Paulk link anti-gay activism and Christian evangelism through their testimonies of per-sonal transformation. The literal meaning of evangelism is to spread the good news that Jesus can save an individual. Through spoken and written testimonies ex-gay men and women communicate the ways that God has come into their lives and that they have transformed their identities through a personal relationship with him. By giving witness to the changes in their lives, they try to convince others that their only option is to disavow their sin of homosexuality. In the case of the Paulks their message moves beyond simple religious evangelism to the idea that ex-gays have an obligation to promote the message that being gay is a choice. Their activism draws on their personal testimonies to lobby against gay-positive school curricula, gay marriage, gay adoption, and partner benefits.

However, the experiences of other ex-gay men and women don't necessarily translate into public activism like that of the Paulks. Men and women in ex-gay ministries like New Hope believe that the idea of change is a much more fraught, fluid, and uncertain process. They readily concede that change is a process that involves identity, behavior, and desires, and they believe that their own conversions are primarily religious. Yet at the same time that they are attempting to transform their own sexuality they are also striving to remain separate from the antigay activism of the Christian Right organizations that sponsored the ad campaign. They are activists who believe they have a right to change their sexuality and participate in ex-gay ministries, but they also feel their stories should not be appropriated by larger organizations to promulgate a message they feel is misleading and false. Although these men and women want to show that change is possible, they also do not want to deprive gay men and lesbians of their rights in the process.

In this essay I first look at how the ex-gay movement emerged through the creation of New Hope Ministry in the 1970s and the ways that they brought together sexual evangelism and political activism. I then explore how some ex-gay men and women have become explicit public activists working directly with Christian Right organizations. Finally I examine how men and women at New Hope ministry, where I spent eighteen months doing fieldwork, often resist the antigay politics of the Christian Right.

NEW HOPE?

The origin of the ex-gay movement is a peculiarly American tale of personal reinvention through religious belief. In 1973 God spoke to Frank Worthen. Frank, a forty-four-year-old gay man and soon to be founding father of the ex-gay movement, had spent twenty-five years living in California's Bay Area as a businessman, participating peripherally in early gay liberation struggles. According to Frank's recollections, after locking his office door and heading for the back entrance of his import store, he planned to visit a new gay bath in San Francisco. "I was leaving my office and the Lord just spoke to me and said, 'I want you back.' I generally don't share that with a lot of people because they don't understand that God can talk to you. It scared the life out of me." With the aid of a young Christian employee, Frank rushed to a nearby chapel where he began confessing and praying the sinner's prayer. He sensed a growing release from what he characterizes as twenty-five years of rebellion during which he had forsaken the conservative Disciples of Christ Church of his childhood.

By attending an Assemblies of God church several times a week, Frank began to rededicate himself to God and minister to other gay men looking for a "way out" of homosexuality. Several weeks later the church challenged him to "reach back to his own people." He placed an ad in a local newspaper and received a deluge of responses from men and women who wanted to leave the homosexual "lifestyle." With the aid of the church, Frank began holding weekly support groups that would eventually evolve into New Hope ministry. A few years later he realized another ex-gay ministry existed in southern California, and he flew down immediately to meet them. The men and women he encountered would become the basis for a national movement that focused on how men and women could become heterosexuals after years of living with same-sex desires. The result of their meeting was the creation of Exodus International, an umbrella organization for the Christian ex-gay movement, in 1976 at Melodyland Christian Center in Anaheim, California with sixty other men and five women.

Today the Christian ex-gay movement, under the umbrella of Exodus, sponsors hundreds of ministries in the U.S. and abroad where men and women attend therapy sessions, Bible studies, twelve-step-style meetings, and regular church services as part of their "journey out of homosexuality."[6] The wider ex-gay movement consists of a network of organizations with overlapping but not necessarily coordinated agendas including Jewish and Catholic groups, psychoanalytic organizations, and independent therapists throughout the world. It has also moved beyond just Christian ministries and now includes Homosexuals Anonymous, Sexaholics Anonymous, Exodus and its legion of Evangelical-based ex-gay ministries, Parents and Friends of Ex-Gays (PFOX), and the National Association for the Research and Treatment of Sexuality (NARTH).

New Hope, the oldest ex-gay ministry in existence, is still directed by Frank, and is one of three residential ex-gay programs in the United States.[7] Located in a Marin County suburb ten miles north of San Francisco, the ministry sits off a suburban main road that is lined with alcohol and drug treatment centers. There are no signs outside the ministry, a low-slung, stucco building almost completely obscured by flowering vines. Their small cul-de-sac ends at discarded railroad tracks. Across the street is an apartment complex where twenty men live during their year in the residential program. From 1999–2001 there were fifteen men in the residential program. They were predominantly white, from working-class and middle-class families, raised primarily in rural areas or small towns of the United States. A similar program for women flourished in the 1980s but was eliminated because of a lack of space and leadership. Instead New Hope currently sponsors Grace, a weekly ex-gay women's support group led by a woman who had spent years at New Hope and eventually married a man from the ex-gay affiliated church called Open Door. Each year there were a few men from Europe, Canada, and other countries who also worked in the New Hope offices across the cul-de-sac from the apartments. Drew, a cheerful South African man in his late thirties, had completed the program three years earlier and was now the New Hope office manager. After people in his small town discovered that he had been having sex with men, he decided an ex-gay ministry was his only option. The other office worker, Curtis, a twenty-one year old former hairdresser from Germany, worked in the New Hope office doing odd jobs like answering the phone. While filing or copying, he moved around the office tethered to a five-foot Walkman cable, listening to Christian technomusic.

With the help of house leaders who have successfully completed the program and a board of directors, Frank oversees New Hope, teaches classes to the men on subjects from theology to masculinity to dating, and serves as a pastor in Open Door church. His wife of eighteen years, Anita, spearheads a ministry for parents of gay children from the same office. She also operates from firsthand experience. Her son is gay and lives with his partner in the same apartment complex as the men at New Hope.

Both she and Frank maintain a close relationship with him despite the fact that he disagrees with the premise of their ministry. After two decades of marriage, Anita and Frank are paragons for other Christian men and women who pray that they will also get married.

HE LOVES ME, HE LOVES ME NOT

"Who do you serve?" was the first question Anita asked me when I came to inquire about doing fieldwork at New Hope. We were sitting in the prayer room, a quiet retreat from the rest of the offices where a placard on the wall read, *Some Facts from God to You*:

1. You need to be saved
2. You can't save yourself
3. Jesus has already provided for your salvation
4. Jesus will enable you to overcome temptation
5. Your part: Repent

After a few moments Anita declared that "we are in a battle," between God and Satan. Never having been faced with that particular choice, I told her that my intention was to understand the worldviews of men and women attempting to change their sexuality. Not yet convinced, Anita explained that the leadership team would convene to decide about my being a researcher at New Hope. After a few weeks of group prayer, Anita let me know that they had determined it was part of God's wider plan for me to come to New Hope. From my own patchwork religious background of lapsed Catholicism and brief childhood forays into New England Congregationalism, Anita read me as a Christian, albeit an unsaved one.

The ministry understood my presence as part of a divine scheme, and they were convinced that God was directing the course of my research. Implicit within their acceptance was the belief that I, too, would be ripe for conversion to a Christian life. Although everyone knew I had come to the ministry to conduct research, many hoped that living so closely among them would encourage me to accept Jesus as my personal savior. Within my first few months at the ministry there were rumors, untrue but well meaning, that Anita had inspired me to pray the sinners prayer. As I left her office the first day, I noticed a bumper sticker on her car: a picture of Jesus over the words "He Loves Me" and a picture of the Devil over "He Loves Me Not." When I knew her well enough to remark on it, she replied, "Well, it does keep my son from borrowing my car."

I had decided to study the ex-gay movement after working as a researcher at a progressive policy institute that monitored the religious right. Many of the exposés I read about ex-gays portrayed them as right-wing bigots. As a political activist committed to the very things the Christian Right seemed to oppose, I felt that leftist scholars and activists too often bandied about the terms *Christian Right* or *Religious Right* without being specific about who or what we were talking about. I hoped that my research would elucidate why certain conservative Christian groups fixated on homosexuality as the most glaring sign of moral decay in the U.S., and, more important, what the social, religious, and economic forces were that compelled ex-gays to attempt to change their sexuality. If we were going to oppose the Christian Right as a political force, it seemed imperative to understand its base of support.

I was utterly unprepared to find that most ex-gays didn't see themselves as part of a wider Christian Right organization, and that religion, not politics, was the driving force in their lives. At the first church services I attended, men and women stood and swayed with eyes closed, waved their arms, called out "Jesus" and "Lord," and prayed by laying their hands on each other's heads and shoulders while a guitarist, keyboardist, drummer, and several singers played what sounded like soft Christian rock music. Nervous and embarrassed, I made myself as inconspicuous as possible in the back of the room, certain that my presence would be viewed with suspicion or even hostility. Instead, I found that their openness and friendliness were disarming, and as I spoke with people it became clear that religious identity and political affiliation are always more complex than left or right, straight or gay, or Christian and non-Christian.

I began to spend up to four days a week in the offices with Frank, Anita, Drew, and Curtis. At night we would eat dinners with the entire house, and I often accompanied them to church, classes, and outings. Around the time I met Anita, the ministry had been praying for someone to help them with their computers. In what I considered a fortuitous confluence of events, but one that Anita considered "God's work," I had done freelance-Web programming throughout graduate school and discovered that helping with their computers would provide a reason to spend time at the ministry. Performing concrete tasks eased my entry into the world of New Hope, and it led to my first meetings with Brian, an ex-gay computer engineer who had designed the Web site, and others who had completed the program several years earlier. My research received a huge boost when Drew mailed a letter I drafted to sixty ex-gay people in the immediate vicinity asking to complete interviews, and it was through these early contacts that I met others. Drew's affability meant that he was in regular touch with dozens of people affiliated with the ministry including men and women who had married, former program participants, and even men and women who had left the program to forge lives as gay men and women. Despite my introduction into this network, it was obvious that the bonds of indebtedness would only grow more complicated as time went on, and they understood, too, that the more obligated I felt toward them the more difficult it would be to criticize the ministry.

RELIGIOUS AND SEXUAL TRANSFORMATION

All the men at New Hope grew up in conservative Christian families and fervently believe that not only is homosexuality a sin according to the Bible but that life as a gay person means being separated from God. Brian had completed the program but still lived in a Christian community house nearby, and he explained how his relationship with his boyfriend interfered with his relationship with God. "So I had a very fulfilling completely faithful, monogamous relationship with Ted. I really loved him, everything about it was great, but I felt that I had sacrificed my relationship with God in order to have it. And it wasn't just something that was in my head. It was in my soul." Like Brian, the men in the program are Christians from Nazarene, Presbyterian, Catholic, Assemblies of God, Baptist, Pentecostal, and Lutheran backgrounds. Although there were a few men from mainstream Protestant denominations and even one or two Catholics, at some point most had become involved in a more charismatic form of Christianity and undergone a born-again experience.

As self-defined Christians, all of them maintain a personal relationship with Jesus and believe in the infallibility and literal truth of Scripture. With few exceptions the nondenominational, informal, experiential religious style of New Hope was familiar to them from childhood. This theological system provides the foundation for their belief that through Christian faith, religious conversion, and a daily accountable relationship with each other and God they could heal their homosexuality. Desires or attractions might linger for years, but they would emerge with new religious identities that helped them to control what they considered the sexually addictive aspects of their lives.

For most of these men New Hope is their last hope. They arrive with tales of sexual addiction, anonymous sex in lavatories, rest stops, and parks, stories of loneliness, and suicide attempts. They come to the ministry because so many conservative Christians and churches remain relentlessly homophobic and hostile to them. Over and over they express a massive sense of relief at finding a place where secrecy, alienation, and self-hatred are unnecessary. Drew explains,

> I didn't feel accepted by the straight world and I was mostly in religious circles and definitely didn't feel accepted there. It was this nonbelonging and the gay world was so anti-Christian, I didn't feel like I belonged there either. There was no little niche where I belonged.

For many this is the first time they've been able to overcome sex addictions, alcohol and drug problems, to keep a job, to maintain accountability and build stability in their lives. They speak of their elation at discovering a community of like-minded ex-gay people who share their experiences and religious beliefs. It is as if they are coming out of the closet with a twist.

Their ideas about change are intimately linked to their religious beliefs. Healing, as it is conceptualized at New Hope, occurs through a conversion process that links sexual and religious identity. Men and women are born-again as sexually and religiously reconstituted people. They emerge as new creations in Christ and take on the identity "ex-gay." For ex-gays Christianity restructures their concept of personhood. Success is predicated on submission to God in all things, and they believe that a personal relationship with Jesus will transform them. New Hope's house leader, Hank, spent twelve years with a male partner before the disintegration of the relationship led him to New Hope. The lover joined New Hope several years later after losing his job, their home, and selling sex for drugs. Hank explains that change is not an overnight process and that many men will never marry or necessarily experience attractions for women. "I tell the guys in this house, If you're coming into the program to be changed from homosexual to heterosexual, you're probably going to be disappointed. If you're coming here to develop a relationship with Jesus Christ, that's what will happen and out of it change happens."

TESTIFYING AS ACTIVISM

When John Paulk testified about "taking off his tiara," he was enacting a common story for most men and women involved in ex-gay ministries. The testimony is the form in which every ex-gay tells the story of their lives before and after becoming a Christian. It is structured as a redemption narrative, and is the mode in which ex-gays describe their "journey out of homosexuality." The testimonies work because they clearly delineate between a previous life of sin and debauchery and a new life in Christ, and the more sordid the previous life the better. As narratives they begin with a dramatic story about past lives of addiction and sin: spending their last dollar on phone sex lines or desperately cruising highway rest stops in search of sex. These testimonies form a technology of personhood, a narrative that reshapes the messiness of life into a coherent story that can be used for sexual evangelization.

The published testimony of Mike Haley, a former New Hope graduate who works alongside John Paulk at Focus on the Family, contains these elements in abundance. "From Prostitute to Pastor: Mike Haley was once addicted to homosexuality. Today he is a fulfilled husband and father. How does he explain the change?" the headline reads. His testimony contains a brief description of his life as a gay prostitute, his sexual relationships with other men, and his experience of being saved by another ex-gay and eventually married to a woman. The ex-gay movement particularly highlights testimonies from those people who were politically active as gay men and women before becoming Christians. One of their most publicized testimonies is that of Amy Tracy, a former communications director for the National Organization of Women (NOW) who organized clinic defense and was a prominent gay activist. In 2000 she spoke as part of New Hope's annual "Pro-Life Night" at a local church. She testified about becoming born again, leaving her lesbian partner, and changing her political views. Amy also now works for Focus on the Family.

As born-again or saved Christians, ex-gays at New Hope become accustomed to continually testifying about the most private, personal, and even harrowing aspects of their lives in public group settings. New Hope expects ex-gays to talk about themselves with others in the program, in published materials, and in front of churches. When a person comes to New Hope, they spend the first week sharing their life story with the rest of the men in the program at a retreat in northern California called the

Lord's Land. Eventually, they learn to hone this story into a dramatic and instructive narrative the ministry will use for publicity materials. After years of being affiliated with an ex-gay ministry, individuals' stories are published as pamphlets or sent to churches throughout the U.S. as tapes. Even the Lord's Land has its own story of transformation. Formerly a hippie commune, it is now a Christian retreat center for the ex-gay movement. Sharing and group process are the centerpiece of the live-in program because Frank and ex-gay leaders believe that public confession is in itself a therapeutic process. Although the ex-gay movement uses surveys as scientific legitimation that change occurs, their main proof is anecdotal.[8] Testimony is the narrative vehicle for a religious and sexual transformation. It is also a form of activism that is necessary to self-healing and to the wider dissemination of the ex-gay movement. Everything becomes a story that can be used to illustrate how Christianity transforms people, and ex-gay men and women become skilled at shaping their lives into this narrative even if their actual experiences overflow the testimonial sin and redemption structure. In a proselytizing community, expressions of public intimacy are the norm. This made interviewing less awkward because of people's willingness to share anything about themselves, but it also made it tricky as I began to witness the ways that the testimonial narrative elided the contradictions in interviewees' lives.

The impetus behind the proliferation of testimonies is not just about saving souls. The goal of the ex-gay movement has always been to communicate these stories to the church and the rest of the world. From the beginning the ex-gay movement has concerned itself not just with rescuing individuals from homosexuality but presenting this message to the church and the wider society. Their mission statement from 1976 reads,

> EXODUS is an international Christian effort to reach homosexuals and lesbians. EXODUS upholds God's standard of righteousness and holiness, which declares that homosexuality is sin and affirms HIS love and redemptive power to recreate the individual. It is the goal of EXODUS International to communicate this message to the Church, to the gay community, and to society.

Since the new president of Exodus took over in 2001, the organization has rearticulated its message to stress that it is "called to encourage, strengthen, unify and equip Christians to minister the transforming power of the Lord Jesus Christ to those affected by homosexuality." The ex-gay movement is invested in promoting their message of change even though many men and women never eradicate same-sex feelings and de-sires and many others leave the ministry to live as gay men and women. In actuality, this message is often quite at odds with the individual expe-riences within the ministry.

ANTIGAY ACTIVISM AND HOPE FOR HEALING

"Hope for healing," has become the mantra of organizations like the CRA ad coalition and Focus on the Family. In promotional ma-terials and church seminars these organizations now regularly feature sto-ries of ex-gay transformation. Rather than overtly condemning gay peo-ple, their new official stance is that Christians must encourage healing and change. Instead of militant, unassimilable homosexuals, conservative Christian organizations speak of compassion for those men and women who can be brought to the Lord and transformed. This idea has become so acceptable to the Christian Right's antigay agenda that even Jerry Fal-well has joined the bandwagon. On "National Coming Out of Homo-sexuality Day," October 11, 1999, Falwell reversed his stance of a dozen years that homosexuality is the scourge of Christianity and told the ex-gays and gay protesters in an unusually conciliatory manner, "Homosex-uality is not more sinful than heterosexual promiscuity."[9] Despite this softer side, the cultural and legislative agendas of Focus and other organ-izations have not altered significantly. The goal is to oppose any local, state, or national attempts to secure civil rights for gay people in the realm of marriage, gay-positive school curriculum, partner benefits, or adoption policy.

People like John Paulk, Mike Haley, and Amy Tracy, who have cho-sen to make their ex-gay identities the public vehicle of their activism, collaborate with James Dobson and the vast financial and media resources of Focus to speak of compassion in the service of antigay activism. In his monthly newsletter to Focus members, James Dobson invokes this anti-gay message combined with the Christian ideas of love and acceptance, "We believe every human being is precious to God and is entitled to ac-ceptance and respect. There is great suffering among homosexuals, and it is our desire to show compassion and concern for those caught in the lifestyle." John Paulk tells readers,

> As the church, we must continue to speak out boldly against the radical ho-
> mosexual agenda while we minister to those who are trapped in the
> lifestyle. Some Christians see an inherent conflict between exhibiting com-
> passion and speaking the truth in love. But it is compassionate to warn
> about the dangers of homosexuality.

Antigay policy decisions are cannily repackaged in the rhetoric of healing, and the stories of people in ministries like New Hope provide the evidence.

Anita's admonition to me that "we are in a battle" is born out through the activism of not only Focus on the Family but ex-gay leaders like Mike Haley and John Paulk as well. Often the site of contestation is the family itself, with homosexuality posited as its foremost enemy. The notion of "family values" has become inextricably linked to antigay politics because of conservative Christian fears about the actual social reproduction of Christian values. The idea that the nuclear family is theologically the only way to lead a Godly life has gained prominence at a historic moment in which the economic rationale for families no longer exists. Groups like Focus now endorse and exaggerate the idea that homosexuality represents a threat to the family in order to galvanize its constituencies into action. Every month Dobson sends out a newsletter, "Family News from Dr. James Dobson," to over two million subscribers. In a folksy tone he comments upon recent political events.

> Homosexuality has become the cause du jour of those who seek to under-
> mine the family. Though homosexuals comprise only 2–3 percent of the
> population, they exert incredible influence over the political arena. Abet-
> ted by a pro-homosexual news and entertainment media, the radical gay
> activists' assault on morality has reached a fever pitch.

Listeners to this radio program have learned to trust his advice on child rearing and other matters, and so when he writes that homosexuality threatens the family they take note. As Ann Burlein writes, this soft-sell approach functions by building an imagined or affiliative community of Christians.[10] Into his radio broadcasts, family magazines, and advice columns Dobson then inserts overt calls to participate in political cam-paigns and information about Christian candidates to listeners and read-ers who are already familiar with him. In one instance, he tells readers that homosexuals achieved "a form of gay marriage in Vermont and are pushing for recognition of same-sex unions in the other 49 states." In the past his newsletters have also endorsed ballot initiatives like Amendment 2 in Colorado.[11]

Ex-gay activists like John Paulk only reinforce the message to Christian supporters that the "gay community" or "radical gay activists" are gaining in numbers, force, and strength. He positions Christians as an embattled minority needing to fight back against a fast encroaching but amorphous gay movement. In a talk at the Exodus annual conference in 2000, "Into His Marvelous Light," Paulk capitalized on this fear of gay takeover. Describing a publication called "Overhauling Straight America," he told all of us in the audience that in this publication gay activists outline how they will gain control of the press and movies. He warns that gays are now visible on television as psychologically sound characters. "What," he asks the five hundred or more ex-gays at the conference, "has Exodus been doing in the nineties to counteract all this?" Paulk exhorts ex-gays to "engage our culture and communicate with conservative Christians. People need to become visible in a culture where they believe we can't change." Although ex-gays like John Paulk continually insist that they aren't a political organization, increasingly they are exhorting ex-gays to take action against the gay forces they believe are marshaled against them.

No one is more interested in encouraging the activism of ex-gays than Joe Dallas, an ex-gay therapist who has written several books.[12] Formerly a member of the pro-gay Metropolitan Community Churches, Dallas believes that the ex-gay movement has to take a stand on social issues. To him the ex-gays have a "prophetic mandate to provide healing and to impact the culture and articulate a standard and uphold that standard." To achieve this end, ex-gay Christians may choose political involvement in issues that include the redefinition of marriage, adoption, public education; freedom of speech such as hate crimes legislation, private associations like the Boy Scouts; and equality and fairness such as antidiscrimination and the issue of gays in the military. Dallas quotes Martin Luther King Jr., "The church must be reminded that it is neither the master of the state nor is it the servant of the state. Rather it is the conscience of the state." To this end he tells listeners that the state requires the operative influence of the church. "The voice of the church is not a law, but in some cases we will fight to make it so." Dallas, despite his proclamations, occupies a more complicated position than that of Haley or Paulk. After participating in a march against antigay violence, he tells the Christians around him that it is important to have regard for the people you oppose. He openly criticized his ex-gay friends who gloated after the Boy Scout's decision to ban homosexuals from its organization. Regardless of gestures to the contrary, Dallas's activism still means working on legislation that will directly impact the quality of life for gay people and ultimately make it more difficult for them to live in the world.

Another ex-gay strategy to spur Christians into action is to portray homosexuality as child endangerment. An age-old tactic, this has been particularly effective in galvanizing Christians to oppose sex education and lobby for the elimination of gay-positive curriculum and books from schools. Mike Haley has spearheaded this campaign in his new position at Focus. At a workshop called "Why Is What They're Teaching So Dangerous?" he highlights pro-gay books like "Heather has Two Mommies" as a threat to children. "To those of you who are parents, I say, 'Be aware!' Your children are being inundated with inaccurate—but enticing—messages about homosexuality. Television, movies, music and an increasing number of public schools constantly reinforce the idea that 'gay is good.'"

Haley is particularly concerned about the "It's Elementary" curriculum, which includes books for children that portray homosexuality as normal, and California's Project 10.[13] He believes these programs give kids the idea that being gay is normal. In addition, Haley rails against school curriculums that undermine parent's moral authority and their ability to decide what a child can and should learn about homosexuality. Hyperbole and overstatement are the basis of both Haley's and Paulk's arguments. During his talk Haley showed a picture of the singer George Michael, who was arrested by police in 1998 for engaging in "lewd behavior" in a public restroom. When he told us, "Our country is fighting to make sex in public restrooms legal," members of the audience gasped. His strategy is effective. People in the audience around me furiously noted the names of the book titles he mentioned in order to demand that their local libraries not stock them.

Ex-gay leaders frame their activism as a necessity against a growing gay movement that has provoked and pushed them until it is their only option to fight back. Being on the defensive enables them to disclaim responsibility for a long history of active political lobbying against gay rights by Christian groups, in which gay rights were defined as either the right to engage in perversion or a demand for special rights. The ex-gay movement

disengages itself from this past by arguing that their activism is only a reaction to a supposedly militant gay community. For example, Janet Folger
argues that gay people are "not advocating tolerance. If that were the case,
they'd live and let live. Instead, they do things like demand that the Boy
Scouts change their position by accepting homosexuality. It's basically
forcing people to embrace their behavior."[14]

Organizations like Focus on the Family and the ex-gay movement reflect the new multiculturalism of the Christian right in which racial differences are acceptable in a way sexual differences are not. Racial pluralism can exist within the framework of Christianity, but homosexuality is
still a difference that is unacceptable. This form of bland multiculturalism
does not extend to rectifying structural and economic inequalities but is
only concerned with Christianizing all people, regardless of race. Frank
and others are intent on disproving the validity of a gay identity and are
quick to pit gay people against what they feel are other legitimate minority groups:

> As homosexuals saw other minorities gain social significance, they were
> tempted with the idea of getting on the minority band-wagon. . . . In the
> last thirty years they have brain-washed almost the entire population of the
> United States into believing that their condition is unchangeable and is
> equally acceptable as heterosexuality.

Joe Dallas, Frank, and others strongly believe that the gay movement celebrates diversity but wants to silence the ex-gay message of the potential
for change. Their argument against the gay rights movement is that if gay
people can be out, then ex-gays should be able to publicly promote their
message as well. While Dallas and other ex-gays refute the validity of a
gay identity or community by citing psychiatric literature that shows homosexuality is only a temporary condition or an arrest in normal development that can be cured, they also lay claim to the same status as an
identity group to argue for their own rights.

Ex-gays leaders like John Paulk and Mike Haley frame their own politics by linking their activism to a lineage of struggle beginning with the
civil rights movement. To them being ex-gay is a matter of social justice.
They appropriate the language of the civil rights movement to argue for
minority status for Christians and ex-gays. That civil rights approach was
most apparent in a speech to over one thousand people given by Micheal
Lumberger, the head of Dunamis Ministries in Pittsburgh and one of the

only African American leaders in the ex-gay movement. In a voice verging on tears, he invoked the history of slavery, saying that Martin Luther King Jr. referred to African Americans as a chosen people, and talked about a holy nation. "African-Americans found freedom because they refused to give up." He declared that gay activists stole the song "We Shall Overcome" from the civil rights movement. Instead he argued that it should be the anthem for ex-gays struggling to overcome homosexuality and committing to a movement to disseminate this message to the world at large. "In the atmosphere of the Exodus conference it is a prophecy." Lumberger and others believe the ex-gay struggle is comparable to the civil rights struggle, and they must fight against gay rights activists and others who believe the ex-gay movement is misguided and dangerous.

As Lumberger spoke, he kept repeating, "We shall overcome," and then he began crying and uttering the words to the song, "Deep in my heart, I do believe, we shall overcome some day. He didn't bring you this far to leave you." Within minutes Lumberger had the entire auditorium, close to seven hundred people, singing "We Shall Overcome." Ex-gays and others clasped hands across the aisles, swayed and sang with heartfelt emotion. While other movements have appropriated the message of civil rights for disparate causes, the sincerity of those in the audience was astounding. They truly believed that they were struggling to overcome a great obstacle, an evil comparable to Jim Crow laws and segregation, and that their message would eventually be supported by the culture at large.

Testifying Against the Christian Right

Not all ex-gay leaders and men and women who join ministries would support James Dobson or John Paulk's proclamations. Although they share conservative Christian theological beliefs about abortion, marriage, and homosexuality with Christian Right organizations, their life experiences have made them wary of the politics of conservative Christianity that would deny rights to gay men and lesbians. Despite the fact that they belief that homosexuality is sinful, they are also aware of the ostracism and rejection they received from conservative Christian groups for most of their lives. Many ex-gays live out a contradiction in that they are devoted to transforming their sexuality, which would seem to align them with Christian Right groups, but at the same time do not advocate an antigay political agenda. Most but not all the men at New Hope balk at the label antigay. Some oppose legislative efforts against gay civil rights and identify with the victims of homophobia. Frank is quick to explain that although "each and every one of us is called to defend the gospel— right-wing groups are not being courteous and respectful." At a New Hope event Worthen discussed the brutal murder of Matthew Shepard and criticized Fred Phelps, the preacher who had protested at Shepard's funeral with signs that read, "God hates Fags." Brian believes that antigay laws like those that Focus and CRA promote are anathema to a Christian agenda. He is strongly opposed to the legislative and public policy agendas of both organizations.

> What I don't like is what I sense is the whole idea that we're going to make you do something, the whole idea that we're going to make it uncomfortable for you socially if you choose to be gay in this society. To the point of taking away your rights or even throwing you in jail. Anything along those lines I believe is repulsive.

This distancing from figures like Phelps helps to bolster ex-gay claims that they are not political, effacing the very real political repercussions of an organization dedicated to the conversion of gay men and women. Unlike Paulk or Haley, Brian has chosen to make his struggle a more private issue. Since completing the program in 1997 he has had what the ministry calls "sexual falls" with other men, but for him trying to change is the only path he can follow and still be true to his faith. Although he theoretically wants to date women, he concedes that he feels no sexual attraction for them. He is the first to admit that the idea of change is a process and that some men and women never change their desires even if they control their outward behavior. For him, the idea of change is primarily religious.

More and more ex-gays like Brian or Drew are worried that an organization they view as a means to change their sexuality has increasingly drawn them into association with the Christian Right. Despite their identification as conservative Christians, not all the men in the New Hope program believe in the idea of a radical homosexual conspiracy. In fact, many find themselves more sympathetic to gay rights than to the agenda of the Christian Right. Curtis felt this way:

> With this whole issue, because you've been ridiculed and mocked and bashed, that's why the pride thing comes in and why gay activists are so in

your face because there's so much anger and bitterness. It's so evil. Their motives come from such a hurt. My whole life was like that.

He had come out to his family at age sixteen as "someone with gay feelings who wants to change." His only same-sex experience was a clandestine relationship with a high school friend. He believed that God wanted him to change his sexuality but that this had nothing to do with being antigay. In fact, one year after finishing the New Hope program, he lives with a gay friend while he continues to try to overcome his same-sex desires and feelings.

What the ad campaign featuring Anne and John Paulk finally brought to light was the shaky and often tenuous association between the ex-gay movement and more influential organizations like Focus on the Family. Although often lumped into the rest of the religious right, Frank and the ex-gay movement had for years sought to gain legitimacy or even a hearing with James Dobson and been ignored. During the 1970s and 1980s James Dobson and people like Beverly LaHaye of Concerned Women for America were wary of getting involved with a movement comprised of former homosexuals. James Dobson and Beverly LaHaye treated Frank and others who had "come out of homosexuality" as outsiders and even as a bit of an embarassment to the legitimate work of conservative Christians. The involvement of the ex-gay movement in the ad campaign emerged from this history of exclusion by James Dobson and others. A desire for validity and publicity led Frank and the president of Exodus at the time, Bob Davies, to allow the Center for Reclaiming America to use their stories. Suddenly, after years of being disregarded, the ex-gays were at the center of a wider Christian coalition. Brian, who was vehemently opposed to the participation of New Hope and the ex-gay movement in the ads, explains,

> The impression that I got . . . was that they were willing to sell out on some of that grayness in order to get some national recognition from these organizations that they've been wanting to get for a long time—some validation. Because Exodus has had trouble. Focus didn't want to touch it for years. It's a weird issue in general, even for Christians, so they were willing to sell out, it was almost like a deal, that's what I saw.

On their end CRA could use ex-gay stories to prove that through Christian love people could change into heterosexuals, cloaking their message in ideas of compassion and change rather than antigay vitriol.

However, after the people from CRA asked for testimonies and pictures, Frank did not hear from them again until the ads were published. No one had asked their opinion about the ad copy or the message they were promoting. Janet Folger, the architect of the ads, appeared on Nightline and ABC evening news, but the ministries themselves were largely forgotten by the larger Christian organizations. Then, when prominent gay organizations like the National Gay and Lesbian Task Force and the Human Rights Campaign responded with outrage, it was the New Hope office and Exodus headquarters that received the brunt of the phone calls and protests. It wasn't the first time New Hope had contended with demonstrations. Gay rights groups had sporadically staged protests at New Hope since its inception in 1973, and the Lesbian Avengers even dumped a box of crickets in the office at one point. This time, however, they were unprepared to handle the deluge of calls and publicity. Frank and the rest of the men at the office found themselves devoted entirely to dealing with the media.

When the men at the ministry read the ads, many were appalled that their stories had been used to argue against civil rights and money for AIDS research. "I got very upset." Brian remembers. " I said to Frank if you want to do advertising, do your own. They are using ministries to promote their agenda." Many like Brian felt that the entire premise of the ads was false."It was too plastic. It wasn't enough. It made it sound like, 'ta da, just walk through our program and it will all be changed. I felt like it wasn't completely honest and it smelled of Christian cheesiness.'" Another man named Evan told Frank, "You're playing in the Republicans' backyard and you're giving them exactly what they want. And you're making yourself look like a fool."

After Brian watched a debate on *Nightline* with Janet Folger of CRA and Andrew Sullivan, his feeling that he was a pawn in a larger political game was confirmed.

> They used them as if to say, "We now have a way for you to change, and if you don't we will pass laws against you." Janet Folger went as far as to refuse to deny that her organization would not defend legislation for the incarceration of homosexuals. In other words, they supported the state's rights to choose to throw people into prison for homosexual behavior. So that didn't sit well with me, and I started to become angry that something I was a part of was going public with a message that I wasn't in agreement with.

Soon after the televised debate Brian and Hank had an argument that created an irreparable rift in the New Hope program. Hank told the men
that he believed states should pass laws to incarcerate homosexuals and
that homosexuality should be made illegal. Brian stormed out of the
meeting in anger and shock. It sparked a personal crisis that made him
question whether he wanted to be part of New Hope. "Suddenly my
whole worldview was turned upside down thinking that maybe everyone
believed that in the church. What was I part of? It was a very hard time
for me."

Although Brian ultimately decided to stay and eventually came to an
uneasy truth with Hank, there was no resolution to the issue. To vent
some of his frustration and anger, he wrote an essay on why he thought
the Bible would oppose legislation for the incarceration of homosexuals.
It wasn't only Brian who defied the political message of the ads and the
uses to which ex-gays' lives were being put. Matt, a thirty-three year old
from Georgia whose father was a Baptist preacher, felt that the ads were
"sneaky and manipulative." However, ultimately he believed that people
would become aware that the message was false. "There's a verse in the
Bible that says, 'What is hidden in darkness will be brought out into the
light.' And that is so true about the ex-gay movement. The ads did not
say, 'It may be a long process, you may always have these sexual feelings
for other men.' They never mentioned that."

THE RIGHT TO CHANGE

The men at New Hope view their own activism as having the
right to participate in an ex-gay ministry and the right to attempt to
change their sexuality, even if they acknowledge the process is more fluid and fraught than the ads proclaimed. They consider change as a process
of religious conversion that affects their identities but not necessarily their
desires or behaviors. Drew defended his position this way,

> I'm all on for these gay guys doing what they like and everything else, but
> I have a right to believe what I believe and not go that way. Why not let
> people, who want to, change. It's not like we're going out there preach-
> ing in the Castro, saying, You must come. We have guys phoning up here
> and they're desperate and suicidal and there's tons of organizations out
> there that are helping people who are gay. Is it wrong for me to not want

to accept the gay lifestyle? Must I do it because everybody else says I have
to do it?

Drew believes that his participation in New Hope is a personal choice
that does not translate to the political realm. Men like Drew, Brian, and
Hank are living as ex-gays, with lingering same-sex desire and attraction,
but firmly believe they are on a Godly path. The ad campaign exempli-
fied to them that the decision to change sexual identity can never be di-
vorced from the realm of politics. At the same time, they showed the
CRA coalition that identities are never stable and that change is an ongoing process. The ex-gay identity is in many ways a queer and liminal
identity that is constantly in flux and incorporates the idea of sexual falls
and subsequent redemption.

The ad coalition was soon to learn this in an extremely public way. In
September of 2001 two men who worked for the HRC recognized John
Paulk in a gay bar in Washington, D.C.[15] Even Paulk—husband, father,
and former drag queen—could not escape the fact that although behavior and identity change, desire, attraction, and old habits might not. What
was common within the ex-gay movement became a national scandal. As
soon as the story broke, Anita told me she wanted to explain her side of
what happened. She'd known John for years through the New Hope program and later as a co-member of the Exodus board of directors. She admitted that, more than his going to a gay bar, what was particularly hurt-
ful and galling was that Paulk initially lied to her and the rest of the
Exodus board, denying that he knew it was a gay bar. He only broke
down and admitted the truth when photographs of him fleeing the establishment surfaced in the press. Anita even added a bit sardonically,
"I'm not gay, but I think you would know it was a gay bar." According
to Anita, the problem the ex-gay movement now faced was whether to
chastise him publicly. By doing so, she felt they ended up siding with the
gay press and media. As a compromise, Exodus required him to temporarily resign from the board of directors. I knew she could have put another spin on the situation to protect one of her own, but she didn't. Anita understood better than anyone that this would irrevocably damage the
credibility of the movement.

Weeks later, Paulk and his wife Anne appeared on the Focus on the
Family radio broadcast with James Dobson. Dobson hadn't fired him, but
he wanted to get the whole incident out in the open. At New Hope we

all gathered around to listen. I'd been sharing articles I'd received with everyone at the office, and we'd been discussing the Paulk incident incessantly. I knew the scandal had deeply affected many men and forced them to question what they were doing. After Curtis's former roommate decided to leave because the Paulk incident discouraged him, Curtis's response was, "You can't put your faith in man. If you do, you'll always be disappointed. I was committed to God before I was committed to change. Without God this would be impossible. You have to put your faith in Him."

On the air Dobson was stern but forgiving. He reprimanded Paulk, but seemed supportive as long as Paulk continued to disavow the gay lifestyle. Paulk told Dobson and the millions of Christians listening that he was curious about the bars since he allegedly hadn't been in them for fifteen years. Justifying his failure to immediately come clean, he claimed he initially panicked and lied because he feared for his job and family. Still he maintained that even his decision to enter the bar couldn't be blamed on his own volition. Satan had been working in his life, he said, and gay activists were calling and threatening to ruin him. This is what lured him into the bar.

When it was over, Anita and everyone else seemed resigned. After all, this wasn't the first time a member of the ex-gay movement had experienced a sexual fall. But, she was upbeat about one thing: the fact that Dobson had supported Paulk publicly. "It couldn't have been easy to stand with him on this issue in front of his entire radio audience." Five years ago Dobson would have kicked Paulk out, and that would have been the end of it. She felt the "Love Won Out" campaign had changed Dobson's perspective from that of an antigay activist to someone with a bit more compassion. In the end even Dobson realized the fallacy of his own activism; some people may purport to change, but their identities often overflow tidy distinctions between heterosexual and homosexual. It was just another battle they had to endure. Eventually, Anita and the others believed, they would overcome.

NOTES

1. A series of ads were placed in the national media beginning with an ad in the *New York Times* on July 13, 1998, followed by an ad on July 14, 1998, in the *Washington Post* and one in *USA Today* on July 15, 1998. The ad campaign continued with

placements in the *Chicago Tribune,* the *Los Angeles Times,* and the *Wall Street Journal.* The ads were sponsored and paid for by fifteen right-wing organizations, Alliance for Traditional Marriage–Hawaii, American Family Association, Americans for Truth About Homosexuality, Center for Reclaiming America, Christian Family Network, Christian Coalition, Citizens for Community Values, Colorado for Family Values, Concerned Women for America, Coral Ridge Ministries, Family First, Family Research Council, Liberty Counsel, National Legal Foundation, and Kerusso Ministries. They were coordinated by Janet Folger of the Center for Reclaiming America who raised $400,000 for the campaign.

2. In this article I refer to public figures by their actual names. I use pseudonyms for the men and women at New Hope ministry where I completed my research since the information they shared with me was often highly personal.

3. See "Ex-Gay Ads Spark Media Firestorm: Millions Hear About Exodus Through *Time, Newsweek,* 'Good Morning America' and a Host of Other Media," *Exodus North America Update,* August 1998.

4. John Paulk, "Sharing the Truth in Love," Focus on the Family pamphlet publication, 1999.

5. Focus, founded by James Dobson in 1977, is a conservative Christian conglomerate with daily radio broadcasts, over sixteen publications geared toward youth, parents, teachers, physicians, and church leaders, overseas missionary organizations, and other media ventures. Dobson also sends a monthly letter to everyone on his mailing list in which he outlines his thoughts on current political controversies. According to Focus, Dobson's syndicated radio broadcast is heard on more than three thousand radio facilities in North America and in nine languages on approximately twenty-three hundred facilities in over ninety-eight other countries. By the mid-1990s Focus had an annual budget of over one hundred million. See Sara Diamond, *Not By Politics Alone: The Enduring Influence of the Christian Right* (New York: Guilford, 1998), pp.30–36. For more information see the Focus on the Family website at www.family.org.

6. Exodus includes over 100 local ministries in the USA and Canada. They are also linked with other Exodus world regions outside of North America, totaling over 135 ministries in 17 countries.

7. Formerly known as Love in Action, New Hope changed its name in 1996. In 1994 Love in Action moved to Memphis, Tenessee where it still runs a residential program for men and women. The other residential program is Freedom at Last in Wichita, Kansas. Most ex-gay ministries are support groups that meet on a weekly basis.

8. In 2001 Robert Spitzer, a psychiatrist at Columbia University and one of the proponents of removing homosexuality from the American Psychiatric Association's *DSM II* in 1973, published the results of his survey of ex-gay ministry leaders to prove that change does occur. See David Elliot "NGLTF Responds to Flawed Spitzer Study on So-Called Reparative Therapy," *National Gay and Lesbian Task Force Press Release,* May 8, 2001; David Elliot, "Snake Oil Versus Science: New Study by New York Re-

searchers on Conversion Therapy Contradicts NARTH," *National Gay and Lesbian Task Force Press Release*, May 8, 2001; Robert Spitzer, "Commentary: Psychiatry and Homosexuality" *Wall Street Journal*, May 23, 2001. NARTH has also published a survey entitled "Retrospective Self-Reports of Changes in Homosexual Orientation: A Consumer Survey of Conversion Therapy Clients" by Joseph Nicolosi, Ph.D., A. Dean Byrd, Ph.D., and Richard W. Potts, M.A.

1. Jerry Falwell, telecast speech, National Coming Out of Homosexuality Day, October 11, 1999, San Francisco.

10. See Ann Burlein, *Lift High the Cross: Where White Supremacy and the Christian Right Converge* (Durham: Duke University Press, 2002).

11. Amendment 2 was a 1992 Colorado ballot initiative that sought to amend the Colorado constitution in order to legally forbid the state, its municipalities, school districts, or agencies from guaranteeing nondiscrimination to those with "homosexual, lesbian, or bisexual orientation." The amendment passed in November 1992 but was subsequently overturned by the U.S. Supreme Court.

12. Joe Dallas is the former president of Exodus and now directs a biblical counseling practice for ex-gays. A frequent Exodus lecturer, he is the author of *Desires in Conflict: Answering the Struggle for Sexual Identity* (Eugene, Ore.: Harvest House, 1991) and *A Strong Delusion: Confronting the "Gay Christian" Movement* (Eugene, Ore.: Harvest House, 1996).

13. Project 10, founded by Dr. Virginia Uribe, is the nation's first public school program dedicated to providing on-site educational support services to gay, lesbian, bisexual, transgender, and questioning youth. Project 10 began in l984 at Fairfax High School in the Los Angeles Unified School District. See http://www.project10.org/.

14. Laurie Goodstein, "Woman Behind Anti-Gay Ads Sees Christians as Victims," *New York Times,* August 13, 1998, p.A10.

15. Joel Lawson, "Ex-Gay Leader Confronted in Gay Bar," *San Francisco Bay Times*, September 28, 2000, p. 3. Exodus also released a public statement regarding this incident. Bob Davies, "Statement by Exodus North America Regarding Chairman John Paulk," September 22, 2000.

6

Sins of Our Soccer Moms:
Servant Evangelism and the
Spiritual Injuries of Class

OMRI ELISHA

On May 3, 2001, Tina Wesson of Knoxville, Tennessee became America's most famous soccer mom. On live television she won the $1 million grand prize on *Survivor II*, the sequel to the popular Reality TV series where contestants try to outwit and outlast one another under "primitive" conditions in harsh, remote regions of the world. After forty-two days of physical and mental hardship in the Australian outback, the forty-year-old Wesson pulled a surprise victory, a triumph of intuition and perseverance over the haughty pretensions of Gen Xers from the coasts. Mother of two and part-time nurse, with a winning smile, southern drawl, and penchant for outdoor athletics, Wesson epitomized the image of an active career- and family-minded soccer mom, the paradigm of twenty-first-century femininity.

Wesson is a self-proclaimed born-again Christian and attends a predominantly white suburban megachurch in Knoxville where I was conducting ethnographic fieldwork on evangelism and church outreach.[1] As *Survivor II* was aired I expected to hear churchgoers excitedly discussing her progress on the show and anticipated that church pastors would at some point publicly acknowledge that a member of their congregation was in the national spotlight. To my surprise churchgoers rarely seemed to bring up the matter at church, and church staff drew no obvious attention to it: no Sunday morning announcements; no blurbs in the church bulletin. Whatever private conversations went on, they generally remained private—that is, until the show was over.

On the Sunday following Wesson's victorious final episode, Pastor Tim began his morning sermon with warm, almost sheepish words of congratulations (despite the fact that she was not present at the time). The two-thousand-plus-seat auditorium erupted in an ovation honoring the sudden spectacular success of a local girl. The congregation's enthusiasm conveyed a sense of relief and gratitude, as if sanctions on a tabooed subject were finally lifted. The last time Pastor Tim had mentioned *Survivor* was several weeks earlier, before Wesson was a contestant, when he criticized the cut-throat competitive ethos of the show and said that a real Christian could never win such a thing. Now, referring back to those comments with charm and humility, he admitted that not only had a Christian won but, to boot, she was a member of his church! "Great things are happening in the Body of Christ!" he joked, to the delight of the congregation. He then proceeded swiftly to preach on a totally unrelated matter: the importance of planting new churches.

Why such a low-key response on the part of this church to the sudden fame of one of its own members? Surely there were mixed feelings about the *Survivor* series itself, being such a "worldly" (and thus morally suspect) media spectacle. Furthermore, the fact that Wesson drew relatively little attention to her Christian faith made her moments in the limelight far less momentous to evangelicals than had she used the opportunity to share the gospel before a national viewing audience. As she traveled the country on a post-*Survivor* publicity tour, small groups of churchgoers prayed that she would find ways to profess her spirituality with confidence. While she did identify herself as a churchgoing Christian, most evangelicals understand that casual spiritual sound bytes can have only minimal impact against the din of secular popular culture.

Most significant, the media image of Tina Wesson—as she skillfully manipulated her temporal circumstances for material rewards—represents at once the yearnings and anxieties of middle-class evangelical identity. Her church's ambivalence is meaningful in light of the fact that most of her fellow congregants are just like her: white, middle-aged suburbanites cultivating comfortable middle-class lifestyles and multitasking their way toward emotional and spiritual fulfillment. They are educated moms and dads, husbands and wives, professionals and homemakers, striving for perfection in a culture of competition and seeking transcendence through born-again spirituality. For suburban evangelicals the relationship between upward mobility and religious piety is a tense one, fraught with ideological contradictions. In many ways entrepreneurialism and material success remain (under the rubric of Western capitalism) standards of moral certification (Weber 1952). Yet much of evangelical Protestantism gives equal weight to New Testament notions of radical humility and self-sacrifice. Contemporary evangelical pastors and theologians reinforce as well as mediate this tension through a densely layered critique of materialism. Churchgoers internalize this critique, in turn, and use it as a framework for continually defining and calling into question their own class identity.

The critique of materialism among conservative evangelical Protestants I observed in Knoxville involves litanies of suburban angst and social commentary that dwell upon what one might call the spiritual injuries of class (paraphrasing Sennett and Cobb 1972).[2] This critique is made up of a diverse array of beliefs and assumptions that nonetheless share a certain ideological coherence in that they blame the culture of modern capitalism for making people—especially upwardly mobile people—more concerned about personal gain than deeper spiritual matters and wider social problems. Though far from an argument against capitalism per se, the critique of materialism targets the norms of selfishness and apathy that advanced wealth and classism engender under the luring guise of earthly—rather than sacred—fulfillment.

In an evangelical worldview, material prosperity is at best a mixed blessing. The ideal evangelical lifestyle requires believers to *submit* material ambitions to God's kingdom, *surrender* earthly assets to the will of God, and *serve* God through acts of evangelism and charity that benefit the poor, needy, and "unchurched." Unbridled materialism threatens personal commitments to such a lifestyle, attaching people to worldly things and alienating them from God even more than they already are. Evangelical theology is based on the idea that believers, through God's grace, overcome alienation by professing faith in the redemptive sacrifice of Christ's crucifixion. Materialism leads Christians to become complacent and spiritually indifferent and distracts them from the theme of radical sacrifice, matters of grave concern especially in suburban megachurches where affluent Christians struggle to reconcile their religious identity with material prosperity.

The all-American soccer mom embodies similar status-related anxieties that vex the moral imagination of suburban evangelicals, especially women. She appeals to conservative family values of motherhood and gendered norms of caregiving, but also exemplifies the pitfalls of materialism and represents "a community of women who are always on the verge of failure" (Rosenbaum 1999). Overburdened but dedicated, she struggles to provide *sacrificially* for her family (see Miller 1998) and nurture them morally and spiritually, while at the same time she aspires to secure material comforts and maintain advantageous social networks. The soccer mom is thus an ambiguous and problematic cultural icon among evangelicals. Her culturally conditioned desires for self-actualization alert suburban evangelicals to their own tendencies to insulate themselves in middle-class "comfort zones" (a phrase that pops up regularly in church discourse), which in turn make them less likely to be involved in evangelistic ministries that serve the welfare needs of communities beyond church walls.

My fieldwork focused on a relatively small contingent of evangelical pastors and lay activists in West Knoxville who are affiliated with large affluent churches and deeply committed to mobilizing these congregations toward greater involvement in charitable social outreach, an area of ministry that many conservative evangelicals do not embrace. In this essay I examine ways that the rhetoric of outreach mobilization draws upon the more widely accepted evangelical critique of materialism and frames that critique as a call to action. By promoting opportunities for churchgoers to do volunteer work in local shelters and charity centers or with disadvantaged people such as new immigrants and high-risk inner-city youth, organizers promote a particular strategy of outreach that has been called *servant evangelism*. The emphasis in servant evangelism—defined as "demonstrating the kindness of God by offering to do some act of humble service with no strings attached" (Sjogren 1993)—is outward compassion and personal sacrifice, a way of performing the gospel rather than merely proclaiming it verbally. Proponents of servant evangelism present it as an effective catalyst for evangelism ("You can't talk to an empty stomach") as well as an antidote to the spiritual injuries that middle-class Christians suffer in pursuit of upward mobility. Familiar images from the landscape of suburbia that signify wealth and consumption are routinely evoked in their rhetorical efforts to stimulate church-based outreach. "When you get involved in the lives of the poor," Pastor Tim once preached, "you experience the love of God in ways that you can never grasp in your West Knoxville soccer games and three-piece suits."

I argue that by infusing the critique of materialism with theological concepts such as "stewardship" and "incarnation" (discussed below) pro-

ponents of servant evangelism navigate churchgoers (including themselves) through the tricky existential contours of religious and class identity. They confront head-on a set of moral dilemmas that orthodox Christians have wrestled with in various forms for centuries: Is it possible to be
"*in* but not *of* this world?" How can suburban churchgoers enjoy their
status achievements and comfort zones while remaining faithful to biblical principles of humility and social responsibility? How does a soccer
mom keep her family on the fast track of upward mobility and still take
time from her busy day to bear the cross for Christ?

MOVEMENTS OF FAITH

Many evangelicals believe that modern America, despite being
founded upon "Christian principles," has become spiritually vulnerable
because of unbridled materialism and idolatry, a situation they believe is
largely exacerbated by liberal government and mass media. Evangelicals
have long struggled to find effective ministry strategies for redirecting the
effects of modernity, especially secularism and social liberalism. Organized
responses over the last century have ranged from the radical separatism of
Christian fundamentalism to more "world-friendly"styles of social engagement (Carpenter 1997). In the 1940s a group of evangelical scholars
and preachers known as the "new evangelicals" began fighting for an ideological middle ground between the fundamentalists on one side and liberal mainline Protestants on the other. Led by figures such as Billy Gra-
ham, Harold Ockenga, and Carl Henry, the neo-evangelical movement
emerged around a network of coalitions, seminaries, and publications that
blended theological conservatism and social consciousness (Stone 1997).[3]
While maintaining orthodox standards on matters of biblical interpretation and individual salvation, neo-evangelicals urged Christians to participate actively in modern life rather than renounce it as had fundamentalists (Henry 1947). They argued that by abdicating social responsibilities
God's people were losing sight of Christianity's social message and would
therefore fail to communicate its redemptive power effectively.

The majority of white conservative evangelicals today associate social
outreach activism with liberal trends of the twentieth century such as the
social gospel movement and the welfare state and thus are likely to resist
the influence of outreach programs in their congregations.[4] Furthermore,
the resurgence of cultural conservatism since the early 1980s that fueled

the Moral Majority and Christian Coalition further marginalized progressive elements in evangelical communities. Conservative evangelicals, who view poverty and homelessness as matters of individual responsibility, are deeply suspicious of church outreach programs that appear to cater to poor people's sense of "entitlement" rather than enforce moral and spiritual accountability. Church leaders have an easier time mobilizing support for politically charged moral crusades about abortion, homosexuality, and prayer in schools than for ministries that target issues related to social injustice and systemic inequality. Nonetheless, moderate to liberal public evangelicals such as Ronald Sider, founder of Evangelicals for Social Action, and Jim Wallis, editor of *Sojourners* magazine, continue to advocate the social consciousness of the neo-evangelical legacy. They promote ministries that make progressive politics and welfare activism integral to the larger project of evangelism and have been active (if cautious) supporters of legislative efforts to expand federal funding for faith-based social services, even though these efforts were built upon the right-wing ideology of "compassionate conservatism."[5]

The widespread proliferation of evangelical megachurches in recent decades is significant in terms of how evangelicals engage modern society.[6] A megachurch may be defined as a congregation with more than two thousand weekly worshippers (well-known megachurches boast records as high as fifteen to twenty thousand on any given Sunday), but megachurches are also defined by stylistic innovations that foster church growth. Influenced by the experiential spirituality of the 1960s and the "restructuring" of American religion away from denominational traditionalism (Wuthnow 1988), megachurches embody the "new paradigm church," which combines high, deeply personalized religiosity with cultural relevance by appropriating the aesthetics and media technologies of popular culture (Miller 1997). To manage growth and recruitment rates, megachurch leaders employ corporate marketing strategies and organization principles adapted from the world of commerce . Such close affinity between religion and business has always existed in the U.S., but it has become explicit in an unprecedented way in the megachurch movement.

Despite their potential for raising the profile of evangelical Christianity in major American cities, megachurches have their share of evangelical critics (see Hart 2000; Horton 2000; and Pritchard 1996). One line of criticism pertains to congregational demographics. The majority of megachurches in the U.S. (nearly three-quarters by some estimates) are commuter churches in affluent suburbs, where resources for ambitious ministries and building campaigns are readily available and potential members (the market "niche") are predominantly white, upwardly mobile professionals. In cities like Knoxville, still plagued by strong social segregation, the self-selectivity of megachurch congregations in terms of race and class is a sore point for evangelicals who desire greater unity among "all God's children." Church-goers often admitted to me that despite all the human and material resources available for social outreach the white-collar ethos that character-izes suburban megachurches reinforces to a fair extent existing economic and cultural boundaries. They worry that their churches look like "social clubs" for affluent Christians rather than outposts of God's kingdom. Pro-ponents of servant evangelism consider suburban megachurches to be "sleeping giants" in terms of social outreach, and they seek to channel the entrepreneurial spirit underlying church growth toward active engagement in local public life, especially with regard to issues of social welfare and racial reconciliation.

My ethnographic research, which took place over fifteen months span-ning 1999–2001, focused on the social outreach work of evangelical ac-tivists from two of Knoxville's most prominent megachurches, Eternal Vine Evangelical Church and Marble Valley Presbyterian Church. Each has roughly thirty-five hundred to five thousand churchgoers and belongs to a conservative evangelical denomination.[7] Despite differences in doc-trine and congregational history, the megachurches are similar in being committed to primary evangelical principles, relatively open to strategic innovations in ministry, and composed almost exclusively of white profes-sionals and their families. Social outreach activities range from financial and volunteer support for local ministries (e.g., shelters, crisis centers, services for refugees or the elderly) to in-house programs (e.g., food pantries, clothing and furniture drives, home and car repair ministries, Christian counseling), plus a host of diffuse and unstructured ministries that rely mostly on individual churchgoer initiatives (e.g., volunteering for after-school programs, taking in foster children, hospital visitations). Outreach activities have gone on for some time, but when it comes to budget allo-cation and member participation they are generally low priorities com-pared to member services and foreign missions.

In efforts to enhance outreach mobilization, proponents of servant evangelism promote interchurch coalition building, Bible classes and workshops dedicated to studies on compassion and stewardship, and social events designed to plug churchgoers into volunteer opportunities. Localized strategies aim to combat what pastors perceive as apathy, materialism, and insularity among middle-class churchgoers, and are grassroots components of a nascent social movement throughout contemporary evangelicalism. Scholarly research on new social movements has largely neglected conservative cultural and religious movements (Pichardo 1997). The emergence of the political Christian Right has received attention, but "these studies have focused exclusively on the national level, leaving unexamined and unexplained the dynamic social base that propelled the movement and gave it its endurance and strength" (McGirr 2001:11). This limited focus may be due in part to the misperception that church-based activism necessarily reflects the political agendas of organized Christian lobbies. Furthermore, since qualitative researchers who study social movements tend to have left-wing sympathies, they may be disinclined to do participant-observational fieldwork with right-wing cultural activists (notable exceptions include Aho 1990; Ginsburg 1989; and Harding 2000).[8] As a result the complexity of conservative movements, including the presence of progressive influences, is grossly overlooked.

My position as a total outsider (a secular non-Christian) to the evangelical faith community limited my active participation in certain programs, especially those with explicitly evangelistic elements. However, as a volunteer for social outreach activities that offer tangible assistance to people in need I could work with (rather than merely observe) the people I studied without being overwhelmed by ideological conflicts of interest. Moreover, the evangelicals I worked with were excited to have an "objective" outsider assessing the quality of their efforts, especially insofar as I was in their eyes another potential convert. The relationships that I formed with evangelical churchgoers allowed me to discover that, contrary to popular views of American evangelicalism as monolithic and unself-conscious, evangelicals are diverse, critically reflexive, and at times even inconsistent in their beliefs and practices. In this sense, conservative evangelicals are much like "the rest of us," and they know it. Indeed it is a truth they find most disturbing. If nothing else, "true Christians" must embody a holy otherworldliness that sets them apart from everything profane and everyone unsaved.

The evangelical critique of materialism exemplifies a complex logic by which middle-class evangelicals assess and renegotiate their status in a material world. What does the rhetoric sound like? What are its theological underpinnings? How does it reflect the cultural and institutional environment where it is produced? I explore these questions by unpacking four central themes in this critique: consumerism, status mobility, time management, and the family.

"WE DON'T WANT PEOPLE TO COME HERE WITH A CONSUMER MENTALITY"

Paul Genero is a young, energetic pastor who has led the formation of a collaborative network of resourceful evangelical churches in Knoxville dedicated to social outreach ministries, named the Samaritans of Knoxville. During one of our many long conversations on the subject of Christian outreach and compassion, he explained the difference between what he termed "biblical Christianity" and "consumer Christianity." Biblical Christianity, he argued, is totally "God-centric," a lived faith completely dependent on and obedient to God's will and expressed through acts of sacrificial compassion toward others. Consumer Christianity, on the other hand, is "egocentric," status driven, and focused on commodities rather than spiritual blessings. Like most evangelicals, Paul sees the effects of consumerism as pandemic in American culture, yet he builds his critique on images of leisure-class privilege.

> What you tend to see is that there is less of a felt need for God. You know how it is. You have money in the bank, all your bills are paid, you got all your scholarship stuff coming in, and you're just sitting fat and sassy. You start to feel smug about life: "Oh, I'm just sitting happy here." You know? It's the same with Christians. Everything's going great and we've got a full staff at church, and our buildings are full of people . . . we have all the felt needs in our life taken care of with money . . . and our kids are all cute and they're doing well in school and there are no *unsolvable* problems. "I'm putting money away for retirement, and maybe I just got a raise at work, and I live in a nice neighborhood, etc." Then why do you need God?

Paul's portrait of consumer culture draws striking parallels between church and society—markedly white-collar society at that—by illustrating that people in both spheres are driven by the same objectives of consumer behavior, namely financial security, property ownership, and quality education. He never means to denigrate wealth per se. After all, his whole ministry strategy is about harnessing upper-class resources and connecting them to communities in need. But first he must convey to others that the desire to do so is a natural outflow of true faith, and for him this is no easy task. "I'm learning to deal with all the casual disinterest I see. We have so many years of church life that have hardened our arteries, because we live in an affluent society that goes against our core principles. . . . It is the rare Christian who can in the midst of his affluence—in his castle—connect himself to the pain-filled world."

The underlying class commentary in this rhetoric reflects, among other qualities, a valorization of the working class. By virtue of their hard work and knowing firsthand what it means to have "felt needs," "blue-collar types" are believed to embody biblical Christianity somewhat more naturally than others. Several church volunteers suggested to me the possibility that people raised in working-class families (as some of them were) develop a knack for compassion. This was one way volunteers rationalized their involvement in social outreach and perhaps also reconciled mixed feelings about their own upward mobility and consumer behavior. During the formative stages (coinciding with my fieldwork) of the Samaritans of Knoxville, there were subtle efforts to identify the movement as blue collar, even though most of the participants were well-educated church pastors, white-collar professionals, stay-at-home suburban moms, and retirees. Invoking such a marker of identity was a strategy to keep participants mindful that they were called by God to break the habits of materialism so inherent to the middle-class comfort zone and rededicate themselves to "rolling up our sleeves" and "keeping it real." A symbolic association between grassroots activism and a blue-collar work ethic stands in opposition to apathy and conspicuous consumption.

The pivotal notion distinguishing biblical Christianity and consumer Christianity is productivity. Consumerism as understood by evangelicals is a corrupting cultural milieu, a system of norms of detachment and self-indulgence. Lost is healthy economic and social entrepreneurialism, not to mention the spiritual work of advancing the kingdom of God. Since megachurches are often compared by critics to commercial shopping malls because they attract members with diverse, multipurpose programs, avoiding an atmosphere of consumerism assumes great importance. Administrators at Eternal Vine voiced this concern frequently: "We don't want people to come here with a consumer mentality, we want them to have a producer mentality." The "product" in question is a world of Christians living out the gospel with conviction and serving God with

humility. "The Father is calling us to transition from being spiritual consumers to being compassionate servants. In other words, God is calling us
to exchange our prosperous, stuff-oriented lives for the life of Christ."[9]

As the emphases on productivity, servanthood, and the move away
from "stuff-oriented lives" suggest, the critique of materialism overlaps
significantly with church discourse about stewardship. Although stewardship commonly refers to the practice of giving money to the church, theologically speaking it is for evangelicals a spiritual discipline that begins
with the recognition that one's assets are not one's own but belong entirely to God. Pastor Jerry of Marble Valley preached that money is dangerous when idolized for personal gain, but "when money is seen as a resource for accomplishing God's purposes on earth, it becomes a useful
part of our stewardship." Consequently "our attitude toward money and
our use of money are prime indicators of our spiritual state." Evangelical
sermons and teachings on stewardship cite a wide range of supporting
biblical texts to impel churchgoers to be "sacrificial" about giving to their
church,[10] thereby reinforcing the authority of churches in mediating capital towards spiritually productive enterprises (see Schervish 1990).

Proponents of servant evangelism build upon notions of stewardship,
but they further encourage churchgoers to grow beyond conventional
church-giving practices by becoming personally active in social outreach
ministry: "The Father is calling us to minister among the poor. . . . We
don't sense he is calling us just to give money to the poor. That is just an
easy, middle-class way to relieve a guilty conscience. We believe God is
calling us into relationship with the poor."[11]

The sentiment represented here is that the average churchgoer is too
complacent with detached, commodified forms of charity, such as simply
writing checks or donating "stuff" out of feelings of obligation (the dread-
ed "guilty conscience"). "In a busy world," Paul Genero once explained,
"the Body of Christ tends to lean toward commodity-based outreach,"
which inadvertently "promotes dependency among needy people and
doesn't get God's people involved relationally." The end result is that the
church becomes, at best, "just a glorified social service agency" and believers remain isolated from hands-on opportunities to "show God's love."

For evangelical baby boomers and busters—generations of people identified as avid consumers in new commercial and spiritual marketplaces—the
critique of materialism expresses a critical self-awareness. Outreach mobi-
lizers use this as a starting point for narratives of radical self-reorientation.

SINS OF OUR SOCCER MOMS

Volunteer testimonies describe churchgoers developing a kind of class consciousness that propels them into outreach activism. These testimonies, especially when delivered from the pulpit, communicate lessons to even the most reluctant churchgoers about making moral decisions regarding how best to spend and invest one's material assets.

"DOWNWARD MOBILITY IS WHAT JESUS WAS ALL ABOUT"

On Christmas Eve Pastor Tim gave a sermon that incorporated symbols of middle-class consciousness into an instructional narrative based on his own volunteer experiences. The sermon, entitled "Christmas: Celebrating the Generosity of God," began (surprisingly) with Pastor Tim defending Christmas consumerism against the common complaint that "Christmas is too commercial." He argued that the commercialism of Christmas is special because gift giving celebrates God's generosity. The incarnation of Jesus Christ was a sacrificial gift from God to humanity. The Bible, Pastor Tim continued, shows a God who "refused to remain cloistered in a walled heaven" (one of the pastor's frequent veiled references to gated residential subdivisions), a God who downgraded to human form in order "to live in relationship with the messy world that He created."

Focusing on the theme of incarnation, Pastor Tim evoked the image of the manger where Jesus was born and framed its symbolism as a call for God's people into direct relational, or "incarnational," outreach ministries. He described with anecdotal flair encounters he had while serving meals to homeless men at a local shelter and said that he has grown to look forward to volunteering because he realized that "God has allowed me to incarnate into a little painful place in the world." He instructed his audience that to truly embody the love and generosity of God, "Find a manger of pain and incarnate yourself into it." In other words, the work of ministry requires believers to literally enter the spaces of physical and spiritual need that surround them. As the example of the homeless shelter suggests, these "mangers of pain" are often unlikely to be found in suburban comfort zones but rather out in the "messy world" of urban poverty.

As I sat with Jackie Sherman, a church staff member, in an office colorfully decorated with holiday ornaments (including her shiny Christmas tree earrings), she spoke of her frustration over affluent Christians who do not follow the footsteps of Christ:

Jesus Christ was for the broken, the oppressed. Foxes have holes, but the Son of Man has nowhere to lay his head.[12] Sometimes when I drive around and look at all the mansions that these Christians live in, and the chariots that they drive up here on Sunday morning, I'm asking, Do you really know the Christ who said, "I came for the poor?" You know? That's the struggle I have. . . . You know, are we really living the radical Christian life in these affluent churches, where we almost have no minorities? We might give money to the church, but do we *sacrificially* give?

I asked how she feels about the fact that the very affluence she denounces as un-Christ-like affords vast resources for church ministries, and she agreed that "there are some good things about having money." But "if Christians were living a radical Christian life," she stressed, "we would have missionaries all over this city and it wouldn't have to take materialism to do it." By way of example, Jackie named a married couple from her church that had recently left the suburbs to purchase a home in a predominantly black inner-city neighborhood where they planned to minister to the needs of the community. "I believe that's the Christian life," she exclaimed. "Just think, that's what it's all about!" Ray Bakke, a popular author on the subject of urban ministry, summed it up for me another way: "Downward mobility is what Jesus was all about."

Practicing one's faith through some form of downward mobility is a powerful theme in Christian evangelism and missiology. Like missionaries abroad, white middle-class Christians who move into low-income neighborhoods to do full-time ministry (which often implies modifying their own incomes and lifestyles) are celebrated as "soldiers at the frontlines" of God's kingdom. At the same time, the prospect of giving up social status and living among the poor in America lacks the romanticism of foreign missions, thus limiting considerably the number of suburban churchgoers who actually do so (I knew of only a handful in Knoxville). Nonetheless, the recognition among churchgoers of their own status anxieties makes the "sacrifice" of those who relocate themselves to inner-city ghettos seem all the more meaningful.[13]

Among proponents of servant evangelism, voluntary long-term relocation into "mangers of pain" is seen as practical as well as exemplary. Following models of urban ministry developed by noted evangelical figures (i.e., Bakke 1997; Lupton 1989; Perkins 1993), they argue that such strategies promote stronger Christian involvement in public life and community revitalization. An evangelical philanthropist who moved his family to the inner city explained to me:

> If you really want to have a significant impact you have to live there, especially as someone who would be characterized as an affluent person. You know, going in and helping, then leaving, that's great, but you don't live here. The school isn't your school, the crime isn't your crime, the drug trade and how it affects everyone isn't affecting you, because you leave. So you need to live there, and all of a sudden the community's issues become your issues and you become enmeshed in the community through that.

Still, most middle-class evangelicals (like most Americans) long for upward mobility and pin their sense of self-actualization on the promise of accumulating rather than sacrificing social and economic capital. The runaway success of Bruce Wilkinson's *The Prayer of Jabez* (2000), one of the biggest best-sellers in Christian publishing (despite being accused by critics of promoting a "gospel of prosperity"), testifies to a climate of material aspiration. Megachurches, arguably, both foster and challenge such sensibilities. Seminars on career edification, professional etiquette, and "financial peace" cater to white-collar ambitions. Fund-raising campaigns to purchase and develop high-end real estate for new sanctuaries, sports facilities, mission houses, and parking lots exemplify the ideals of property ownership and social entrepreneurialism. And yet, while evangelical megachurches encourage members to construct comfort zones of personal and spiritual growth, the evangelical critique of materialism and promotion of servant evangelism simultaneously caution them against getting too comfortable there. Maintaining a proper balance becomes the burden of middle-class faith.

"There's Something About How God Blesses When People Are Willing to Give Their Time"

When I asked outreach ministry workers about the biggest obstacles to mobilizing church volunteers, nearly every one complained that no one seems to have any time. Evangelical activists see middle-class "busyness," however unavoidable, as part of the pathology of materialism. Their critique is at once about the amount of time that churchgoers allocate for social outreach and about the quality of activities that take up the rest of their day. The more time people spend running around doing "stuff" of minor spiritual significance, the less time they have to "seek God's face" through prayer and acts of compassion. Busy Christians are encouraged at church to set aside "quality time" for family, study, and prayer, but even this is sometimes criticized insofar as it compartmental- izes spirituality, separating religious faith from areas of everyday life where it should have a direct impact.

Ministry professionals who depend on volunteer labor as much as char- itable donations are particularly bothered by suburban busyness. Because of other religious, professional, and recreational activities available to up- wardly mobile evangelicals, ministries are forced to compete for people's time and energy. This is often a losing battle, as Carol Farlan, an urban ministry worker, explained, referring to larger societal trends:

> The biggest problem, not just here in Knoxville but in general, is that time is one of the most valuable assets we have these days, and there just does- n't seem to be enough of it for anybody. The years of people having a nine-to-five job are over. . . . So time becomes this very very valuable commodity, and you're in there fighting for the same bit of time that's left over *after* somebody has worked all those hours and had their family time and taken all the kids to soccer practice and Brownies and Boy Scouts and all of that stuff and has spent time with their spouse kind of working on their marriage. There isn't a lot left over.

The speaker (who happens to attend a megachurch) never challenges the validity of parents taking their children to "soccer practice and Brownies and Boy Scouts." Indeed, few of the many allegorical references to soccer that I heard were explicitly opposed to such uses of one's time. Rather, these references are used to signify metonymically "all that stuff"—those material indulgences that improve physical bodies and strengthen egos but detract people from obedience to the mandates of God's kingdom.

Raymond Andrews, a wealthy businessman who does volunteer work with inner-city families, describes his commitment to the principles of so- cial outreach as a process of reorganizing his personal priorities. He insists that a Christian must not only give up time and money but also learn to do so in "radical ways" and with a "denial of self." Otherwise the believ- er is indistinguishable from anyone else who "lives in a big fancy house" and "goes to soccer games." In his efforts to get churchgoers to give rad- ically of themselves, Raymond encourages interpersonal rather than purely financial modes of charity because of his belief that "there's *something* about how God blesses when people are willing to give their time."

As with personal finances, the discipline of regimenting one's time "biblically" is addressed in sermons and topical workshops. The subject is especially relevant in the current cultural climate where time itself is a scarce resource that career- and family-minded people must learn to invest and manage efficiently (Hochschild 1997). For evangelicals, mundane time constraints of modern society devalue spiritual life, which in turn affects the quality of work and family life. Megachurch services and programs, offered daily, are designed to help churchgoers break the binds of secular time. Ironically, these activities are time consuming in their own right and create yet another layer of resistance that proponents of servant evangelism must negotiate in order to convince churchgoers to commit more time to social outreach and less time to themselves.

"GOD JUST WANTS TO LOVE PEOPLE THROUGH MY FAMILY"

Family egoism is an especially loaded topic in the polemics of antimaterialism and servant evangelism. Devotion to one's family is highly esteemed as virtuous and essential to Christian living, but to the extent that one may become consumed by family affairs at the expense of larger Christian duties it may be viewed as problematic. Given the patriarchal traditionalism of evangelical gender ideology, this area of critique implicitly draws attention to women's roles in the domestic sphere. Idealized as custodians of good Christian homes, women bear the bulk of responsibility for activities that constitute family life. In many ways evangelical households reveal a tendency for "pragmatic egalitarianism" between husbands and wives (Gallagher and Smith 1999), and divisions of family labor are actually quite varied, reflecting attitudinal diversity and the fact that many wives and mothers are themselves wage earners (Bartkowski 2001). However, recreation and community socialization continue to be seen as chiefly the domain of female decision making. Consequently the pressures to raise families that live out a Godly faith on a daily basis are most immediate for middle-class evangelical women, regardless of whether they are homemakers, homeschoolers, or salaried professionals.

American evangelicals have always positioned themselves as passionate advocates for the sanctity of the traditional nuclear family. Many conservative Christian social and political movements have crystallized around issues regarding sexual morality, abortion, feminism, and other controversial subjects that fuel ongoing "culture wars" over the terms of kinship, reproduction, and domestic life (see Bendroth 1993; Ginsburg 1989; Harding 2000; Kintz 1997). Feminism, in particular, is reviled by conservative evangelicals, who see it as consistent with the Godless self-indulgence and unbridled materialism of modern culture. They believe that women have been misled to desire material prosperity and career ambitions outside the home, resulting in widespread devaluation of the family. Women's "natural" caregiving virtues, it is argued, have been undermined, and family life—where religious and economic values are learned and reproduced—has become "egocentric."

Because of the expectations that evangelical gender ideology place on family life, many women choose to work in the home, and a smaller but not insignificant number homeschool their children. Several of the suburban mothers I met who identified themselves as "stay-at-home moms" were college educated (some with graduate degrees) and had given up professional careers to commit their time and energy entirely to the edification of their families. Their sacrifice of career ambitions was for many a difficult but principled decision that signaled their commitment to serve God. Even for them, however, the danger of being consumed by the busyness, frivolity, and isolationism of the suburban comfort zone can be a source of spiritual anxiety. Even a practice as religiously motivated as Christian homeschooling (often done with the aid of church-based curricula and support groups) can serve as a poignant illustration of the dilemmas that evangelical parents face. Homeschooling is popular (along with private Christian education) among conservative evangelicals as a way of ensuring that children are continually exposed to Christian rather than secular (immoral/amoral) influences. But many evangelicals also believe that keeping children isolated from the world goes against the principle of "engaged orthodoxy" that suggests that Christian families should improve school systems from within rather than abandon them (Smith 2000:131).

Proponents of servant evangelism, as they seek to mobilize the potentially vibrant volunteer force of stay-at-home and homeschooling moms, find themselves caught in the middle of counterposed evangelical notions of domestic protectionism on one hand and family-based evangelism on the other. Managing this ideological tension involves the use of rhetoric that is intended to remind busy parents that outreach activism will "radically" transform their priorities and improve their emotional, spiritual, and family lives. As one activist explained:

> My family isn't the end all and be all of my religion anymore, but my family becomes part of what God wants to use to actually *bless,* to reach out to the rest of those who don't know Him. . . . God just wants to love people through my family, which is not to say my family doesn't get totally blessed and loved in the process, because they do. That's all part of the *secret* of the whole thing. . . . They get filled up and overflowed by God and that overflow gets out to the community and the community feels the impact.

In short, servant evangelism brings one closer to the realization that God, not you or your family, is the center of the universe. The fulfillment of the kingdom of God requires Christian families to be *in* their communities, spreading the gospel intentionally and selflessly. Suburban households are encouraged to affect a "paradigm shift," as I often heard it expressed, away from leisure and security and toward active compassion and service for people in need. The ideal model for the family, in this sense, resembles the sacrificial ideal of Christian motherhood.

Servant evangelism also invites middle-class evangelical women into a specialized (and spiritualized) area of productivity that is alternative to the male-dominated spheres of business and commerce. Women are believed to be somewhat better suited or "wired" for compassion than men, a logic that is used to explain the preponderance of women among lay churchgoers who volunteer in outreach ministries.[14] Most of the organized social outreach in the churches I studied was coordinated by women volunteers and women's ministry staff. Consequently women are more regularly encouraged to find ways of incorporating ministry opportunities into family routines, ways of instilling evangelistic values in their children while concentrating their parental energies more efficiently. Mothers who homeschool and also have a "heart" for servant evangelism find it especially rewarding to make social outreach activities (e.g., visiting poor families and nursing homes) an essential part of the homeschool curriculum. This allows them to keep family at the forefront of their commitment and still participate in church activities that bring them out from the home and into the public or civic sphere. They can be good Christian mothers and dedicated volunteers and activists, inching themselves away from the loaded cultural stereotype of the suburban soccer mom.

Conservative evangelicals in the U.S. are more "worldly" than most Americans, including evangelicals themselves, care to acknowledge (Smith 1998; Warner 1998). Despite certain doctrines and qualities that give them the appearance of a distinct subculture, evangelicals are mainstream in many ways. They are subject to modern sensibilities and lifestyles and therefore susceptible, in their eyes, to modern sins. Evangelical preaching, contrary to stereotypes, is not solely a rhetoric of accusation directed at the sinful, unchurched world outside. It is rather a medium of moral instruction often directed squarely at the people in the pews. The reflexive evangelical critique of materialism is a glaring testimony to this understanding.

During the final episode of *Survivor II*, Tina Wesson was asked what she would do with the $1 million prize. She said she would pay off her house and her best friend's house and set up a fund for families in need. She also said she had never earned more than minimum wage and looked forward to making a major a contribution to her family's finances. In a nutshell, Wesson articulated personal ambitions that epitomize popular American notions of self-fulfillment. Her message was simple and familiar to people just like her, including the roughly five thousand born-again Christians who every Sunday fill the vast parking lot of her church back home. The Gospel of Tina struck a culturally resonant chord. But its lack of spiritual resonance tempered the enthusiasm of her fellow believers.

The intimate imagery of an SUV-driving soccer mom is central to a complex, agonized rhetorical movement calling conservative Christians back into local public spheres in order that they be "conquered in God's name." As Americans turn in growing numbers toward new forms of religious practice and cultural activism, and as evangelical Christians struggle to regain prominence in public life, social outreach ministries take on a sense of urgency. Proponents of servant evangelism capitalize upon this sense of urgency and define faith-based activism as an expression of spiritual fulfillment as well as a specialized alternative space of productivity, especially for overburdened family women. Tina Wesson's iconic significance in her church (demonstrated by its notable muteness) is thus interwoven with a distinctly white, middle-class evangelical style of self-abnegation with increasingly political overtones. In addition to feeling partly complicit in a culture of materialism, evangelicals lament modern Christianity's failure to assert itself as the socially relevant institution it once was. They yearn for a past age when they believe local churches took care of all community needs, a time when Christians practiced active compassion before the intervention of government programs (see Olasky 1992). The recent decline of state welfare and growing popularity of faith-based social services have raised the stakes of community voluntarism (Cnaan 1999), and churchgoing Christians are positioning themselves to seize the opportunity. A critical area for further study is how servant evangelists encounter other cultural activists and social service providers who occupy those same spheres, each defining for themselves the terms of civic engagement.

NOTES

1. My research was supported by grants from the Social Science Research Council, Louisville Institute, and Department of Anthropology at New York University.

2. The term *evangelical* is applied to diverse Christian communities and traditions. My use refers primarily to mainstream evangelical Protestantism, which came out of early American revivalism. Conservative evangelicals share basic doctrines regarding the importance of "born-again" conversion, proselytization, lay spirituality, biblical infallibility, and the deity of Jesus Christ.

3. The National Association of Evangelicals, Fuller Theological Seminary, and *Christianity Today* magazine are among the most prominent outflows of the neo-evangelical movement.

4. By contrast, the black evangelical tradition in America is historically strongly committed to social action, a characteristic that has contributed to the powerful racial divide within evangelicalism (Emerson and Smith 2000).

5. The chief proponent of "compassionate conservatism" is Marvin Olasky, a conservative evangelical ideologue and editor of *World* magazine.

6. Scott Thumma of the Hartford Institute for Religion Research (at Hartford Theological Seminary) has done extensive research on megachurches. See Thumma 1996, and his on-line database: http://hirr.hartsem.edu/.

7. Eternal Vine belongs to the Evangelical Free Church of America. Marble Valley changed its affiliation during my research from Presbyterian Church of America to Evangelical Presbyterian Church.

8. See Ginsburg 1993 on the difficulties of writing about cultural conservatives and having one's own convictions misidentified by people at both ends of the spectrum.

9. *Eternal Vine Sunday Morning Bulletin*, April 29, 2001.

10. Texts cited include Luke 16:1–15, Mark 12:41–44, 1 Timothy 6:6–10, and Matthew 6:24, to name just a sample.

11. *Eternal Vine Morning Bulletin*, April 22, 2001

12. See Matthew 8:20.

13. Ethnographers have shown that pressures of upward and downward status mobility greatly influence how Americans define themselves and evaluate experiences of social dislocation. See Dudley 1994, Ehrenreich 1989, and Newman 1988.

14. National survey statistics on civic voluntarism show that men and women participate equally in nonpolitical voluntary activities, but women do considerably more voluntary activities with religious institutions (Verba, Schlozman, and Brady 1995: 257–259). Regarding the historical alliance between women and clergy in American Protestantism, see Douglas 1977.

Works Cited

Aho, James A. 1990. *The Politics of Righteousness: Idaho Christian Patriotism*. Seattle: University of Washington Press.

Bakke, Ray. 1997. *A Theology as Big as the City*. Downers Grove, Ill.: InterVarsity.

Bartkowski, John P. 2001. *Remaking the Godly Marriage: Gender Negotiation in Evangelical Families*. New Brunswick, N.J.: Rutgers University Press.

Bendroth, Margaret. 1993. *Fundamentalism and Gender, 1875 to the Present*. New Haven: Yale University Press.

Carpenter, Joel A. 1997. *Revive Us Again: The Reawakening of American Fundamentalism*. Oxford: Oxford University Press.

Cnaan, Ram A. with Robert J. Wineburg and Stephanie C. Boddie. 1999. *The Newer Deal: Social Work and Religion in Partnership*. New York: Columbia University Press.

Douglas, Ann. 1977. *The Feminization of American Culture*. New York: Knopf.

Dudley, Kathryn Marie. 1994. *The End of the Line: Lost Jobs, New Lives in Postindustrial America*. Chicago: University of Chicago Press.

Ehrenreich, Barbara. 1989. *Fear of Falling: The Inner Life of the Middle Class*. New York: Pantheon.

Emerson, Michael O. and Christian Smith. 2000. *Divided By Faith: Evangelical Religion and the Problem of Race in America*. Oxford: Oxford University Press.

Gallagher, Sally K. and Christian Smith. 1999. "Symbolic Traditionalism and Pragmatic Egalitarianism: Contemporary Evangelicals, Families, and Gender." *Gender and Society* 13(2): 211–233.

Ginsburg, Faye D. 1993. "The Case of Mistaken Identity: Problems in Representing Women on the Right." In Caroline Brettell, ed., *When They Read What We Write: The Politics of Ethnography*, pp. 167–176. Westport, Conn.: Bergin and Garvey.

—— 1989. *Contested Lives : The Abortion Debate in an American Community*. Berkeley: University of California Press.

Harding, Susan F. 2000. *The Book of Jerry Falwell: Fundamentalist Language and Politics*. Princeton: Princeton University Press.

Hart, D. G. 2000. "The Techniques of Church Growth." *Modern Reformation: The Malling of Mission* 9(3): 20–25. Special issue.

Henry, Carl F. 1947. *The Uneasy Conscience of Fundamentalism*. Grand Rapids: Ecrdmans.

Hochschild, Arlie Russell. 1997. *The Time Bind: When Work Becomes Home and Home Becomes Work*. New York: Holt.

Horton, Michael. 2000. "The Ethnocentricity of the American Church Growth Movement." *Modern Reformation: The Malling of Mission* 9(3): 15–19. Special issue.

Kintz, Linda. 1997. *Between Jesus and the Market: The Emotions That Matter in Right-wing America*. Durham: Duke University Press.

Lupton, Robert D. 1989. *Theirs Is the Kingdom: Celebrating the Gospel in Urban America*. San Francisco: HarperCollins.

McGirr, Lisa. 2001. *Suburban Warriors: The Origins of the New American Right*. Princeton: Princeton University Press.

Miller, Daniel. 1998. *A Theory of Shopping*. Cambridge and Ithaca: Polity and Cornell University Press.

Miller, Donald E. 1997. *Reinventing American Protestantism: Christianity in the New Millennium*. Berkeley: University of California Press.

Newman, Katherine S. 1988. *Falling from Grace: The Experience of Downward Mobility in the American Middle Class*. New York: Free.

Olasky, Marvin. 1992. *The Tragedy of American Compassion*. Washington, D.C.: Regnery.

Perkins, John M. 1993. *Beyond Charity: The Call to Christian Community Development*. Grand Rapids, Mich.: Baker.

Pichardo, Nelson A. 1997. "New Social Movements: A Critical Review." *Annual Review of Sociology* 23:411–30.

Pritchard, G. A. 1996. *Willow Creek Seeker Services: Evaluating a New Way of Doing Church*. Grand Rapids, Mich.: Baker.

Rosenbaum, Susanna. 1999. "Embattled, Uncertain, and Exhausting: Motherhood and Work in the 1990s." Master's thesis, Department of Anthropology, New York University.

Schervish, Paul G. 1990. "Wealth and the Spiritual Secret of Money." In R. Wuthnow and Virginia A. Hodgkinson, eds., *Faith and Philanthropy in America: Exploring the Role of Religion in America's Voluntary Sector,* pp. 63–90. San Francisco: Jossey-Bass.

Sennett, Richard and Jonathan Cobb. 1972. *The Hidden Injuries of Class*. New York: Knopf.

Sjogren, Steve. 1993. *Conspiracy of Kindness: A Refreshing New Approach to Sharing the Love of Jesus with Others*. Ann Arbor: Vine.

Smith, Christian. 2000. *Christian America? What Evangelicals Really Want*. Berkeley: University of California Press.

—— 1998. *American Evangelicalism: Embattled and Thriving*. Chicago: University of Chicago Press.

Stone, Jon R. 1997. *On the Boundaries of American Evangelicalism: The Postwar Evangelical Coalition*. New York: St. Martin's Press.

Thumma, Scott L. 1996. "The Kingdom, the Power, and the Glory: The Mega-church in Modern American Society." Ph.D. diss., Graduate Division of Religion, Emory University.

Verba, Sidney, Kay Lehman Schlozman, and Henry E. Brady. 1995. *Voice and Equality: Civic Voluntarism in American Politics.* Cambridge: Harvard University Press.

Warner, R. Stephen. 1988. *New Wine in Old Wineskins: Evangelicals and Liberals in a Small-Town Church.* Berkeley: University of California Press.

Weber, Max. 1952. *The Protestant Ethic and the Spirit of Capitalism.* New York: Scribner's.

Wilkinson, Bruce H. 2000. *The Prayer of Jabez: Breaking Through to the Blessed Life.* Sisters, Ore.: Multnomah.

Wuthnow, Robert. 1988. *The Restructuring of American Religion: Society and Faith Since World War II.* Princeton: Princeton University Press.

7

Food Fights: Contesting
"Cultural Diversity" in Crown Heights

HENRY GOLDSCHMIDT

In August of 1991, the Afro-Caribbean, African American, and Hasidic Jewish communities in the Brooklyn neighborhood of Crown Heights were engulfed in a violent conflict that a government report later called "the most widespread racial unrest to occur in New York City in more than twenty years" (Girgenti 1993:132). The violence began on the evening of August 19 with the deaths of a seven-year-old Black boy from Guyana named Gavin Cato and a twenty-nine-year-old Australian Orthodox Jew named Yankel Rosenbaum—the former struck by a car in the motorcade of the Lubavitcher Rebbe (the spiritual leader of the Lubavitch Hasidic community), the latter stabbed by a Black rioter hours later. Over the following three days, Blacks and Jews faced off in angry demonstrations—hurling rocks, bottles, slogans, and slurs. A half-dozen stores were looted, and a few predominantly Black youths assaulted Jews, journalists, and police. In the years that followed, the dramatic story of "Crown Heights" became a potent symbol of racial tension in New York and throughout the United States.[1]

In the wake of the violence of 1991, a number of government agencies and community organizations established forums for "dialogue" across the social divide between the neighborhood's Blacks and Jews.[2] More often than not, participants in these forums were encouraged to share their "customs" and "traditions" with their neighbors and embrace their neighborhood's "cultural diversity." In the course of their everyday lives, Black Crown Heights residents tend to view the difference between Blacks and Jews as, in essence, a "racial" difference between Blacks and

Whites, while their Jewish neighbors tend to view Black-Jewish difference as a "religious" difference between Jews and Gentiles.[3] But organizations working to build bridges between these communities tended to focus instead on what they viewed as "cultural" differences between two of Brooklyn's many ethnic groups. *Culture* was invoked as both a mediating and depoliticizing term—in between race and religion. Activists and officials encouraged Blacks and Jews to exchange customs and traditions, rather than accusations of racism and antisemitism. Drawing on a conceptual model of "multiculturalism" that has shaped recent state interventions in community relations, as well as educational programs in public schools, universities, and elsewhere, many felt that ritualized discussion and exchange of foods, music, holiday observances, or what have you would help ameliorate conflict in Crown Heights.

For an anthropologist like myself, it is tempting to imagine that the concept of culture—a concept at the heart of American anthropological thought—might provide a conceptual and political common ground for Crown Heights residents divided by race and religion. Yet, as it turned out, "culture" was not the neutral term that activists, officials, and some neighborhood residents hoped it would be. Although many Black Crown Heights residents were eager to participate in forums for cultural exchange, most of their Jewish neighbors did so only reluctantly, or refused to do so at all. As I hope to show here, the reluctance of most Lubavitchers to participate in cultural exchange raises far-reaching questions about the concept of culture itself and the increasingly significant role of this concept in American political life.

But before I develop this argument any further, let me first provide an ethnographic introduction to the uses of "culture" in Crown Heights politics by describing one of the first public programs for cultural exchange organized after the violence of 1991. On September 27, 1991, the Brooklyn borough president and the Crown Heights Coalition (a group of community leaders the borough president's office had just organized) invited 150 Black public school students to visit a large sukkah erected by a Lubavitch community organization. Every fall during the holiday of Sukkot, Lubavitch Hasidim, like other orthodox Jews, build outdoor booths, or sukkahs, in which they eat all their meals for eight days—filling the streets with the smells of kosher foods, and generating no little curiosity among Black Crown Heights residents. The Crown Heights Coalition saw this as an ideal opportunity to bridge the gap between

Blacks and Jews. While visiting the sukkah, the children learned about the ancient harvest festival of Sukkot and had a snack of soda and cookies. Long-time Borough President Howard Golden then exhorted the children—and their hosts—with words of multiculturalist wisdom. Golden told them:

> So much of bias and bias-related violence stems from fear and ignorance. We can break down these barriers by learning about the cultural traditions of our neighbors. The joyous holiday of Sukkot—marking a new harvest, a new beginning—is the perfect time for the people of Crown Heights to work toward a unified and peaceful future. (Crown Heights Coalition 1992:22)

But some in the audience did not share Golden's optimistic enthusiasm for "break[ing] down . . . barriers." One Lubavitcher I knew, whose family had been attacked in the violence of the previous month, attended the event and was horrified by what she considered kowtowing to Black antisemitism. Years later she asked me rhetorically, "We should invite them into our sukkahs, and give them snacks so they won't kill us?"

Though I cannot pass judgment on this Hasidic woman's anger, given the violence she suffered in August of 1991, I do not intend to endorse her bigoted generalizations about "us" and "them." I do, however, intend to take her resistance to dialogue quite seriously—and listen to her concerns with a sympathetic ear. For her reluctance to invite Black children into a Jewish space reflects a broader tension in the social life of Crown Heights—a neighborhood where a large Black majority and a small Jewish minority live together on integrated city blocks but spend their days in segregated social worlds.[4] Like the former borough president, many Black neighborhood residents see this social segregation as an impediment to "a unified and peaceful future." The Reverend Clarence Norman, a long-time local pastor and community activist, told me, "The tragedy [in Crown Heights] is we're living side by side—two communities living side by side—with no interrelation, no relationship with each other, except when there's an explosion. That's the only time we talk, or dialogue, is when something happens." But efforts to integrate Crown Heights in ways that go beyond physical co-presence are often frustrated by the different view of community held by most Hasidim. Another Hasidic woman—a grandmother in her fifties and a community activist who participated, with increasing frustration, in many of the Black-

Jewish dialogues of the early 1990s—cast doubt on the basic premises of such efforts. I asked her if Blacks and Jews in Crown Heights would benefit from an "open and honest dialogue," and she replied:

> We don't want it. They don't want it either. There's no point in it. Because the issues that we have, that are problems, are not issues that are gonna be solved that way. For instance . . . I've heard, at different things that I've gone to—y'know: "You don't eat in my house" or "You don't say hello to me" or "You won't let my kids play"—so what? *So what!?* So what if I don't let my children play with your children? Does that make me a bad person? No. It just means we're different. . . . Y'see that's what also makes me upset, that there really is no respect for diversity, that there's always a lot of pressure on the Jews to come across, and be open, and share. . . . We're not interested. We're just insular. You don't like my being insular, that's your problem. It's not my problem. And the pressure from the city and from different agencies to try and overcome that is insulting!

This insularity stems, above all, from a widespread Lubavitch concern that social contact with Gentiles will undermine the religious life of their community—a concern sometimes, though by no means always, coupled with varying amounts of racial bigotry. But as I have begun to argue, it also reflects the distance between most Lubavitch Hasidim and the widely shared assumptions of American multiculturalism. Although this Lubavitch activist invokes a key term of multicultural rhetoric when she appeals for "respect for diversity," her refusal to "share" her culture with others violates a central principle of multicultural politics.

My own understanding of this refusal to "share" has shifted quite dramatically over the course of my engagement with the people and politics of Crown Heights. When I began my field research in the neighborhood, in the summer of 1996, I was inspired to learn of the forums for Black-Jewish dialogue that had been organized since 1991. I was eager to explore how such programs might foster respect between Blacks and Jews, and perhaps blur the lines between Black and Jewish identities. I too saw Hasidic insularity as an impediment to peaceful coexistence. Yet, as I spoke to a broad range of Black and Jewish Crown Heights residents, I came to understand and respect the depth of my Lubavitch informants' concerns about Black-Jewish dialogue and cultural exchange. By the time I finished my research, in the summer of 1998, I was thoroughly—if a bit reluctantly—convinced that these multiculturalist ideals are not, in fact, particularly good ways to improve Black-Jewish relations in Crown Heights.

And in the years since, as I reflected on my experiences in Crown Heights, my grudging respect for Hasidic sensibilities has gradually evolved toward a fundamental—though somewhat ambivalent—critique of the underlying assumptions of American multiculturalism. Is it, in fact, always necessary to "break down [the] barriers" between diverse communities if they are to share "a unified and peaceful future"? And, if so, is the best way to do so through "learning about the cultural traditions of our neighbors"? Like many Lubavitch Hasidim, though for somewhat different reasons, I think the answer to these questions may be no.

I will explore these questions here by examining efforts to promote cultural exchange between Blacks and Jews in Crown Heights in the wake of the violence of 1991. I will focus, above all, on moments when Black and Jewish "cultures" were defined by distinctive cuisines, and "cultural exchange" was thus linked to the sharing of food. As we will see, this popular equation of culture and food was especially problematic in Crown Heights, as it placed the political project of cultural exchange in tension with the Jewish dietary laws of *kashrus*.[5] But before I turn to Lubavitch understandings of kashrus and kosher food, I will examine the popular understandings of culture and cultural food that set the terms for cultural exchange in Crown Heights.

THE POLITICS OF "CULTURE"

Over the past thirty or forty years, a number of intersecting social movements and trends have placed "culture" and "cultural identity" increasingly close to the heart of American political life. These have included, among others, the African American civil rights struggles of the 1950s and 1960s, the turn toward Afrocentrism in the Black Power movement of the late 1960s and the subsequent "ethnic revival" among many White Americans, the concurrent emergence of second-wave feminism, gay liberation, and similar social movements, the dramatic increase in migration to the United States that followed the 1965 reform of U.S. immigration law, and, perhaps above all, the growing commodification of "culture" and "heritage" throughout the world. As a result of these tumultuous trends, multiculturalism has emerged as a dominant model for understanding and negotiating America's diversity.[6]

Multicultural programs by educators and activists usually invoke a more or less anthropological concept of culture—loosely defined as the shared beliefs and practices of a community—and they generally encourage Americans to celebrate their cultural traditions while gaining an appreciation of the traditions of others. So far, so good—a cultural anthropologist could hardly disagree, although a Lubavitcher Hasid might. But most contemporary anthropologists describe culture as a fluid *process*, constituted in everyday life, that transgresses the boundaries of clearly defined communities, while multicultural programs tend to focus on static *objects*, like distinctive clothing or foods, that are often taken as self-evident signs of membership in clearly defined social or political interest groups. The Black and Jewish communities of Crown Heights, for example, may thus be distinguished as Kwanza is from Hanukkah—or dreadlocks from yarmulkes, or jerk chicken from gefilte fish—without making much of an effort to understand the meanings and textures of Black and Jewish lives. Although multicultural programs tend to encourage "cultural exchange," the ritual exchange of these decontextualized objects tends to eclipse, or even displace, the more fluid and prosaic realities of a shared social world. And here, oddly enough, I think an anthropologist and a Hasid may find common cause for concern.[7]

Despite such concerns, the objectification—or reification—of culture has profoundly shaped the ways many Americans, and others, experience collective identities and differences. For some individuals and communities, though not all, this limited concept of culture has served a strategic purpose or struck a distinctive chord. For many Black Crown Heights residents, for example, discussions and celebrations of "African culture" form a potent rhetoric of self-making and community building—and a refutation of the longstanding charge that the peoples of the African diaspora were stripped of all autonomous traditions in the cruel course of plantation slavery. And for many Afro-Caribbean Crown Heights residents, more specifically, celebrations of Caribbean "cultures" form enduring links to their childhood or ancestral homes. The objectification of culture in multicultural programing thus marks an unstable confluence between the political rhetorics of Black Crown Heights residents and the state—a seemingly odd intersection, given the persistent marginalization of Brooklyn's Black population in both local and national politics. Yet the Lubavitch Hasidim—an equally marginalized population, though in different ways—have largely resisted incorporation into American understandings of cultural difference. Where Black Crown Heights residents, and many other Americans, might invoke their "cultures" or "traditions"—for example, as explanations of distinctive holidays or foods—Lubavitchers would more likely invoke the commandments of the Torah or the will of their God. And these religious objectifications of everyday practice are not so easily incorporated into multiculturalism's "culture."

The political project of "cultural exchange" rests upon a fundamental assumption that the heterogeneous practices of diverse communities may all be subsumed within the concept of culture. Kwanza and Hanukkah, dreadlocks and yarmulkes, jerk chicken and gefilte fish, may all be exchanged for each other because all are equivalently "cultural." But the Lubavitch Hasidim—and other sectarian communities—disrupt this chain of equivalence by insisting on the categorical uniqueness of their own distinctive practices. This resistance to "culture" complicated the process of Black-Jewish dialogue following the violence of 1991, as will be clear when we examine the tensions between cultural and kosher food.

CULTURAL FOOD, CULTURAL EXCHANGE

An extremely broad range of objects and practices are taken to represent culture in multicultural programs, but a particularly intimate connection is often established between culture and food. From university dining halls to national folk-life festivals, from street corner take-out joints to haute cuisine fusion menus, the experience of cultural diversity is often equated with the consumption of diverse foods. With the rise of multiculturalism and the increasing commodification of culture, people around the world—including many Black Crown Heights residents—have come to see "cultural foods" as symbolically charged vessels for collective identity.

Though culinary differences have long been used to define social solidarities and distinctions, the static link between food, culture, and identity seems to be a rather recent historical development.[8] The anthropologist Richard Wilk notes, for example, that when he first conducted fieldwork in Belize in the early 1970s, most people told him there was no such thing as "Belizean food" (Wilk 1995:112). But by the early 1990s

a Belizean cuisine has appeared, first in expatriate Belizean restaurants in New York and Los Angeles, then in the form of a "Belizean Dish of the

Day" at tourist hotels. Belizean cookbooks were produced by the Peace
Corps, and today almost every eatery [in Belize] which isn't Chinese is advertising "authentic Belizean food." (113)

In twenty short years, writes Wilk, "dishes that were once markers of rural poverty [have] been converted into national cuisine" (1999:251). According to Wilk, this new understanding of "authentic Belizean food" has
been popularized in large part by educated elites self-consciously attempting to construct a national culture (244). Somewhat similarly, I
think, American understandings of "authentic [ethnic] food" have been
popularized by authors and activists working to promote racial harmony
and cultural diversity.[9] Yet even in this class-specific milieu, these newfound culinary identities leave a funny taste in many mouths. The legal
scholar and activist Patricia Williams recalls, for example, being invited to
a book party:

> The book was about pluralism. "Bring an hors d'oeuvre representing your
> ethnic heritage," said the hostess, innocently enough. Her request threw
> me into a panic. *Do I even have an ethnicity?* I wondered. . . . What are the
> habits, customs and common traits of the social group by which I have
> been guided in life—and how do I cook them? (Williams 1998:34)

Williams concludes that her West African ancestry has probably had the
greatest impact on her life in America's racialized society, but unfortunately, she writes: "I haven't the faintest idea what they do for hors
d'oeuvres in West Africa" (ibid.).

Although there are undoubtedly many Black Crown Heights residents
who share such reservations, the concept of cultural food has clearly
shaped Black imaginations of identity in Crown Heights. For example, at
the Crown Heights Youth Collective (an Afrocentric private school and
influential community organization led by the activist and educator
Richard Green) an elementary school science class on seeds and germina-
tion was organized around a student project to grow collard greens—a
typically "Black" food in popular imagination. Green began the class by
reminding his twenty or thirty African American and Afro-Caribbean students that the collards they were going to grow "had a big part to play in
our whole mission as a people." "Back when we were slaves," he explained, "whenever our great-great-grandmothers had to make a meal
they went outside and collected collard greens."

The complex intersections of race and culture around foods such as collard greens allow older Black Crown Heights residents to articulate a broad range of culinary identities. For example, one Black woman (a member of the Black-Jewish women's group Mothers to Mothers, which I will discuss below) drew on her favorite foods to define her own identity as a "Black American" rather than an "African American"—an identity she considered stridently separatist. Although she told me, in an interview, that the heritage of ancient Africa was "in [her] bloodline," she insisted that she does not consider herself "African" in any way: "Because of my culture and the way I'm brought up—I been brought up in America. My culture is American, Southern American. I cook with pork. I season with fatback. . . . I make collard greens and candy yams. All of that's part of my cultural food."

This woman thus defines herself as one sort of Black person rather than another by drawing a distinction between race and culture—or rather between her circulatory and digestive systems. Through a process of cultural objectification (cf. Handler 1988) her "cultural foods" stand in for the histories that produced them. The history of slavery in the American South is collapsed into collard greens and fatback, just as Jewish life in eastern Europe may be stuffed (in Yiddish, *gefilte*) into thinly sliced patties of fish topped with horseradish.

This transformation of history into recipe facilitates cultural exchange across communal boundaries by distilling identities into portable and edible objects—locating culture in products rather than processes, on the plate rather than in the kitchen. Much as "an hors d'oeuvre representing [one's] ethnic heritage" may be brought to a book party, these cultural foods are made to be shared. Indeed the process of exchange is often central to their status as "cultural." The historian Donna Gabaccia has shown, for example, that many of the foods associated with American ethnic groups took on their "ethnic" character through interethnic exchange. Bagels, she writes, "became firmly identified as 'Jewish' only as Jewish bakers began selling them to their multi-ethnic urban neighbors" (Gabaccia 1998:5).

And in multiethnic Crown Heights, my African American and Afro-Caribbean acquaintances often took pride in their knowledge of "Jewish" foods, and expressed pleasant surprise that I had heard of—let alone ate and enjoyed—"Black" foods. For example, an Afro-Caribbean woman I once chatted with in a grocery store almost fell down laughing when I told her I was buying ingredients for a curry—then made me promise I'd come visit her in Trinidad. In this and many other cases, Black Crown Heights residents viewed cultural foods as crucial ingredients of their identities, but took pleasure in sharing both food and identity with others. For many Black Crown Heights residents, culinary exchange thus suggests—and helps produce—communal harmony. For example, an African American activist I spoke to recalled, with giddy nostalgia, the meals he had shared with secular Jewish friends as a child growing up in Brownsville in the 1950s. He described his Jewish friends coming over to his home for collard greens, then rattled off a long list of the "Jewish foods" he used to eat in their homes: bagels, gefilte fish, whitefish, kugel, pastrami, tongue, matzah ball soup, and many more I can't remember. His voice rose and his smile widened as he built to a poetic crescendo recalling all these foods, until finally he slapped his knee, burst out laughing, and cried with delight, "A lot of times when I shitted, I shitted Jewish! And they shitted South!"

This heartfelt vision of Black-Jewish unity through collards and kugel was at once shared and co-opted by the activists and officials who developed programs for Black-Jewish "dialogue" after the violence of August 1991. Borough President Golden's 1991 Sukkot speech marked the beginning of a concerted effort—on the part of city agencies, museums, local and national organizations, and a few neighborhood residents—to improve Black-Jewish relations by teaching Crown Heights residents about "the cultural traditions of [their] neighbors." The programs these organizations developed generally took the salutary effects of cultural exchange for granted, and often—though not always—linked culture to food.

Over the course of the 1990s Crown Heights residents witnessed, and occasionally even participated in, more programs for dialogue and exchange than I can describe here. Some—like the basketball games, discussion groups, and rap concerts organized by the community organization Project CURE—had little or nothing to do with food. In some—like the Hanukkah-Kwanza celebrations held for a number of years at the Crown Heights Youth Collective or the ambitious series of exhibits and programs at local museums known as the Crown Heights History Project—food was one topic of discussion and exchange among many. And some—like the annual picnic organized by a local police precinct—were centered around the sharing of food, but drew links between food, culture, and identity only loosely or not at all.

These links were made explicit, however, in the programs and publications of the Crown Heights Coalition. The coalition, as I noted above, was
organized by the Brooklyn borough president's office, just days after the
violence of August 1991, and brought together a broad range of Black and
Jewish community leaders—rabbis and pastors, educators and activists,
elected officials, community board members, and the directors of prominent local organizations. The coalition's programs, however, were largely
conceived and developed by staff-members and consultants of the borough
president's Office of Ethnic Affairs, and these pluralism professionals tended to draw on multiculturalist models of cultural food and exchange.[10]

For example, the coalition's Cultural Awareness and Interaction Committee published and distributed a booklet for neighborhood youth entitled *Who Are My Neighbors? Answers to Some Questions About the Many Cultures of Crown Heights*. The anonymous authors of this booklet explain to
their young readers: "Culture is the way that you, your family and friends
do things. It includes the foods you eat, the holidays you celebrate and the
languages you speak" (26). To illustrate the links between culture and
food, they tell their readers: "Every Caribbean country has national dishes
which form the regular diet of its people" (29). The authors then ask, with
disarming simplicity, "What kinds of things do Jewish people like to eat?"
and answer: "Many Jewish people in Crown Heights have family roots in
Europe, so foods that originated in Poland, Hungary, Germany, Russia
and other Eastern European countries are very popular" (ibid.). They give
examples of "special Caribbean foods," like jerk chicken (from Jamaica),
roti (from Trinidad and Guyana), and fried pork (from Haiti). These are
mirrored by "Jewish foods" like gefilte fish, chicken soup, and kugel.

This booklet was only one part of a broader educational campaign.
Coalition members visited local public schools and yeshivas, making "cultural heritage presentations" (Crown Heights Coalition 1992:20). As I
have described, the coalition hosted Black public school students visiting
a Lubavitch sukkah. And finally, the coalition met on April 15, 1992, for
a Passover "Seder of Reconciliation," in which Black and Jewish community leaders "shared the traditional Jewish meal of matzah and bitter
herbs" (ibid.:22). Inspired by multiculturalist ideals, the coalition hoped
that by breaking bread—or matzah—together, and sharing each other's
cultures, Crown Heights residents might learn to live in peace.

There was a striking asymmetry, however, in the Crown Heights
Coalition's program of cultural exchange. Black school children visited a

sukkah, but Lubavitch yeshiva students never attended, say, a baptism or a revival meeting. The Passover "Seder of Reconciliation" was not followed by an Easter "Feast of Renewal." Black Crown Heights residents were eager—or at least willing—to sample their neighbors' "cultural foods," but Jewish Crown Heights residents were not. To understand this Lubavitch resistance to culinary and cultural exchange, we must examine Lubavitch understandings of kosher, rather than cultural, food.

KOSHER FOOD, KOSHER SELVES

Lubavitch participation in culinary and cultural exchange is limited in significant ways by Lubavitchers' careful adherence to the dietary laws and symbolic principles of kashrus, which tend to require boundaries between both foods and communities—milk and meat, Jews and non-Jews. Indeed, many Hasidim in Crown Heights see the requirements of kashrus as a primary explanation of the social distance between the neighborhood's Blacks and Jews. According to most Hasidim, the boundaries established by kashrus secure the essence of Jewishness itself, because kosher food makes kosher, observant Jews, while nonkosher food makes nonkosher, apostate Jews. As a rabbi once told me, during an informal kashrus course for newly orthodox Jews: "We are what we eat." This basic principle links the laws of kashrus to the construction of Jewishness in a way that parallels—yet diverges from—the links between food and culture outlined above.

Rabbi Shea Hecht, a Lubavitch community leader, highlighted the exclusionary aspects of kashrus in an interview with Anna Deavere Smith, for Smith's play *Fires in the Mirror*. Though Hecht was the founding cochair of the Crown Heights Coalition, he told Smith bluntly: "My goal is not to give anybody a message that we [in Crown Heights] plan on working things out by integrating our two things" (Smith 1993:109). Like most Hasidim, he argued that such integration is impossible, given the difference between Blacks and Jews. He argued that although Blacks and Jews must grant each other mutual respect as "children of God"

> that does not mean that I have to invite you to my house for dinner, because I can't go back to your home for dinner, because you're not going to give me kosher food! And I said, so, like one Black said: "I'll bring in kosher food;" I said: "Eh-eh." We can't use your ovens, we can't use your

dishes. It's not just a question of buying certain food, it's buying the food, preparing it in a certain way. We can't use your dishes, we can't use your oven! (110–111)

Hecht's response points to specific aspects of kashrus that help maintain the boundaries between Blacks and Jews. It is not, he notes, "just a question of buying certain food." Indeed, the laws of kashrus touch on many aspects of orthodox Jewish life.

The Hebrew Bible establishes the foundations of kashrus in two main ways. First, a number of animals are described as "abominations" unfit for Israelite consumption. Best known among these forbidden foods are all varieties of pork and shellfish.[11] Second, the Israelites are forbidden to "boil a kid [a young goat] in its mother's milk" (Exodus 23:19 and elsewhere), a prohibition Talmudic sages later reinterpreted to outlaw the mixing of milk and meat and require the use of separate utensils for milk and meat meals. A contemporary kosher kitchen thus requires two sets of dishes, cutlery, pots, pans, tupperware, tablecloths, and most everything else—and four sets of many such items, including additional milk and meat utensils for Passover, during which orthodox Jews may not eat leavened bread. The Talmudic sages and rabbinic authorities also established detailed procedures for the slaughter of kosher animals and strict requirements for foods deemed particularly subject to impurity. Many contemporary orthodox Jews do not keep these stringent standards of kashrus, but Lubavitchers and other Hasidim do. Milk, for example, must be produced under the supervision of an orthodox Jew, so a number of companies supply Hasidim with carefully supervised milk, known as *Chalav Yisroel* (literally, "Jewish milk").

This intricate web of law and custom lies behind Rabbi Hecht's skepticism of his neighbor's offer to "bring in kosher food." Indeed, with the sometimes crucial exception of packaged foods bearing kosher certifications, Lubavitchers simply cannot eat in their Black neighbors' homes— or most anywhere else outside of their community. But the significance of kashrus in Hasidic life is hardly limited to these legal and practical considerations. For most Hasidim, as I have noted, the everyday practice of cooking and eating is tied to broader concerns with personal and communal purity.

The rabbi who taught my informal kashrus course stressed the significance of these concerns by telling me what he described as "a famous story." He recounted how, some years ago, a non-Hasidic orthodox family called on a prominent Lubavitch rabbi, Nissan Mangel, to ask his help with their son, who was getting involved with Jews for Jesus. Rabbi Mangel agreed to study Torah with the boy, in an effort to debunk the Christian literature he had been reading. After a year of study, I was told, the boy was convinced that these books and pamphlets were "full of baloney," and agreed to burn them—"the whole suitcase full, everything." But unfortunately, according to my narrator, the young boy was irresistibly drawn to heresy. Though "he under[stood] logically that . . . the Torah is the true way of life," he wept as his Christian pamphlets burned. At this point Rabbi Mangel decided to write to the Lubavitcher Rebbe, to ask his advice and blessing. The Rebbe responded that the boy's family should be careful in their observance of kashrus, and though Rabbi Mangel was reluctant to broach the topic with the boy's father—whom he knew to keep kosher "one thousand percent"—he felt compelled to convey the Rebbe's message. When he told the boy's father that the Rebbe had warned him about kashrus, the father immediately started to cry. He confessed that although his family still kept kosher in every other way, not long before his son's troubles began they had started drinking regular milk instead of Chalav Yisroel. Following this revelation, his family returned to Chalav Yisroel, and his son soon returned to yeshiva. As my narrator reassured me, "The whole story straightened out."[12]

This narrative establishes symbolic links between the laws of kashrus and other aspects of Jewish life that I cannot address here.[13] But beyond such associations, the story also envisions a concrete, causal link between kosher food and Jewish identity. An orthodox family stops drinking Chalav Yisroel and their son strays from the Torah. By drinking nonkosher milk the boy sinks into nonkosher Jewishness. He doesn't make a conscious choice to believe in Jesus, but is forced into this belief— like an addict—by the nonkosher milk he's been drinking.

When the protagonist, Rabbi Mangel, told his own version of the story in a lecture to a class of newly orthodox yeshiva students, he situated the plight of the wayward yeshiva boy in a broad historical and theological account of the significance of kashrus. Mangel argued that the decline in orthodox Jewish observance over the past few hundred years—a shift in Jewish practice that secular scholars often attribute to "modernity"— has in fact been caused by nonkosher food. He explained that, despite their intellectual justifications, the primary reason so many contemporary

Jews fail to keep the laws of the Torah is that their souls have been "de-filed from trefa [nonkosher] food." Even the seemingly minor transgres-sion of drinking what Mangel described as "Goyishe [non-Jewish] milk" can have disastrous consequences:

> You can't imagine how many Jews, precisely for this reason, either they
> marry shiksas [non-Jewish women], or become dope addicts, or become—
> all the mishegas [craziness] they went through in the sixties and seventies—
> precisely for this reason: because they did not use Chalav Yisroel!

In sum, according to Rabbi Mangel and many other Lubavitchers, nonkosher food is a "virus" that "contaminates" the Jewish soul—and thus the Jewish people. By contrast, kosher food helps the Jews to fulfill their God-given mission as a chosen people. As the editor of a well-known kashrus manual for newly orthodox Jews reminds her readers: "The kosher diet . . . is designed to bring refinement and purification to the Jewish people" (Emmer 1989:5). Indeed, she promises that "meticu-lous care in kashrus will bring redemption in our time" (7).

This link between kosher food and Jewish peoplehood rests, in part, on a central theme of Hasidic thought: the distinctively Hasidic emphasis on the spiritual dimensions of everyday life and the ability of average Jews to commune with God through work, food, sex, and so on. Like much of Hasidic thought, this "sanctification of the concrete" builds on the kabbalistic theology of Isaac Luria, a famous sixteenth-century mystic. In Lurianic cosmology, creation is shot through with "sparks" of divine en-ergy, exiled from their source by a cataclysmic shattering of the cosmic order that followed its creation. According to both Lurianic and Hasidic thought, the God-given purpose of the Jewish people—the essence of their "chosenness," and their unique contribution to the messianic re-demption of creation—is to liberate these sparks of godliness from the physical world and thus return them to God. Jews accomplish this task by using material objects for spiritual purposes, according to the standards of religious law—by eating kosher foods, for example, and using their suste-nance for Torah study and prayer.[14]

However, these sparks of divine energy enter the material world in a number of different ways, and don't all maintain the purity of their source. Kosher and nonkosher foods—like Jews and non-Jews, for that matter—are all sustained by the energy of God; but the divine energy of kosher foods enters the world from an elevated spiritual realm, close to the essence of God, while the divine energy of nonkosher foods enters the world from an impure realm, far from its ultimate source. According to Hasidim, the body absorbs these pure and impure energies whenever one eats. As Rabbi Mangel explains, "It's not the potato itself, or the chicken itself . . . but the Word of God, which comes from the mouth of the *Abeshter* [the One Above]. This divine energy, this *nitzus eloki* [godly spark]—this spark is in the food. And this food—this divine energy—is what can influence a person." The impure energy of nonkosher food thus led to "all the mishegas [of] the sixties and seventies," while the godly energy of kosher food "will bring redemption in our time."

These threats and promises demonstrate the widespread Hasidic belief in the power of food to produce and sustain—or pollute and undermine—Jewish identity and community. In Lubavitch eyes, nothing a Jew eats or does can make him or her into a non-Jew; but the food one eats can still influence the nature of one's Jewishness in far-reaching ways. There are a number of important parallels between this Hasidic understanding of kosher food and Black Crown Heights residents' understandings of cultural food. The claim, quoted above, that collard greens "had a big part to play in our whole mission as [Black] people" resonates with the claim that kosher food "is designed to bring refinement and purification to the Jewish people." Much as fatback and candied yams mark the difference between a "Black American" and an "African American," Chalav Yisroel marks the difference between a yeshiva student and a Jew for Jesus. As signs and performances of authenticity, both cultural and kosher foods help construct collective identities, and define one's relationship to Blackness or Jewishness. In each case "We are what we eat."

But these parallel links between food and identity function in substantially different ways. For Lubavitch Hasidim and other orthodox Jews, the "Jewishness" of kosher foods generally inheres in the preparation and consumption of the food according to religious law, not in the food itself. As Shea Hecht noted, "It's not just a question of buying certain food, it's buying the food [and] preparing it in a certain way" (Smith 1993:110–111). There are a number of foods that are inherently nonkosher and non-Jewish, but no food is inherently kosher or Jewish. A hamburger or jerk chicken or Peking duck can all provide the godly energy needed to sustain a Hasid's Jewish soul—and Jewish identity—if the meat is slaughtered, prepared, blessed, and consumed appropriately. And a bowl of cholent (a traditional and highly symbolic beef stew eaten on the Sabbath) can pollute one's Jewish soul if accompanied by a glass of milk. By contrast, according to agencies and organizations working in Crown Heights in the 1990s, as well as many Black Crown Heights residents, cultural foods such as jerk chicken and cholent crystallize and inculcate collective identities, more or less regardless of how they are prepared and consumed. Distinctive ingredients and techniques are no doubt required to make a "Haitian" fried plantain, for example; but once it is produced, this "Haitianness" is largely independent of the codes that governed its production. A kosher chicken soup, however, will likely become tainted—and lose its "Jewishness"—if removed from a kosher home or served with Haitian plantains. Kosher food is inextricably tied to social practices that cultural food may transcend.

The Blackness and Jewishness of cultural and kosher foods are thus produced by two comparable, yet quite different, systems of objectification—two different systems for the production, and consumption, of identity. In each case, elements of everyday life are transformed into symbols of identity and community. But cultural foods are created when specific culinary *objects* are taken to represent the complex histories that produced them and diverse people who eat them, while kosher foods are created when specific culinary *processes* are taken to represent the authority of religious law and the cosmological significance of God's chosen people. The difference is crucial, because the definition of cultural food in terms of portable, edible objects facilitates culinary and cultural exchange across communal boundaries, while the definition of kosher food in terms of a web of standards and practices inhibits just such exchange.

BLACKS AND JEWS AT A BARBECUE

Yet over the course of the 1990s Crown Heights residents made quite a few efforts to overcome these social and conceptual differences by sharing meals of various kinds. In addition to one-time programs like those hosted by the Crown Heights Coalition, two annual events have brought Blacks and Jews in Crown Heights together for meals: a picnic sponsored by a local police precinct and a barbecue organized by the Black-Jewish women's group Mothers to Mothers. These meals have subjected the tensions between kosher and cultural food to the complex negotiations of everyday life and political practice. I will examine these complexities by taking a brief look at the Mothers to Mothers barbecue.

Mothers to Mothers was founded in 1992, as a response to the violence of August 1991, by a Lubavitch woman named Henna White and an Afro-Caribbean woman named Jean Griffith Sandiford (for profiles of Mothers to Mothers see Pogrebin 1997; Safer 1997). Over the next few years the group grew to include some fifteen to twenty women, most of whom, though not all, live in or near Crown Heights. The Mothers (as they tend to call themselves, though they aren't all mothers) began meeting each month and talking—talking about religion, politics, and, above all, family life. One African American member told me the conversations that had the greatest impact on her were

> the ones where we got to share our cultures, and the [Jewish] women shar-
> ing their culture, which is wrapped around their religion . . . that helped
> me to understand some things [about the Hasidic community]. And just
> being around, y'know, different people.

Over time, personal friendships took the place of formal dialogue. And in the summer of 1993, after a year and a half spent building trust, the Mothers decided to hold the first of their annual barbecues. Given the widely assumed links between women and domestic life—and the Mothers' own claims that their shared experiences as women help them transcend divisions between Blacks and Jews—they considered it uniquely appropriate to share a meal.

The Mothers' barbecue menu tends to avoid the "cultural foods" of Crown Heights residents. Rather than serving "Black" or "Jewish" foods like jerk chicken or pickled herring, they meet on the shared and familiar terrain of "American" foods like hamburgers and potato chips. But there's no way to avoid kosher food, which makes planning the barbecue a bit of a project, as the Mothers go out of their way to make sure each and every member can contribute something to the meal. I asked Henna White how Mothers to Mothers dealt with Hasidic members' concerns about kashrus, and she replied, "Well it wasn't very complicated. . . . The [Black] women had to learn about kashrus. So everybody had to buy po-tato chips with [a kosher certification] on it, and nobody had a problem with it." Another Hasidic member, who coordinated the barbecue for a number of years, told me there has never been a problem with kashrus. She described the planning process:

> I called up—I think Ann [an African American member] was bringing
> pickles this year—and she asked me, "Ben's Pickles [a brand] OK? I think

it's got [a kosher certification]." And y'know, like, everybody knows already! We've learned about each other's culture, and everybody respects it.
Nobody—there was not one person, and we've been doing this a number
of years—has brought anything that they shouldn't have.

I asked this woman what she thought when other Lubavitchers explain
Black-Jewish tensions by claiming that "we can't eat together," and she
replied simply, "That's garbage." And indeed, at the Mothers to Mothers
barbecue I attended in July of 1998, a dozen or so Black and Jewish women sat comfortably in a Brooklyn backyard—chatting, laughing, and en-
joying hot dogs, hamburgers, potato and macaroni salads, vegetables,
tabouli, pickles, chips, soda and beer.

But the culinary divide between Blacks and Jews still lingered beneath
the surface of this bucolic scene. As in every meal shared by Blacks and
Jews in Crown Heights, culinary authority and decision making must ultimately rest with the Jews. Blacks must simply accept the requirements
of kashrus and buy the right brands of pickles and chips. Most Black
members of Mothers to Mothers are more than happy to do so, out of respect for their Hasidic friends' beliefs—and, perhaps, for their "culture."
But some are not so thrilled with this arrangement. The same member of
Mothers to Mothers who told me her "cultural food" includes pork and
fatback said she understands, from her reading of Scripture, why the Jews
in Mothers to Mothers refuse to eat these foods, but has nevertheless been
frustrated by what she considers their stubbornness in planning the barbecue. "It's all kosher food," she complained, "so in a sense you feel
that—well, it's a one-way street when it comes to food."

Like the Crown Heights Coalition's interfaith seder, Mothers to
Mothers' annual barbecue thus establishes an asymmetrical pattern of exchange. It often is, in fact, "a one-way street" when Crown Heights activists strike a balance between kashrus and culture.

THE LIMITS OF "CULTURAL DIVERSITY"

This balance is hard to strike because Black and Jews in
Crown Heights are not simply different—they are different in different
ways. Unlike most of their neighbors, most Lubavitch Hasidim do not
have "cultural" differences. In a certain sense of the word, the Lubavitch
Hasidim don't have a "culture." Or, rather, they don't experience themselves as "having a culture" in the same ways that many other Americans

do. Lubavitchers have commandments from God that govern nearly every aspect of their lives, including what they eat. But this is substantially different from having a culture. One's commandments from God may not, for example, be shared in the same ways one's culture may be. Yet, in the wake of the violence of August 1991, government agencies, community organizations, and others called on the Lubavitch Hasidim to have a culture and exchange it with their neighbors. Some were happy to do so. But many complained, in the words of the activist quoted above, that "there really is no respect for diversity, that there's always a lot of pressure on the Jews to come across, and be open, and share."

This pressure stemmed, in large part, from a laudable concern for the troubled state of Black-Jewish relations in Crown Heights. But it also reflected the increasing hegemony of what Richard Wilk has aptly described as "global systems of common difference," which "celebrate particular kinds of diversity while submerging, deflating or suppressing others" (Wilk 1995:118). According to Wilk, the equation of culinary and cultural difference is produced within

> [a] new global cultural system [that] *promotes difference* instead of suppressing it, but difference of a particular kind. Its hegemony is not of content, but of form. . . . while different cultures continue to be quite distinct and varied, they are becoming different in very uniform ways. The *dimensions* across which they vary are becoming more limited, and therefore more mutually intelligible. (ibid.)

Of course in a neighborhood like Crown Heights, where dramatically different people share busy streets, limited housing, and overtaxed public facilities, a bit of mutual intelligibility may be a very good thing. Within a multiculturalist understanding of cultural food, the Blacks have their collard greens and jerk chicken, the Jews have their matzah balls and gefilte fish, and even if they don't usually eat together they can at least conceptualize each other's lives. But when state agencies and elite institutions work to promote cultural exchange in places like Crown Heights, I start to worry about this act of translation and the "hegemony of form" it supports. I worry that "cultural diversity" may ultimately subsume the complex differences of Crown Heights residents, and others, within a state-sponsored regime of mandated difference—forcing Blacks, Jews, Catholics, Queers, Hindus, Muslims, and most everyone else to structure their identities and communities in equivalent and interchangeable ways.

This structural containment of difference is no doubt attractive to many state actors and social activists, who seem to have an easier time dealing with diverse communities that are formally identical. More broadly, and loosely, it may be appealing to "mainstream" Americans, who have developed a taste for differences that come in easily digestible forms. But in the long run, I think, it is not in the best interests of Blacks or Jews in Crown Heights, or anyone else who wants to define their own differences on their own terms. Although some minority communities—like the Black communities of Crown Heights—have their own distinctive investments in the concepts of culture and cultural diversity, the rhetoric and practice of multiculturalism may nevertheless facilitate their incorporation in the conceptual grid and political projects of the state and social elites. And for other minority communities—like the Jewish community of Crown Heights—the concepts of culture and cultural diversity may deny them the ability (dare I say the right?) to imagine their collective identities and conduct their social lives in terms that are meaningful to them. In this sense, I think, my Lubavitch friend was right when she argued that "there really is no respect for diversity" in programs of cultural exchange.

But what are the alternatives to such programs? How else might neighborhood residents, and others, work to improve Black-Jewish relations in Crown Heights? These practical questions must at least be raised, although I will not be able to address them here in adequate depth. A number of organizations founded in Crown Heights in the late 1990s are, in fact, working to bring Blacks and Jews together to address their shared concerns, without calling much attention to their "cultures" or "identities." The Crown Heights Community Mediation Center, for example, enlists Blacks and Jews from the neighborhood—and others like myself—to work as volunteer mediators who help resolve everyday conflicts between landlords and tenants, parents and children, and neighbors of all kinds. And a new coalition of Black and Jewish community leaders, called Project CARE, has worked in recent years to develop housing and improve city services for all Crown Heights residents.[15]

Organizations like these have fostered relationships between Blacks and Jews in Crown Heights in a prosaic yet profound way—not by teaching neighborhood residents about each other's cultures but by getting them involved in each other's lives. Their modest efforts offer us a glimpse of a truly multicultural American society in which complex coalitions reach out across radical differences.

NOTES

My research and writing have been funded, in part, by the International-
al Migration Program of the Social Science Research Council, the Lucius N. Littauer
Foundation, Phi Beta Kappa of Northern California, the National Foundation for
Jewish Culture, and the Institute for the Advanced Study of Religion at Yale University. I received invaluable feedback on this essay, in its various incarnations, from
my dissertation committee at the University of California at Santa Cruz; from the
members of my dissertation writing group, especially Ben Chesluk and David Valentine; from the editors of this volume, Melissa Checker and Maggie Fishman; and from
Nina Schnall and Jillian Shagan. This essay is dedicated—with ambivalent solidarity
and unambivalent respect—to Rivka, who refuses to "share."

1. The factual details of these events are extremely complex and often hotly contested. For more information and multiple perspectives see Girgenti 1993; Goldschmidt 2000:52–92; Smith 1993; Rieder 1995.

2. Like most Crown Heights residents, I usually use *Black* as a catchall term for
people of recognized African descent—including both native-born African Americans
and Afro-Caribbean immigrants. I usually capitalize terms denoting racial and religious categories, because standard English usage requires me to capitalize *Jew* and simple fairness requires me to treat Blacks and Jews alike in such textual details.

3. For analyses of the tension between race and religion in Crown Heights residents' constructions of Black-Jewish difference, see Goldschmidt 2000.

4. In 1990 some twelve thousand Lubavitch Hasidim made up about 8 percent of
the total population of Crown Heights, as the boundaries of the neighborhood are
semi-officially defined. Though there are a few blocks in south Crown Heights that
are predominantly Jewish, the Hasidim do not form a clearly defined "enclave" within this larger community. For a detailed picture of the social geography of Crown
Heights, see Goldschmidt 2000:93–158.

5. My spelling of the term *kashrus* follows the Ashkenazic pronunciation of most
Lubavitch Hasidim. Many other contemporary Jews refer to the dietary laws as
"kashrut" or "kashruth."

6. For a broader account of the historical context of American multiculturalism,
focusing on global trends in the organization of capital and communities, see Turner
1993, especially 423–424.

7. My critiques of multiculturalism, and the distinctions I have made between anthropological and multiculturalist concepts of "culture," draw on a number of intersecting literatures. Above all, my arguments rest on recent analyses of the uses of culture in contemporary politics, including: Baumann 1996; Gilroy 1987; Handler 1988;
Stolke 1995. These analyses speak, in turn, to recent debates over the culture concept
by anthropologists, multiculturalists, and others. For useful introductions to these on-

FOOD FIGHTS

going discussions see: Borofsky, et al. 2001; Goldberg (ed.) 1994; Gordon & Newfield
(eds.) 1996.

8. There are extensive scholarly literatures on the social life and cultural significance of food. Unfortunately, most authors on the subject simply restate the com-
monsense equation of food and identity in authoritative scholarly garb. Others, however, offer subtle analyses of the diverse ways this equation is produced. Texts that
have been particularly helpful to me include Diner 2002; Gabaccia 1998; Mintz 1996.
For a broad overview of the literatures on food and culture see Counihan and Van
Esterik 1997. For the classic analysis of the role of "commensality" in cementing relationships between individuals and groups, see Robertson Smith 1972 [1889].

9. Donna Gabaccia also highlights the role of state-sponsored "folk-life" festivals
and commercial cookbooks in popularizing regional and ethnic foods as central components of the "new ethnicity" of the 1960s and 1970s (Gabaccia 1998:175–201).

10. Despite my best efforts, I was never invited to attend meetings of the Crown
Heights Coalition, and I was not privy to the inner workings of the organization. My
account of its top-down style of program development rests on the comments of a
number of coalition members but would no doubt be disputed by others.

11. These lists of forbidden beasts are the subjects of Mary Douglas's justly famous
analysis of the laws of kashrus (1966). See Douglas 1975.

12. Elements of this narrative that may seem remarkable at first glance—like the
miraculous powers attributed to the Lubavitcher Rebbe, and the unique relationship
between the Rebbe and his Hasidim—are, in fact, quite commonplace in Hasidic life.

13. For the full text of this narrative, and a more detailed analysis, see Goldschmidt
2000:184–186.

14. For a sketch of Lurianic cosmology, see Scholem 1971:43–48. For discussions
of Hasidism's "sanctification of the concrete," along with other elements of Hasidic
thought, see Hundert 1991.

15. For more information on the Mediation Center see: http://www.courtinno-
vation.org/demo_06chcmc.html. For more information on Project CARE (not to be
confused with the early nineties' Project CURE), see http://www.project-care.com.

WORKS CITED

Baumann, Gerd. 1996. *Contesting Culture: Discourses of Identity in Multi-Ethnic London.*
Cambridge: Cambridge University Press.
Borofsky, Robert, Fredrik Barth, Richard Shweder, Lars Rodseth, and Nomi Maya
Stolzenberg. 2001. "WHEN: A Conversation About Culture." *American Anthro-
pologist* 103(2): 432–446.
Counihan, Carole and Penny Van Esterik, eds. 1997. *Food and Culture: A Reader.*
New York: Routledge.

Crown Heights Coalition. 1992. *Crown Heights: A Strategy for the Future.* Report prepared in cooperation with the Brooklyn Borough President's Office.

—— N.d. *Who Are My Neighbors? Answers to Some Questions About the Many Cultures of Crown Heights.* Booklet prepared in cooperation with the Brooklyn Borough President's Office.

Diner, Hasia. 2002. *Hungering for America: Italian, Irish, and Jewish Foodways in the Age of Migration.* Cambridge: Harvard University Press.

Douglas, Mary. 1975. "Deciphering a Meal" and "Self-Evidence." In *Implicit Meanings.* pp. 249–318. London: Routledge and Kegan Paul.

—— 1966. "The Abominations of Leviticus." In *Purity and Danger,* pp. 42–58. London: Routledge.

Emmer, Tzivia. 1989. "The Kashrut Connection: Does G-d Really Care What I Eat?" In Kashruth Division of the Lubavitch Women's Organization, eds., *Body and Soul: A Handbook for Kosher Living,* pp. 3–8. Brooklyn: Lubavitch Women's.

Gabaccia, Donna. 1998. *We Are What We Eat: Ethnic Food and the Making of Americans.* Cambridge: Harvard University Press.

Gilroy, Paul. 1987. *"There Ain't No Black in the Union Jack": The Cultural Politics of Race and Nation.* Chicago: University of Chicago Press.

Girgenti, Richard. 1993. *A Report to the Governor on the Disturbances in Crown Heights.* Vol. 1: *An Assessment of the City's Preparedness and Response to Civil Disorder.* Albany: New York State Division of Criminal Justice Services.

Goldberg, David Theo, ed., 1994. *Multiculturalism: A Critical Reader.* Cambridge: Blackwell.

Goldschmidt, Henry. 2000. "Peoples Apart: Race, Religion, and Other Jewish Differences in Crown Heights." Ph.D. diss., Board of Studies in Anthropology, University of California at Santa Cruz.

Gordon, Avery and Christopher Newfield, eds. 1996. *Mapping Multiculturalism.* Minneapolis: University of Minnesota Press.

Handler, Richard. 1988. *Nationalism and the Politics of Culture in Quebec.* Madison: University of Wisconsin Press.

Hundert, Gershon David, ed. 1991. *Essential Papers on Hasidism: Origins to Present.* New York: New York University Press.

Mintz, Sidney. 1996. *Tasting Food, Tasting Freedom: Excursions into Eating, Culture, and the Past.* Boston: Beacon.

Pogrebin, Letty Cottin. 1997. "The Twain Shall Meet." *New York Times.* March 16, p. 17.

Rieder, Jonathan. 1995. "Reflections on Crown Heights: Interpretive Dilemmas and Black-Jewish Conflict." In Jerome Chanes, ed., *Antisemitism in America Today,* pp. 348–385. New York: Birch Lane.

Robertson Smith, William. 1972 [1889]. *The Religion of the Semites: The Fundamental Institutions.* New York: Schocken.

Safer, Sarah. 1997. "Mothers Reshuffle the Race Card in Crown Heights." *Lilith* 22(1): 8.

Scholem, Gershom. 1971. *The Messianic Idea in Judaism, and Other Essays on Jewish Spirituality*. New York: Schocken.

Smith, Anna Deavere. 1993. *Fires in the Mirror: Crown Heights, Brooklyn, and Other Identities*. New York: Anchor.

Stolke, Verena. 1995. "Talking Culture: New Boundaries, New Rhetorics of Exclusion in Europe." *Current Anthropology* 36(1): 1–24.

Turner, Terence. 1993. "Anthropology and Multiculturalism: What is Anthropology That Multiculturalists Should Be Mindful of It?" *Cultural Anthropology* 8(4): 411–429.

Wilk, Richard. 1999. "'Real Belizean Food': Building Local Identity in the Transnational Caribbean." *American Anthropologist* 101(2): 244–255.

—— 1995. "Learning to Be Local in Belize: Global Systems of Common Difference." In Daniel Miller, ed., *Worlds Apart*, pp. 110–133. London: Routledge.

Williams, Patricia. 1998. "Ethnic Hash." *Transition* 7(1): 34–39.

8

FOBby or Tight? "Multicultural Day" and Other Struggles at Two Silicon Valley High Schools

SHALINI SHANKAR

In a packed gymnasium at Mercer High School in Silicon Valley, California eleven hundred students and their teachers rise as a student sings the "Star Spangled Banner" with electric guitar accompaniment. In the adjacent locker rooms girls fidget with their shiny golden head jewelry and generously applied makeup while boys enact mock sword fights with their *dhandiya*, or decorated sticks, which they will use shortly in their dance. The national anthem ends and students settle onto the bleachers in noisy anticipation of the hour-long multicultural program that has replaced their third and fourth period classes today. Elaborately costumed groups of enthusiastic students begin to perform their prepared dances and martial arts routines.

When the Indian Student Club is introduced, six South Asian American (hereafter *Desi*) girls strike a pose in a circle at the center of the gym; thirty-four other performers—of South Asian, East Asian, Middle Eastern, and European descent—stand poised and ready to enter on cue.[1] The inner circle of Desi girls begins dancing gracefully to *Taal*, the title song from a popular recent Hindi film.[2] Fourteen more girls in coordinated green and gold skirts join in, soon followed by their twenty male partners. The gym echoes with reverberating bass and howls of kids cheering for their friends while the performers enjoy their moment in the limelight. The music quickly segues from one lively Hindi film song to another as the choreography includes bhangra and hip-hop influenced moves and *filmy* flirting and courting rituals.[3] The dance closes with a dramatic pose that sends the audience into wild appreciation.

This celebratory seven-minute performance, like myriad other multicultural programs in U.S. high schools, is beautifully performed by students and audibly appreciated by audiences. The choreography and music—painstakingly selected by students to incorporate both international and local cultural forms—flow seamlessly together. What is obscured in these short performances, however, is a broad range of enduring inequalities of ethnicity and class that dominate the everyday lives of students.

Although multiculturalism's ideologies of equal rights and representation grew out of various civil rights and postcolonial struggles, they often lose their potency when they are implemented. The schools' initiatives reflect the egalitarian spirit of multiculturalism, but the inconsistent ways in which they are executed offer little support to ensure this outcome. The rhetoric that all students are able to participate in these programs and, more broadly, in the culture of high school itself masks the exclusion of many interested kids; moreover, it overshadows historically produced systems of advantage and disadvantage that favor particular ethnic groups and ignores socioeconomic cleavages that exist within them.

Yet, to consider these events as a predictable case of haves and have-nots would obscure another type of struggle enacted in these spaces—namely, a politics of representation. Ideologies of multiculturalism—especially the inclusion of non-European cultural expression—are important to Desi kids, as they are the only school forum dedicated to exploring cultural difference. Kids invest considerable time and energy in casting, choreographing, and outfitting these dances in order to define who they are to a broader audience. Their agency, however, is circumscribed in the reductive arena of multicultural programs, where tradition and authenticity are imagined in different ways by performers and audiences. While kids fashion performances according to their notions of "FOBby" (unstylish) versus "tight" (cool, fashionable), this cultural logic often gets lost in translation for audiences of school peers and faculty in search of an idealized, authentic performance.

In this essay I focus on Desi students' attempts to take part in multicultural programs at two different Silicon Valley high schools where students of color are the majority. By going backstage, so to speak, to examine the casting, creating, and rehearsing of these performances, I will illustrate how these celebrations are far less inclusive than they appear on stage. At Mercer High School struggles to participate occur between various ethnic groups; at Greene High School they take place among Desis themselves.

My interest in how kids develop a sense of ownership over their high schools grew out of an initial observation in my research—it seemed that most kids who did not participate in mainstream school programs such as multicultural celebrations were genuinely uninterested in these activities. As I tracked the preparation for these programs during daily fieldwork in these two schools, I soon realized the situation to be far more complex. Thus I became committed to investigating how and why some kids dominate school activities while others who are interested remain unable to do so. Relatedly, I sought to better understand the nuanced meanings of kids' attempts at self-expression and how they are received in school contexts. In this case, if kids are investing great care and effort to craft cultural identities for performance, what are some of the dynamics that contribute to their being so easily misunderstood by high school audiences?

The examples I present in this essay address these points. Both cases—fraught with a similar twofold tension of students vying against one another for performance time while being judged according to essentialized notions of cultural identity—illustrate local processes of ethnic formation.[4] Moreover, we can better understand these struggles over public representation in the context of larger historical shifts and inequalities of ethnicity and class prevalent in this region of California.[5]

TRANSFORMATIONS OF THE CATEGORY "SOUTH ASIAN"

In California, as in other parts of the U.S., ethnic groups have had drastically different experiences with economic and political success depending on the time period and conditions under which they emigrated. Even within some ethnic populations these experiences have been anything but consistent (cf. Brodkin-Sachs 1994; Ignatiev 1995), emphasizing the fluidity of meanings around ethnicity (Sollors 1989). For example, what it means to be of South Asian descent has changed significantly in California over the past century. Early South Asian immigration consisted primarily of male farmers from Punjab during the late nineteenth and early twentieth centuries (Leonard 1992). These immigrants were portrayed in local newspapers as lacking morals, literacy skills, and personal hygiene. Proclaimed "the most undesirable immigrant in the state,"[6] they were denied citizenship and landownership rights. Yet, in the present-day sociopolitical climate of Silicon Valley, Desis' prestigious positions in the high-tech industry and elsewhere offers many of them ac-

cess to land and wealth unimaginable a century ago. Rather than potential miscreants, the recent visibility of post-1965 professionals immigrants
has earned Desis the honor of being considered "part of a solution"
(Prashad 2000) in the public imagination as well as public policy. Such a
drastic reversal of fortune highlights how local definitions of ethnicity are
shaped by specific configurations of capital, opportunity structures, and
socioeconomic backgrounds with which groups enter the American
economy at different historical moments.

This positive casting can, however, obscure cleavages of class, educational level, and immigration background among Desis. Scholars of the
South Asian diaspora emphasize the growing divide between early post-
1965 immigrants and the often less skilled immigrants they have subsequently sponsored (Khandelwal 1995; Leonard 1998; Lessinger 1995). In
Silicon Valley this population is further diversified not only by the slew of
highly skilled, "body-shopped" computer programmer labor of the 1990s,
but by a largely unacknowledged population of Punjabis whose relatives
have lived in California since pre-1965.[7] As all of these different types of
Desis move to Silicon Valley seeking employment ranging from assembly-
line work to white-collar jobs, ever deepening rifts of inequality have tak-
en hold in this seemingly homogeneous community. These differences are
especially salient for Desi kids in Silicon Valley high schools, where varying notions of entitlement, belonging, and influence create complex dynamics of inclusion and representation. They translate into various positions from which Desi kids approach multicultural programs.

MULTICULTURALISM IN THE U.S.: IDEOLOGIES AND INITIATIVES

Multiculturalism emerged in the U.S. in the late twentieth
century as a response to "European monoculturalism" (Goldberg 1994:3)
and Eurocentricism (c.f. Stam and Shohat 1994), an ideology pervasive in
American universities from the late nineteenth century. Such European
hegemony was in harmony with prevailing policies and attitudes toward
immigrants during that period. Rather than the concerted attempts to acknowledge and respect diversity that mark present-day multiculturalism,
immigrants were encouraged to relinquish any cultural values or language
practices that conflicted with Anglo-European monoculturalism and English monolingualism (Silverstein 1996).

This "melting-pot" model of assimilation (Glazer and Moynihan 1963) came under increasing attack during the latter part of the twentieth century, a period marked by emerging postcolonial nations worldwide and ardent civil rights movements in the U.S. as well as a relaxation of U.S. anti-Asian immigration laws (Lowe 1996). Further, since the mid-1960s the now commonplace realities of globalization—ease of travel and communication and a proliferation of media and images (Appadurai 1996; Harvey 1990; Jameson 1991)—encouraged the commodification of cultural difference in previously unimagined ways.

No sooner had these agendas and aspirations been announced than they came under intense debate. Outright opponents of multiculturalism have thwarted the movement's call for deeper economic, political, and social change with vilifying critiques of curricular reform, affirmative action, and other social changes (see Hu-DeHart 2001). More constructive critiques assert that the purely celebratory character of multicultural initiatives—such as festivals and fairs consisting of "ethnic" food, music, and performance—highlight the ways in which immigrants add color and diversity to an otherwise static American society while failing to address embedded power relations that contribute to inequality among these groups (McLaren 1994; Takaki 2001; Wallace 1994). Notably such celebrations are premised on the elision of whiteness as an ethnic category, wherein being "ethnic" is predicated on the existence of an unmarked white majority (Frankenburg 1993; Winant 1997; Waters 1990).

While multicultural agendas have been examined in colleges, less attention has been directed toward high schools, where there is less activism and organizing. Yet, students' everyday struggles around rights and representation is an important arena of social justice. "Cultural citizenship" (Rosaldo and Flores 1997), or "the right to be different (in terms of race, ethnicity, or native language) with respect to the norms of the dominant national community, without compromising one's right to belong, in the sense of participating in the nation-state's democratic processes" (ibid. 57), offers a framework for understanding how kids attempt to participate in the public culture of their high schools—in other words, how they exercise agency. Agency—social actors' ability and impetus to engage in acts that challenge dominant values and beliefs—is intricately linked to cultural citizenship. Although agency is seemingly boundless, it is also circumscribed within particular structures that govern thoughts and actions (Ahern 2001; Bourdieu 1977; de Certeau 1984; Giddens 1979). Indeed the desire to participate in a multicultural program does not ensure inclusion; rather the very process of getting into the program requires sophisticated knowledge of the interworkings of school activities. I refer to this complex intersection of social class, educational background, and immigration history as "cultural capital" (Bourdieu 1984). Kids who have cultural capital are better able to manipulate school systems to their advantage than kids who do not. For example, to gain entry into a multicultural program individuals as well as groups of kids have to feel comfortable asserting themselves in school activities, become familiar with the interworkings of this program, and be able to mobilize a group into practice and performance. While many kids may strive for greater cultural citizenship, only some have the cultural capital to fulfill their goals. As I will describe below for each school, some groups of students are far more successful at working the system than others.

MULTICULTURALISM IN TWO SILICON VALLEY HIGH SCHOOLS

Enrollment in Silicon Valley high schools has burgeoned over the past several decades. Such populations include kids of immigrants and refugees from South and East Asia as well as a significant Mexican/ Chicano community. No longer characterized by one minority group in a white majority environment, these schools must balance complex dynamics among Asian, Latino, African American, and white students, as well as between students and teachers.[8] The high-tech boom of the 1980s and nineties also contributed to a general overcrowding, and both high schools in this study are now enrolled 75–125 percent over capacity. School faculty and administrators—who are overwhelmingly white—have had an exceedingly challenging time dealing with the religious, linguistic, and cultural diversity of their students. Along with increased enrollment, this predicament has reprioritized administrators' agendas and led them to focus on basic tasks such as maintaining disciplinary order and ensuring appropriate classes, desks, and books over initiatives such as multiculturalism.

Both Mercer and Greene High Schools lack "formal" multicultural efforts in their curricula. While discussing ethnicity through an occasional project, presentation, or report is an option, multicultural programs stand alone as the prescribed space where issues of racial difference receive public attention. When public expression of difference is abbreviated to a single day or week, all "cultures" are presented as existing in harmony next to one another rather than as having to interact on an everyday level, in effect erasing large- and small-scale distinctions (c.f. Abercrombie 1991, Rogers 1999). These productions, along with ethnic food and music, are displayed as representative of entire countries and even continents (i.e. "African culture" or "Latin American culture") when they barely represent the diversity of the students of that group in that school.

At Mercer High School multicultural initiatives consist of a week-long festival culminating in a final assembly during class time on Friday. Located in Fremont,[9] it includes grades 9–12 of 2,250 with an ethnic breakdown of 54 percent Asian American (about one-third South Asian American), 41 percent white, 3 percent Latino, 1 percent African American, and less than 1 percent Native American. White, African American, and Latino families once dominated this area but have become increasingly marginalized by hundreds of Asian families who have flocked to the area to send their kids to this top-ranking public high school. Nearly all the Desi kids at this school are from upper-middle-class families, are relatively high achievers, and participate in a wide range of school activities.

One such activity, multicultural week, consists of four days, each of which is dedicated to a different racial group—African American, Asian American, Latino, and European American—and students are encouraged to dress in corresponding ethnic clothing. Friday is "Unity Day," and the week's events culminate in an hour-long assembly of performances held in the gym. During lunch, student clubs are invited to play music and sell ethnic foods and crafts. In this carnival-like atmosphere students can stroll around to different tables, snack on egg rolls and kabobs, and even get a "henna tattoo" at the Muslim Student Association.

In contrast, celebrating multiculturalism at Greene High School is a one-day affair. Like Mercer, Greene High School has also undergone a type of gentrification that has exacerbated inequalities. Located in East San Jose, Greene High School has 2,648 students—53 percent Asian, 28 percent Latino, 12 percent white, 6 percent African American, and less than 1 percent Native American. Greene High School has both Desi kids whose parents are high-tech professionals as well as a growing population of working- and middle-class kids whose parents relocated from other regions of the U.S., or directly from South Asia, to seek blue-collar employment during the economic growth of the mid to late 1990s. While wealthier South Asian students tend to participate in school activities and student leadership, middle- and working-class kids form their own groups and are less inclined to participate. To celebrate multiculturalism the school sponsors "International Day," which features an extended lunch period for students to play music, sell ethnic food, and have staged student performances in the center of the quad.

At both schools students themselves are inclined to regard multicultural programs primarily as entertainment. Still, students of color at both schools described them as the one event they felt was their own and compared it to other school productions such as homecoming and school dances—often referred to as "white" events. As one Desi boy commented, "I think MC week is cool because we can express ourselves in another angle that people usually don't see us through. . . . We're able to dress up—it helps show who you are." In this sense cultural performance is linked to cultural citizenship—it is a means for groups of students to represent themselves in the public arena of their schools. The processes by which this happens raise challenging questions as to how to translate multicultural ideologies of access and representation for all into equitable programs for students; the following discussions explore two such examples.

INTERGROUP TENSIONS:
A CASE FROM MERCER HIGH SCHOOL

Should students from all ethnic groups be included in Multicultural Week? This issue—about whether the program should take to heart multicultural ideology about equal access and representation or instead prioritize pleasing the majority of the student body—spawned debates and newspaper editorials during the 1999–2000 Mercer High School year. The issue began with the way the student committee handled auditions for the multiculturalism program, which were necessary to manage the overwhelming student interest in participating in the hour-long program. The planning committee appointed an all-white panel of teachers to judge the auditions, scheduled three months before the performance.[10] Chosen primarily based on their willingness to stay after school for the auditions, judges were asked to evaluate each act on content, choreography, and overall "entertainment value" of each group—equal representation of each interested ethnic group was not deemed an important criterion. Although students were alerted about the audition in early November, they received little information about how to prepare.

From this early stage onward, differences in cultural capital among students began to surface. Some hopeful participants were able to draw on the preparation experiences of friends and siblings in past assemblies, community dance programs, and their overall involvement in a wide range of school activities. The group of Desi girls I followed—one of several at the audition—were nonplussed by the lack of directives on how to ready themselves. Tara and Meena, two close friends, asked several of their Desi female friends to join their dance. Having won several South Asian community dance contests, they were no strangers to how dances are choreographed, rehearsed, and costumed. This, coupled with their love of Hindi films, left Tara and Meena to choose from literally thousands of Bollywood dance sequences upon which to model their dance. Motivated by the prospect of representing themselves to their school, they invested significant time and effort to procure what they knew would be a highly coveted spot. They successfully trained and costumed ten girls into nearly flawless audition material.

Only some groups, however, were able to access such a wide range of experiences and skills. The relative lack of cultural capital of African American and Latino students became apparent on the day of the audition. During this lengthy event, in which ten groups vied for four places, a number of Asian groups arrived with costumes and props alongside a smaller number of representatives from the Black Student Union (BSU) and the Latino student group (MECHA).[11] Their audition—earnest and creative but without costumes and their full cast of performers—was passed over in favor of ten Desi girls in matching outfits, the Chinese girls who performed a traditional ribbon dance using props owned by their families, the Filipino boys and girls who did a dance with lit candles that they had performed at community shows, and the uniformed Japanese Martial Arts group.

In contrast to the heightened visibility that many East and South Asians have experienced in recent decades in Silicon Valley, Latinos and African Americans have yet to be similarly acknowledged. What they lacked in cultural capital—the social knowledge, background, and experience to secure a place in the program—they sought to gain in their struggles for cultural citizenship. Although these African American and Latino groups were excluded, they still exercised agency and made their voices heard through writing to the school newspaper and trying to raise awareness about the exclusionary dynamic of the audition process. The BSU faculty adviser wrote a letter to the school newspaper arguing that although BSU was a relatively new student group and therefore unprepared, the exclusion of MECHA was inexcusable and signaled the declining rights of Latinos at the school—a predicament compounded by the absence of Latino teachers or faculty to advocate on students' behalf. The all-Asian multicultural student planning committee (in a school that was 54 percent Asian), however, was unsympathetic to this plea, asserting the judges had chosen performers according to proscribed criteria. To add insult to injury, the committee proceeded with their plan to hire two troupes of professional adult performers—a move to enhance entertainment value. The student committee leader justified the decision to include a dance troupe from Bolivia and a Chinese Acrobat show by arguing that student-only performances "can't hold the audience's attention," and the budget included funds to hire two outside acts.

The African American and Latino students I spoke with magnanimously supported the chosen performers. Yet they took issue with the school administration for not advocating on their behalf over professional adult performers and for leaving the program in the hands of four Asian students who did not prioritize inclusion of all interested student constituencies. The student president of MECHA submitted a provocative letter to the school paper, asserting that "if students are proud of their heritage and are willing to share it with their fellow students, they should be allowed to." Both groups argued that audition flyers did not call for costumes and polished pieces and questioned the underlying assumption that multicultural week is inherently less interesting and requires entertainment value to make it more appealing.

What emerged from these events is that the very unity Multicultural Week is intended to foster was undermined by disagreement over its goals and poorly publicized expectations about performance and entertainment. When asked about the controversy, the student activities coordinator asserted that this was the first year he had received complaints and that they were primarily from excluded students. Defending his stance in support of the committee's actions, he offered his interpretation: "Their viewpoint was that we do a quota type thing, that you take people regardless of how well they perform and put them in because you want to get *all* the ethnicities that you can. For us to be able to put every single group in there is impossible." The director's reluctance to include "*all* ethnicities" resonates with many opponents of affirmative action who equate inclusion with compromise of quality and substance. Although African American and Latino students voiced their objections and exercised cultural citizenship through the means available to them, they were further marginalized by being denied a place in a program purported by the school principal to "unite the community." Their unfortunate lack of cultural capital, coupled with larger contention about the underlying purpose of this multicultural initiative, ultimately denied these students a place in the program.

Multicultural Week proceeded on schedule, and although most were appreciative of the assembly (described in the opening of this article), many had mixed responses. Some found multicultural week entertaining but were unsure of whether it had a larger purpose. Jose, a member of MECHA, raised questions of fairness and equity: "There are hardly any black and Latino students in the school, so it isn't surprising that they are underrepresented at the assembly . . . but they should still be allowed to perform." Likewise, Shaniqua and Alicia, two students from the BSU, commented that being a minority does not diminish a group's desire to represent itself. Alicia recounted that the leadership committee refused her plea to include an African American group, maintaining it would be "redundant" to have something from African American culture "two years in a row." When asked how the problem could have been handled better, she reflected for a minute and replied, "I think instead of having the Chinese acrobat people—because they didn't represent any culture, it was more just a goofy sideshow—that's where *we* could have . . . not *we* . . . *there* could have been an African or African American anything." Alicia's comment, especially her shift from "*we*" to "not *we* . . . *there*" is indicative of how little ownership African American and Latino students feel over school activities and functions.

Mercer High Schools's multicultural program inadvertently reinforced existing race-based hierarchies in the school. Rather than attempt to include African American and Latino students—a minority at this high school, but a significant presence in American society and in California especially—the students in leadership chose to have the program correspond with current school composition. Since the administration did not intervene, representation became contingent on knowledge and resources available only to groups like the Desi kids, who were able to manipulate the system. In the next example, International Day at Greene High School presents related yet distinct issues that challenge established discourses of unity and multiculturalism.

INTRAGROUP STRUGGLES:
A CASE FROM GREENE HIGH SCHOOL

Should members within an ethnic group be assured equal access to multicultural programs? While Desi kids at Greene High School did not face competition from other ethnic groups such as African Americans or Latinos, they did end up competing with one another to perform in International Day 2000. Although not raised publicly, this issue was problematic all the same. In this case there were no auditions, nor were there any restrictions against having two dances to represent the same ethnic group; in fact, performing groups did not necessarily have to be affiliated with a student club. Yet a perplexing situation resulted from this seemingly open invitation: although there was plenty of room for all interested students to participate, only some were able to do so. When the program was announced, there was widespread interest among Desi kids. Yet, it was two upper-middle-class sisters—Jaspreet and Amanpreet—who first announced that they were planning to do a Desi dance. Other groups of Desi kids, despite their interest, had nary a clue as to how to procure a program slot.

That Desi kids at the same school should have such vastly different experiences with their multicultural program points to larger dynamics of cultural capital that stem from class and immigration history. Jaspreet and Amanpreet, daughters of well-educated, professional immigrants, "kick it" (hang out, spend time with) in the quad—the center of the schoolyard dominated by popular kids involved in a variety of school activities. Drawing on the cultural capital of their upbringing along with expertise and experience from school performances past, the sisters easily began to organize a dance. In contrast, "back-corner" (my term) kids who kick it in the periphery of the schoolyard and are generally uneasy about many school activities found International Day to be no exception. These working- and middle-class Desi kids outnumber the handful of upper-middle-class Desi kids who kick it in the quad. Many are third- and fourth-generation Punjabi kids whose families moved to Silicon Valley from other parts of California (see Gibson 1988). For many of these kids school and its programs

seem like obstacles to be overcome rather than potential enrichment opportunities. With little cultural capital and even less clout in school, their
ability to plan a dance was limited from the outset.

A few daring back-corner girls did, however, attempt to join the dance
with Jaspreet, Amanpreet, and their friends. While one girl who was not
easily intimidated and knew Amanpreet from her classes convinced her
three friends to join, others in the back corner were less successful. As one
girl commented, "I wanted to join a dance, but Jaspreet and Amanpreet
are kind of snobby and live way up in the hills, so I don't really want to
do it with them." Three different groups of girls expressed interest in doing dances but shied away at the prospect of visiting the leadership office
for information. Some of the Punjabi-speaking boys discussed the possibility of doing a *bhangra* dance, yet none took initiative. One by one,
back-corner kids let go of the idea of doing their own dance, and soon
the sisters' dance became the only Desi entry.

Although Jaspreet and Amanpreet initially had an easy time, problems
soon arose that highlighted socioeconomic differences separating them
from the back-corner girls. For example, rather than holding afternoon
practices at school, the sisters chose to hold them during the evening at
their home. Back-corner girls with especially religious parents—mostly
Sikh—had trouble attending these rehearsals. With considerable limitations on their movements outside school and home, they felt extremely
uneasy approaching their parents for permission and transportation to a
stranger's home in the evening. Although the sisters were also from a Sikh
family, their liberal upper-middle-class parents placed fewer constraints on
their social lives and clothing options. Their family moved in an elite social circle and seldom attended *Gurdwara* (Sikh temple) where the middle-
class kids' parents came to know each other.

Issues of gender-based propriety posed even greater challenges. The
sisters choreographed and outfited a dance that conflicted with the standards of the back-corner girls and even some of their more conservative
friends. Gurinder, a back-corner girl in the dance, objected, "You have
to do all this motioning across your chest and spread your legs. It's, like,
some kind of seduction dance." To make matters worse, the "slut dance,"
as it was quickly dubbed, was to feature excessively revealing outfits. Another back-corner girl commented: "The *lehengas* have slits in them up to
here [pointing to her mid thigh], the blouses have a hole cut out of
them.[12] I told my mom about these *lehengas* and she asked why they don't

just wear miniskirts." With choreography and costumes they regarded as too sexually suggestive, several girls, including some of the sisters' friends, decided to drop out. The sisters were frustrated yet felt strongly about being in the program. Rather than cancel the dance altogether, they compromised by toning down the dance and letting performers wear their own *lehengas*, leaving the choice up to each girl to cover or reveal as much as she pleased.

On a warm spring day in April the event at Greene High School proceeded as planned. The quad was adorned with a colorful banner that read "International Day 2000" surrounded by hand-painted flags from various countries and framed by an arc of balloons stretched across the concrete stage. As the bell rang to signal the start of a lunch period specially extended for this event, students packed onto the steps surrounding the quad and spilled over onto the grassy area facing the stage. After about half of the twenty-five hundred student body had assembled, students rose for the American national anthem, and for a brief minute the restless swarms of teens managed to stand relatively still. The Indian Club's dance was announced, and eight Desi girls in uncoordinated but colorful *lehengas* took their places, their backs to the audience. As the bass from their remixed music reverberated, they demurely lifted their *duppatas* to uncover their faces and began to sway—some suggestively, others uneasily.[13] The two sisters wore alluring outfits that would make any Bollywood costume designer proud and relished the enthusiastic audience cheers. Other back-corner dancers seemed less comfortable being the center of attention in the quad. The music quickly segued into a second Hindi song, and the girls spun around and slithered to the ground in a series of coiling, serpentine moves. Their five-minute dance ended dramatically, and the girls exited the stage onto the grass. Looking pleased and relieved, they sat and laced up their sneakers while watching the remainder of the program.

Responses to International Day were decidedly mixed. Although friends of Jaspreet and Amanpreet were extremely appreciative, only a handful of the back-corner Desi students even attended the program. Some came as a show of support for the few friends who made it into the dance. Others who skipped the performance crowded around the small LCD screen on my camera to watch the video I had just taped. A barrage of critiques ensued: it was too slow, it contained slutty, hootchy moves, and it was not nearly as good as past years. One back-corner girl announced, "It would have been amazing if *we* had done bhangra," and others nodded in agreement. The girls who participated were hurt when they overheard friends saying, "It sucked." Had the dance been more inclusive, perhaps the back-corner Desi kids would have been less critical. Unfortunately, those responsible for the artistic content of the dance—Jaspreet and Amanpreet—were far out of earshot, leaving the scathing remarks of the excluded back-corner kids to fall on the ears of their own friends who had struggled to gain entry into the dance.

That the sisters and their friends—far outnumbered by back-corner kids—dominated the dance reveals the way in which some students feel a sense of ownership and privilege over school events while others shy away from this public arena, even as they would desire the option of inclusion. This struggle over cultural citizenship between Desi kids of different class backgrounds occurred without any public airing of issues. Unlike the disenfranchised students at Mercer High School, these excluded Desi kids did not feel confident or comfortable enough to approach school faculty to intervene on their behalf, and they had no experience to draw on. Their only recourse was to retaliate through gossip and criticism. This multicultural program, then, only deepened fissures of class among Desi kids. Rather than offering more inclusive opportunities, it reinforced existing hierarchies of power among these students. Both this and the earlier example from Mercer High School point to the broad range of differences among and within ethnic groups. This diversity not only complicates issues of equity but, as I will discuss in the next section, also questions of representation.

AGENCY, REPRESENTATION, AND RECEPTION

Should multicultural programs be about performing something "traditional," or should they reflect dynamic, locally constructed ethnic identities? This thorny issue underscores ways that audience expectations can clash with performers' agendas. In everyday school settings students and faculty rarely take the opportunity to examine what it means to be, for example, Pakistani, Bangladeshi, or Indian. Through multicultural performances, however, kids may challenge and potentially redefine dominant ideologies otherwise implicit in such overarching categories. By exercising agency, kids are able to disrupt the stability of seemingly fixed categories such as *Desi*, albeit in limited ways. As I will discuss below, kids innovate to create these meanings—a process seldom appreciated in the depiction of culture—and are accordingly constrained by one another as well as the audience.

Indeed, while kids use this program as an expressive space in school, faculty and other students perhaps still look to it as a way to learn about "Indian culture," considered a monolithic category. Notions of what it means to be Desi from an outsider's perspective—whether from a different ethnic group or even another generation—generally draw on clear-cut distinctions of "South Asian" and "American," of "traditional" and "Westernized." Especially during multicultural programs, essentialized, timeless notions of culture triumph as authentic—effectively bounding them into homogeneous, separate units that raze their texture and difference (Turner 1994:407). Often, larger audiences with expectations of how a multicultural performance should appear do not consider cultural expression that is meaningful to kids to be authentic .

For Desi kids at Mercer and Greene High Schools an intricate cultural logic governs the process of crafting representations. This dynamic is captured by kids' fluid use of the terms *FOBby* and *tight*.[14] A self-reflexive and group-reflexive term, *FOBby* is the adjective form of *FOB,* which stands for "Fresh Off the Boat." *Tight* is California slang for cool. *FOBby* and *tight* are kids' terms, and provide a way of redefining the social category Desi. At first glance it might be easy to associate FOBby with things South Asian and tight with anything American. Yet, while FOBby generally refers to a set of cultural and linguistic practices associated with those who are recently arrived from South Asia, kids' use of the term is quite specific. Their quickness to admire certain styles generated in South Asia and displayed in Bollywood movies or Desi clothes in their local store as tight or even *hella tight* (really cool), indicates that FOBby does not simply define anything South Asian. Likewise, tight does not blindly praise all things American. Desi kids draw on numerous sources in constructing identities (Maira 2002); in Silicon Valley these include both Bollywood films—their songs, actors, and narratives—as well as local television programming, Hollywood, and music such as hip-hop and pop.

In these ways kids have reclaimed *FOB,* a term that initially mocked immigrants, to make it a dimension of their identity and one they manipulate (cf. Butler 1993). While being FOBby is undesirable, being FOBulous is tight—a metacommentary on this larger semiotic system that indexes insider knowledge. The term *FOBulous* is generated out of this wordplay—a term I borrow from a clique of stylish Desi girls who call themselves "The FOBulous Six." Such terms enable kids to differentiate themselves from parents and peers while simultaneously showing connections to both. A shifting balance of FOBby and tight shapes local meanings of Desi that integrate a wide range of cultural forms and verbal practices.

Creating a tight dance is a complex project. Performing to a predominantly South Asian community audience means catering to people accustomed to the finer aspects of a regional dance form (i.e., *garba, bhangra,* and other South Asian folk or classical dances). In contrast, pieces choreographed for school audiences incorporate several regional styles and also borrow from other genres such as hip-hop and modern dance. The latter feature remixes or medleys of songs rarely displayed in community performances. Costumes and accessories are important as well, and the overall process of deciding how to select and display elements of global and local culture at schools is an important site of student agency.

At Mercer High School, negotiation centered around outfits and performers. Tara and Meena, the two organizers, created a medley incorporating three different songs and dance styles. While it would have been far simpler to perform a "traditional" village folk dance, they opted for the more challenging task of melding several different styles. Rather than wear typical South Asian outfits, girls wore a black top of their choosing with either a green or gold piece of fabric to be tied like a sarong. To accessorize, they crafted head jewelry from plastic bead curtains tied together and spray-painted gold. Each girl paid $10 for her costume and outfited her partner in *kurta-pyjama* sets borrowed from male family members.[15] Such close attention to detail and careful planning underscores kids' reliance on this space as an important, if not singular, site of agency around cultural representation. At the same time, these decisions, though generally acceptable to most participants, drew a variety of critiques from other Desi girls in the dance. Other cliques, especially The FOBulous Six, took issue with these aesthetic selections. They asserted that the outfits "don't look very Indian"; further, they were frustrated that costume design was dominated by two Indian girls and did not seek the input of Pakistani and Afghani girls who sought equal representation under the category Desi.

Another contentious decision was to make the dance co-ed and include kids of other ethnicities. This move occurred because many Desi boys scoffed that dancing in school was FOBby and refused to join. Only a few were willing to participate, even though many knew how to dance from community festivals. Determined to have a co-ed dance despite these apathetic Desi boys, the girls broke from the previous years' tradition and opened the dance to girls and boys of any racial background.

While the audience certainly enjoyed the dance, including participants of various ethnicities, using remixed music and a range of innovative dance steps, and wearing nontraditional costumes raised questions of authenticity. James, a participant in the dance, expressed this doubt: "[The dance] seems a little whitewashed. The ending that they have now seems a little less *cultural* than I hoped. It seems like it's been dumbed-down, Whitified. I don't know if I know what I'm talking about, but that's what it seems like." Interestingly, this ending typified male-female interaction and flirting in Bollywood movies, which borrow from a number of contemporary film genres, including Hollywood (Ganti 2000). Yet James and others expected something quite different, something "traditional," without being able to articulate or imagine it specifically. Although they were somewhat disappointed with these critiques, the girls stood by their decisions to prioritize being tight over catering to their audiences, proving that one person's authentic is another person's FOBby.

At Greene High School gender-based notions of propriety surfaced as the main point of contention. When the two sisters began choreographing the dance, they alone made the choices about the types of music and the steps. Here, too, Hindi films were a prominent influence, and the sisters also chose to splice together a medley of Bollywood songs and choreograph a dance. Although some back-corner girls initially argued for the inclusion of a more traditional *bhangra* song, they gave in—in part out of their own love of Bollywood.

Even though the sisters were in charge of the dance, their agency was circumscribed by larger social codes about what is proper for Desi girls. Such notions are closely linked with class, wherein many upper-middle-class girls are often far less constrained by strict rules around dress and comportment than middle- and working-class girls. Desi girls who came from wealthy families (like the sisters) by and large had less restrictions placed on their movements and choices. Amanpreet explained, "We want to do something that represents our culture, but something cool—not something FOBby and boring." The sisters' version of tight, however, crossed a line for back-corner girls, who were raised to adhere to more rigid standards of propriety and found the dance slutty and inappropriate.

Here the wide socioeconomic gap between Desi kids made the process of agreeing on what is tight far more challenging.

Excluded Desi students seized upon this disjuncture in aesthetic vision as a means of critiquing the program from which they were excluded. Asserting that the risqué nature of the sisters' dance made it altogether inauthentic, the performance became a source of amusing gossip for the back-corner Desi girls. They began to feel vindicated in their decision not to participate; as one girls smugly remarked, "It's, like, become an *American* dance." While there were countless things American that were highly valued by these Desi and used in representation, appearing "slutty" was not among them. Although the sisters regarded this degree of modesty FOBby, they were outnumbered by girls who were able to deflect this criticism back at the sisters and their "slut" dance.

Considering their lack of access to the program, it is not surprising that back-corner kids would criticize it in any way possible—authenticity provides an accessible and meaningful trope. Had they the cultural capital to put together a performance of their own, they may have been more charitable in their review of the other dance. Being appreciated for being FOBulous, then, turned out to be far more challenging than simply being FOBby.

Returning to broader debates about cultural citizenship, I conclude with a discussion of the finale from the Mercer High School multicultural assembly. The final act was a "flag parade," in which students paraded flags from various countries around the gym while the emcee announced the corresponding country names. The last flag stood in sharp contrast with the others carried by a diverse range of students. As the finale, five white boys carried a giant U.S. flag accompanied by the song "God Bless the USA."[16] This portion received both wild cheering from the general audience and visible waves of discomfort among many students of color.

These five white boys—serving as the unmarked majority—paraded the American flag as an authoritative end to what was already an exclusive program. As if to reclaim control of a space that had been temporarily surrendered to other groups, the boys asserted what they considered rightfully theirs. Many students felt this gesture undermined the entire program. As Alicia from the Black Student Union expressed, "It pissed me off because the whole point is that even though we are different cultures and even though we're not all white, we're still Americans. So I think instead of having the big four [*sic*] white guys go up there and parade around with the flag they should have had students to represent different races." A number of other students also felt that this finale belittled other performers' efforts at cultural expression.

As the flag parade and other examples I have discussed illustrate, cultural citizenship remains a highly contested process. Kids exert a wide spectrum of efforts—both successful and not—to claim a space for themselves in the public sphere of their high schools. The first example from Mercer High School underscores how ethnic groups in an advantageous position are able to operationalize their cultural capital to ensure their inclusion. Others who have fewer resources available were still able to publicly voice their discontent. Unfortunately, their actions did not achieve their goal of greater representation; in fact, African American and Latino students were even overlooked for the Desi dance, as participants mainly asked friends from their own cliques and seemed largely unaware of the absence of these other minorities. The second example, International Day at Greene High School, illustrates struggles among Desis that emerge from sharp differences of cultural capital due to differences in class and immigration history. Excluded kids did not even consider writing to the school paper—a forum that most found entirely off-limits. In both examples the ideology of multiculturalism based on unity, equality, and cultural understanding, in implementation, exacerbated race, class, and gender-based divisions between students.

In this essay I focused on the preparation, presentation, and reception of five to seven minutes of allotted performance time. These quick snapshots provide a window into the dynamic interworkings of ethnicity, class, and gender and, relatedly, cultural capital through which kids develop a sense of ownership and entitlement over school time and resources. While it may seem coincidental that only some kids participate in these programs, the reasons are, in fact, deeply rooted in larger social processes such as immigration history, class, educational background, and the larger sociopolitical climate—all of which shape everyday processes of ethnic formation for kids.

Though somewhat rhetorical, the questions I raised earlier as to whether multiculturalism should offer equal opportunities to all interested groups as well as individuals are addressed by these problematic outcomes. The question whether tight or FOBby performances are more appropriate—that is, whether they are to reflect locally crafted ethnic

identities or depict a timeless, traditional culture—remains ambiguous. The
unfavorable reception of these expressions by non-Desi peers and faculty,
however, serves as a reminder that agency is circumscribed by audiences
and contexts. In this active struggle categories such as South Asian reflect
the lived experiences of those encompassed by such a grouping. It is precisely because of these daily struggles that a category such as Desi means
anything at all and being FOBulous, rather than FOBby, matters.

NOTES

1. *Desi* means "countryman" and is a used by South Asians to refer to each other.
Based on the way kids in my study use the term, it includes people originally from
South Asia who have immigrated to the U.S. from Bangladesh, India, Nepal, Pak-
istan, Sri Lanka, as well as Africa, the Caribbean, Fiji, and Great Britain.

2. Released in 1999, *Taal* is a Bollywood movie about an aspiring dancer and was
a popular choice for many performances. The word t*aal* means "beat" or "rhythmic
cycle."

3. *Filmy* is a common adjective used by Hindi film viewers to describe a song,
dance, or attribute resembling a Bollywood movie.

4. Borrowing from Omi and Winant's (1994) process "racial formation," I here
use the term *ethnic formation* to discuss those cultural, religious, and linguistic differences that can contribute to local inequalities for Desi kids.

5. This examination is part of a larger project for which I conducted sixteen
months of ethnographic and sociolinguistic research (from September 1999 to August
2000 and February through May 2001) in three high schools that serve different socioeconomic strata of Silicon Valley across school, family, and community settings.

6. This excerpt is part of a larger passage from the 1920 report of the California
State Board of Control, quoted in Leonard 1992, p. 24.

7. Hundreds of laborers were literally "body-shopped," from East and South
Asia—i.e., brought over on H1-B visas for short-term work as programmers and engineers in Silicon Valley companies. See Mankekar 2002 for a discussion of the cultural politics and practices of these immigrants.

8. These schools also contained about 1 percent Native American students (about
twenty students). They were seldom able to make their presence felt in these arenas.

9. Fremont has evolved into a bedroom community for Silicon Valley.

10. The faculty was nearly all White, so this selection was typical.

11. Mecha (Movimiento Estudiantil Chicano de Aztlan) is a movement of Chicano groups organizing on California campuses statewide. For a detailed discussion,
see Rodrigues and Trueba 1998.

12. A *lehenga* is the skirt part of a coordinated women's outfit and is mainly worn for festivals or special occasions.

13. A *dupatta* is a coordinated strip of cloth worn with various South Asian women's outfits. As a garment of modesty, it is intended to cover the head, neck, and bust.

14. These terms were current during 1999–2001 when I conducted my fieldwork.

15. These are ethnic clothes from North India used both for daily wear and festivals.

16. A modern-day version of "God Bless America," this song was released during Operation Desert Storm.

WORKS CITED

Abercrombie, Thomas. 1991. "To Be Indian, to Be Bolivian: 'Ethnic' and 'National' Discourses of Identity." In Greg Urban and Joel Sherzer, eds., *Nation-States and Indians in Latin America*. Austin: University of Texas Press.

Ahern, Laura. 2001. Language and Agency. *Annual Review of Anthropology* 30:109–137.

Appadurai, Arjun. 1996. *Modernity at Large: Cultural Dimensions of Globalization*. Minneapolis: University of Minnesota Press.

Bourdieu, Pierre. 1991. *Language and Symbolic Power*. Cambridge: Harvard University Press.

—— 1984. *Distinction: A Social Critique of the Judgement of Taste*. Cambridge: Harvard University Press.

—— 1977. *Outline of a Theory of Practice*. Cambridge: Cambridge University Press.

Brodkin-Sachs, Karen. 1994. "How Did Jews Become White Folks?" In Steven Gregory and Roger Sanjek, eds., *Race*, pp. 78–102. New Brunswick, N.J.: Rutgers University Press.

Butler, Judith. 1993. *Bodies That Matter : On the Discursive Limits of "Sex."* New York: Routledge.

De Certeau, Michel. 1984. *The Practice of Everyday Life*. Berkeley: University of California Press.

Flores, William and Rita Benmayor, eds. 1997. *Latino Cultural Citizenship*. Boston: Beacon.

Frankenburg, Ruth. 1993. *White Women, Race Matters: The Social Construction of Whiteness*. Minneapolis: University of Minnesota Press.

Ganti, Tejaswini. 2000. "Casting Culture: The Social Life of Hindi Film Production in Contemporary India." Ph.D. diss., Department of Anthropology, New York University.

Gibson, Margaret. 1988. *Accommodation Without Assimilation: Sikh Immigrants in an American High School*. Ithaca: Cornell University Press.

Giddens, Anthony. 1979. *Central Problems in Social Theory*. Berkeley: University of California Press.

Glazer, Nathan and Daniel Moynihan. 1963. *Beyond the Melting Pot*. Cambridge: MIT Press.

Goldberg, David. 1994. "Introduction: Multicultural Conditions." In David Goldberg, ed., *Multiculturalism: A Critical Reader*, pp. 1–44. Oxford: Blackwell.

Harvey, David. 1990. *The Condition of Postmodernity*. London: Blackwell.

Hu-DeHart, Evelyn. 2001. "Ethnic Studies in U.S. Higher Education: The State of the Discipline. In Johnnella Butler, ed., *Color-Line to Borderlands: The Matrix of American Ethnic Studies*, pp. 103–112. Seattle: University of Washington Press.

Ignatiev, Noel. 1995. *How the Irish Became White*. New York: Routledge.

Jameson, Frederick. 1991. *Postmodernism, or the Cultural Logic of Late Capitalism*. Durham: Duke University Press.

Khandelwal, Madhulika. 1995. "Indian Immigrants in Queens, New York City." In Peter van der Veer, ed., *Nation and Migration: The Politics of Space in the South Asian Diaspora*, Philadelphia: University of Pennsylvania Press.

Leonard, Karen. 1998. *The South Asian Americans*. Westport, Conn.: Greenwood.

—— 1992. *Making Ethnic Choices: California's Punjabi Mexican Americans*. Philadelphia: Temple University Press.

Lessinger, Johanna. 1995. *From the Ganges to the Hudson: Indian Immigrants in New York City*. Boston: Allyn and Bacon.

Lowe, Lisa. 1996. *Immigrant Acts: On Asian American Cultural Politics*. Durham: Duke University Press.

McLaren, Peter. 1994. "Multiculturalism and the Postmodern Critique: Toward a Pedagogy of Resistance and Transformation." In Henry A. Giroux and Peter McLaren, eds., *Between Borders: Pedagogy and the Politics of Cultural Studies*. New York: Routledge.

Maira, Sunaina. 2002. *Desis in the House: Indian American Youth Culture in New York City*. Philadelphia: Temple University Press.

Mankekar, Purnima. 2002. "'India Shopping': Indian Grocery Stores and Transnational Configurations of Belonging." *Ethnos* 67:75–98.

Omi, Michael and Howard Winant. 1994. *Racial Formation in the United States*. New York: Routledge.

Prashad, Vijay. 2000. *The Karma of Brown Folk*. Minneapolis: University of Minnesota Press.

Rodriguez, Cirenio and Enrique T. Trueba. 1998. "Leadership, Education, and Political Action: The Emergence of New Latino Ethnic Identities." In Yali Zou and Enrique T. Trueba, eds., *Ethnic Identity and Power: Cultural Contexts of Political Action in School and Society*. New York: SUNY Press.

Rogers, M. 1999. "Spectacular Bodies: Folklorization and the Politics of Identity in Ecuadorian Beauty Pageants." *Journal of Latin American Anthropology* 3:54–85.

Rosaldo, Renato and William Flores. 1997. "Cultural Citizenship." In William Flores and Rita Benmayor, eds., *Latino Cultural Citizenship: Claiming Identity, Space, and Rights.* Boston: Beacon.

Silverstein, Michael. 1996. "Monoglot 'Standard' in America: Standardization and Metaphors of Linguistic Hegemony." In D. Brennis and R. Macauley, eds., *The Matrix of Language*, pp. 284–306. Boulder: Westview.

Sollors, Werner. 1989. "Introduction: The Invention of Ethnicity." In Werner Sollors, ed., *The Invention of Ethnicity*. New York: Oxford University Press.

Stam, Robert and Ella Shohat. 1994. "Contested Histories: Eurocentricism, Multiculturalism, and the Media." In David Goldberg, ed., *Multiculturalism: A Critical Reader*, pp. 296–324. Oxford: Blackwell.

Takaki, Ronald. 2001. "Multiculturalism: Battleground or Meeting Ground?" In J. Butler, ed., *Color-Line to Borderlands: The Matrix of American Ethnic Studies*, pp. 3–17. Seattle: University of Washington Press.

Turner, Terrence. 1994. "Anthropology and Multiculturalism: What Is Anthropology That Multiculturalists Should Be Mindful of It?" In David Goldberg, ed., *Multiculturalism: A Critical Reader*, pp. 406–425. Oxford: Blackwell.

Wallace, Michelle. 1994. Multiculturalism and Oppositionality. In Henry A. Giroux and Peter McLaren, eds., *Between Borders: Pedagogy and the Politics of Cultural Studies*, pp. 180–191. New York: Routledge.

Waters, Mary. 1990. *Ethnic Options: Choosing Identities in America.* Berkeley: University of California Press.

Winant, Howard. 1997. "Behind Blue Eyes: Whiteness and Contemporary U.S. Racial Politics." In M. Fine, L. Weis, L. Powell, and M. Wong, eds., *Off White: Readings on Race, Power, and Society*, pp. 40–56. New York: Routledge.

9

Gathering "Roots" and Making History in the Korean Adoptee Community

ELEANA KIM

My own awareness and consciousness was raised with great pain, isolation, and alienation. I have been rejected by the local Korean community because I have white parents, and I have been rejected by the white society because I am Korean.
—ANNE MI OK BRUINING, 1991

With this anthology, we seek to break a certain silence—silence from our land of origin, silence from the lands we now inhabit—tongues tied by racism, some external, some painfully internal; tongues tied by social mores, codes, and contradictions; tongues tied by colonialist myths of rescue missions and smooth assimilations.
—TONYA BISHOFF, 1997

I was adopted from Korea, and all I got was this lousy T-shirt, 12 years of education, 4 years of college, food and a roof over my head, and I'm Still Bitter.
—SNAPSHOT EXHIBIT T-SHIRT, July 1999, Korean American Museum, Los Angeles

On a clear September morning in 1999, nearly four hundred Korean émigrés gathered at the Korean War Veterans Memorial in Washington, D.C. Hailing from thirty-six states and several European countries, they had come to honor and remember the sacrifices of soldiers who served and died in the first major military conflict of the cold war. Although none were veterans, and few had memories of that time, the commemoration was powerful enough to move many to tears. In acknowledging the brutal human consequences of war—massive social dislocation, divided families, orphaned and abandoned children—they recognized the tragic roots of their own histories. For these were not immigrants in the traditional sense of people motivated by a desire for a better life or desperate to escape calamitous political situations in their home countries. Rather each had left Korea as a child, as a real or legal "orphan," at the mercy of political, economic, and social conditions beyond his or her grasp. They were transported across borders and emerged at airport arrival gates around the world, to be embraced by new families, given new names and the identities that came with them.

The children adopted shortly after the war were the pioneers of what grew into the largest and longest running transnational adoption program in the world. Since 1953 families in the West have adopted more than 150,000 South Korean children, and, of those, Americans have adopted more than 100,000. Although today annual adoptions of Chinese and Russian children by Americans significantly outnumber those of South Korean children, throughout the 1960s, seventiess, and eighties South Korea was the major sending country for overseas adoption. In the U.S. Korean adoption accounted for over half the total international adoptions during the mid-1970s and 1980s.

The adoptees at the memorial had met just two days earlier, convening in Washington, D.C. for the Gathering of the First Generation of Korean Adoptees, or what is now simply known as the Gathering. Heralded as a "historic event," the "first significant and deliberate opportunity for the first generation of Korean adult adoptees to come together," this three-day conference included adult adoptees, ranging in age from their early twenties to late fifties, and their spouses or partners, along with several adoption researchers and adoption agency observers. The coordinators celebrated it as the first conference organized by and exclusively for adult Korean adoptees, and for many in attendance it symbolized an important moment of self-determination. For the first time they collectively asserted autonomy from families, agencies, and governments—institutions that had, for much of their lives, decided their fates and mediated their realities.

From a young age these adoptees contended with being constant sources of curiosity to others ("we were all novelties," according to a Gathering participant), object lessons in race relations and multiculturalism, or, as adults, "cultural ambassadors." In the words of adoptees at the Gathering, the conference was a time to "speak for ourselves, not as children without a voice." Or, as another attested, "We can share with each other without having to do so much explaining."

European adopted Koreans first began meeting in small numbers in Sweden, and adopted Koreans in Minnesota were gathering in 1991. By 1998 similar groups had mushroomed throughout Western Europe and the U.S. and even in Korea.[1] The Gathering thus represented the culmination of more than a decade of such activities by adult adopted Koreans around the world, consolidating what had been relatively localized phenomena into a major public event. It also marked a significant turning point for a nascent Korean adoptee movement, bringing adopted Koreans into national and international visibility as adults, and made it abundantly clear that adopted Koreans have reached a critical mass.

Historically, adoptees and adoptive parents, especially mothers, have been overtly pathologized in the popular media. In the recent pro-adoption, and especially pro-international adoption, climate, however, these images of deviancy have faded somewhat, though now they tend toward another extreme: Asian children with white parents now appear in advertisements and magazine articles as adorable model-minority adoptees.

Korean adult adoptee narratives implicitly speak against these stereotypes. These stories are shared at conferences, organization meetings, and on the Internet, and through expressive work, in the form of novels, films, poetry, spoken word, visual, and cartoon art.[2] This cultural work presents a diversity of Korean adoptee experiences while at the same time drawing out common threads among these differences. In this essay I combine ethnographic data from the Gathering with my analysis of recent autobiographical films by adopted Koreans to explore how adult adoptees are empowering themselves and producing their own discourses, cultures, and alternative social spaces that allow them both to speak among themselves and to engage a wider public.

In the course of my research, particularly at the Gathering (where I both volunteered and observed), I found I could identify with many of the stories I heard about coping with racism and struggling with identity issues. Yet the circumstances of these adoptees, while on the surface parallel to my own upbringing in a middle-class white suburb, were radically different because it was transnational adoption, not simple immigration, that brought them to this country. On the one hand, Korean Americans like myself and adopted Koreans share a history of migration—our lives coincided with the large influx of Asian immigrants to the U.S. after 1965—on the other hand, the historical and political differences in our displacements make any simple equation between our life experiences superficial at best. My observations at the Gathering made it clear to me that transnational, transracial adoption presents a complex intertwining of race, ethnicity, and culture, as well as kinship—both biological and social—that also refracts intricate dilemmas of cultural belonging and citizenship.

The adult adoptees who meet with some frequency today often grew up without the adoptive family networks that have become de rigueur for families adopting Chinese children today. Many rejected parental attempts to connect to the Korean American community or to other adoptees in their adolescent pursuits to "fit in." Now, they actively seek each other out, sharing stories of isolation, assimilation, and loss. Their narratives represent a new sense of agency and growing solidarity among adopted Koreans, and they not only articulate an untold collective history but also have the potential to affect the course of transnational adoption in the U.S. and elsewhere.

REPAIRING THE BROKEN NARRATIVE

In 1993 filmmaker Me-K. Ahn was producing her video *living in halftones*, an experimental short that poetically composes a "memory-archive" of her experiences as a Korean adoptee returning to Korea. Around the same time, Kim Su Theiler was finishing her film *Great Girl*, also an experimental piece that probes questions of memory, identity, and history for an adoptee seeking information about her adoption. Remarkably, these two filmmakers were utterly unaware of each other until they both received notice from artist and film communities and thus heard about the similarities in their work.

Ahn and Theiler were harbingers of what, in the years that followed, has grown into a kind of minigenre of Korean adoptee films and videos. At least a dozen experimental films, personal documentaries, and narrative films have been produced in the past decade, and they share themes of identity, family, and history, foregrounding the ambiguity of ethnic, biological, and social relatedness. In recognizing the larger social and historical processes in which the personal lives of the filmmakers are implicated, these works are both autobiographical and ethnographic and thus a kind of "journey of the self" that media scholar Catherine Russell calls "autoethnography."[3]

Until recently these films and their makers had primarily received individual attention in mainstream or alternative art venues as well as from Korean American or Asian American organizations. In 1998, however, Me-K. Ahn curated a film event called Evenstill at the Minneapolis College of Art and Design. Along with films by second-generation Korean Americans, it featured a program of eight films by or about adopted Koreans. Then, in 2000, Deann Borshay Liem's *First Person Plural* made an impressive debut at major international film festivals and screened several times on PBS. Her outreach to adoptive family and adoptee groups led to subsequent screenings at adoption conferences, adoptee group meetings, and adoption agencies. Korean adoptee creative work is now regularly featured at adoption conferences, and the circulation of the films in particular is helping to forge community while it also serves to contribute to the broader representation of adopted Koreans nationally and internationally.

These films share common themes with other adult adoptee personal narratives in which a desire for coherence and authenticity is enacted through the writing and telling of stories. As Korean adoptee Kimberley SaRee Tomes says in her film *Looking for Wendy*, "A sense of natural family and history is available in daydream and fantasy. I repair the broken narrative by dreaming it along." This sense of being cut off from a genealogical history is coupled with the inescapable issues of race and social belonging for transracial and transnational adoptees. How do families construct the inalienable relationships of sameness assumed by the word *family* when the possibility of "passing" is foreclosed by the starkly visible racial differences between parents and children? No matter how supportive their domestic lives may be, adoptees, their parents, and siblings, as "conspicuous families," must confront confused, insensitive, or bigoted responses from friends, neighbors, and strangers. Moreover, despite a century or more of Asian immigration to the U.S., Asian Americans continue to be perceived as being from somewhere else, or, as in the title of sociologist Mia Tuan's book, as "Forever Foreigner or Honorary Whites." Korean adoptee autoethnographies show how, for adoptees, "fitting in" at school, and even at home, meant "forgetting" about race or denying the gap between their identities as "one of the family" and the assumptions made about them when they left the security of home.

Especially for adoptees who arrived in the U.S. before the rise of American multiculturalism, pressures to assimilate required a repression of racial difference in order to achieve, or approximate, the ideal image of the "American family." Deann Borshay, who was adopted in 1966 at the age of eight, states in her film, *First Person Plural*, "There was an unspoken contract between us which we had all agreed upon, but never discussed, that I was an orphan with no family ties to Korea. . . . I belonged only to my American parents. It meant I didn't have a Korean history or a Korean identity."

Adoptees were by and large encouraged to become "American," often meaning the wholesale embrace of a new identity, family, and history. For many their "arrival day"—the day they were picked up at the airport—became as significant as their birthdays. Even if the possibility for exposure to Korean culture was available, many adult adoptees now admit that they were resistant to being identified as "other." In *Crossing Chasms* Jennifer Arndt describes her feelings about going to Korean culture camp in junior high school: "I resented my Asian identity and going to camp reinforced my Koreanness when I wanted to be quote-unquote white."

In Korean adoptee films family photos are used to visually represent the dissonance between the adoptee's seemingly "smooth assimilation" and her internal conflicts. The photos show the adopted child as a smiling, happy member of the "all-American family," yet the racially different adoptee also disturbs that idealized vision. Like the unexpected jolt that comes from discovering that a "white" person's name is attached to an "Asian" face, family photos present a challenge to assumptions about what families should look like. For the filmmakers, undergoing a search for an authentic self and scrutinizing their pasts, the family snapshots stand as a kind of false consciousness. They speak to the adoptee's complicity in the suppression of her difference to be one with the "American family."

Filmmaker Nathan Adolfson interrogates the myth of assimilation in his personal documentary, *Passing Through*. He matches images of himself as a child, looking like a "normal kid" in elementary school classes and family photos, with an interview with his mother who describes the lack of awareness that she and her husband had of the problems he faced as an Asian child in small-town Minnesota: "We really didn't think it was that you were having problems. You never *said* anything. Never said a *word*. . . . We probably did try to raise you as being too American, or too. . . . Maybe we weren't sensitive enough to your heritage . . . tried to turn you into a little Scandinavian."

These autoethnographies resonate with stories from the Gathering. For many there it was the first time they had met a large group of other adoptees, and some had never really thought about their ethnicity or spent much time with other Korean Americans. Some didn't even know what other Koreans might look like: a self-described "tall and skinny" adoptee admitted that he "came out of curiosity to see other Korean people. Are all Koreans tall and skinny? I didn't know!"

A survey of the Gathering attendees found that 40 percent of respondents said they identified as Caucasian in their adolescence and would perceive Asians as "the other." For these adoptees who grew up fully identifying as (white) Americans, racial discrimination provoked a particularly difficult form of double consciousness. Even the most empathetic parents were perceived as unable to fully relate to the experience of racism, thereby intensifying feelings of alienation and racial difference.

The Gathering participants divided up into seven concurrent workshop sessions, according to the years in which they were adopted. In these workshops adoptees' stories—intimate and painful memories of Korea, their childhoods in America, and their negative experiences with discrimination and racial difference[4]—complicated the official narratives of "success" and "achievement" that characterized the speeches by adoption agency professionals and representatives of the Korean government in the opening plenary. I sat in on one workshop with around fifty adoptees in their late twenties and early thirties who were adopted in the late 1960s.

In the workshop adoptees questioned the amount of "culture" that should be presented to a child who may be resistant to identifying at all as the other. Some adoptees felt that the pushing of culture on them was "overdetermined," as if they (and not their adoptive parents) were the "only ones with an ethnic identity." One thirty-something male adoptee said in reference to the racist caricature of an Asian exchange student, Long Duk Dong, in the teen movie *Sixteen Candles*: "We were Anthony Michael Hall in that movie; we weren't Long Duk Dong. . . . When our parents were pushing culture on us, that was making us into Long Duk Dong." At the same time, although many parents attempted to incorporate Korean culture into their children's lives, many others did not, or even denigrated Korean culture and society.

Typical adolescent growing pains are difficult to separate out from adoptee- or Korean-adoptee-specific issues, but there was general agreement that cultural belonging was a problem in a dominant white society that equated "American" with being visibly "white." Some described it as a pendulum swinging back and forth between "Korean" and "American" sides. Many agreed with one attendee's sense that "Koreans reject the American side, Americans reject the Korean side," adding, "Koreans reject the adoption side. For them, I ha[ve] no family, no history." Another adoptee described her identity as being "about culture, and your culture is not your face—but you're pinpointed for that all your life." But the recognition of a broad historical and cultural shift was clear—as one adoptee stated, an "international identity is emerging," and another commented, "We grew up in a Cheryl Tieg era; now we're in a Connie Chung era." Or, as another informed his cohort, "Don't you know? Asian people are 'in' now."

"KOREA"

American multiculturalism and cultural globalization have created an atmosphere in which it is now acceptable, if not fashionable, especially in certain cosmopolitan circles, to be "different," hybrid, or nomadic. These developments have perhaps made it easier for adopted Koreans to embrace their own racial difference and to explore their cultural and emotional relationships to Korea. Although some adoptees may have little or no interest in their biological families or country of birth, it is undeniable that "Korea" holds a central place in many adoptees' imaginations about who they are, where they came from, and what they might have been. Many have always felt a yearning, laced with fear, to return to the country of their birth, to explore their cultural and biological roots, and perhaps to locate missing pieces of themselves.

Following the 1988 Seoul Olympic Games, Korean adoptees began returning to Korea in increasing numbers. Today, an estimated twenty-five hundred adopted Koreans return every year, some to take language or cultural classes, others to actively search for their birth families, and some to go on Motherland tours, organized by the Korean government or adoption agencies. There are also approximately two hundred long-term sojourners who are living and working in Korea.

Adoptees at the Gathering who had traveled to Korea, mostly without language skills, social connections, or cultural knowledge, described their experiences there as being marked by frustration and sadness. As would be the case for many travelers, they suffered from culture shock and basic discomforts of being a stranger in a strange land. But, as adoptees, the country bears a heavy symbolic load, embodying for them memories, lost or too distant to retrieve, unknown histories, and severed biological connections.[5] In *Great Girl* Kim Su Theiler says she went back to Korea "in a way to make my own documents of memories that exist now only in my mind."

Adoptee accounts of their experiences in Korea reflected feelings of disappointment as the fantasy of "home" failed to live up in reality. In Korea they confronted feelings about being adopted and worked out complicated issues about race, ethnicity, and culture. Their amazement at finally being in a place where they looked like everyone else was coupled with the difficulty of not "relating" to Koreans or Korean culture. Others had more positive experiences, with one attendee insisting that one or two trips would not be enough, but rather, having himself been back to Korea six times, that "you have to go several times to understand your relationship to [Korea]."

Jennifer Arndt's film *Crossing Chasms* provides useful ethnographic information about adult adopted Koreans living and working in Korea. In an interview Me-K. Ahn notes about Korea, "It's a difficult place to be. . . . So many adoptees dream of being part of the mainstream, but you have to cultivate your own space to feel comfortable [here]." Later on in the film she adds, "[Korea]'s so nationalistic. If you're not *really, really* Korean you're looked down upon. At the same time, so many people have shameful feelings about sending us away. . . . Circumstances surrounding adoption are pretty taboo."

This perception of being "looked down upon" was shared by adoptees at the conference and linked to interactions with Korean nationals who tend to view adoptees as objects of pity. They assume tragic backgrounds for them, not comprehending that they may have had relatively positive and supportive family lives. Other adoptees have mentioned meeting Koreans who were surprised at how well they had grown up, for they had only heard sensationalizing stories about sexual abuse and slavery among adopted children by foreigners. Furthermore, the primacy of "blood" in Korean cultural understandings of individual disposition and national character has been rejected by adoptees who cannot accept the essentializing assumptions of Koreans who subscribe to a strong ethnic nationalism. As another adoptee in Ardnt's film declares, "People here say, 'You have Korean blood.' . . . It's such b.s. It doesn't make me *feel* Korean. I don't think 'blood' means anything."

Korean adoptee autoethnographies explore this complex relationship to Korea as country of birth, culture, and "home." For adoptees who were old enough when they left to have some memory of Korea, the films reveal the deep sense of alienation produced by this process of forgetting, in the sense that the only thing remembered is the forgetting itself, leaving a trace of memory that, never fully forgotten, cannot, at the same time, be entirely remembered. Borshay, for instance, recalls her desperate attempts as a newly adopted child to retain a singular memory of her home in Korea: "It was getting more and more difficult to remember how to get home. I remember closing my eyes and saying, OK, don't forget, but the last memory of Korea was starting to fade. . . . I forgot everything. I forgot how to speak Korean; I forgot any memory of ever having had a family, and I even forgot my real name." Borshay and Adolfson's videos attempt to reconcile long-held fantasies about "Korea" and their Korean families with their reality. After reuniting with their birth families, they return "home" to the U.S., to a stronger sense of self and a greater appreciation for their "real" or "true" American families. In these adoptee autoethnographies "family" is represented as an achievement, something that cannot be taken for granted by either adoptees or adoptive parents, given the very different path the adoptee's life may have taken in Korea. For some at the Gathering, experiences in Korea visiting orphanages "put their [lives] in perspective," especially when they learned how others from similar circumstances, but who had not been adopted, had suffered difficult fates, without the emotional support, comforts, or privileges of having a family.

Yet the gratitude adoptees feel toward their parents for having been "rescued" from a possible life of disenfranchisement is oftentimes also felt as a barrier to expressing other painful aspects of their experience or as a burden that holds them in perpetual debt to their parents. Filmmaker Borshay describes herself as being so eager as a child to please her new parents that she made herself ill. Any sign of unhappiness or anger would shatter the image of the well-adjusted adoptee fully integrated into her American home, and thus many adoptees, if they did not rebel, had the "will to be the best we could be." For one adoptee the Gathering was a "statement to our parents that we didn't get what we needed then, and we're getting it now."

UNEARTHING THE PAST

Experiences of adoptees who suffered doubly because of abuses by their adoptive families speak to the lack of adequate accountability on the part of adoption agencies. Harry Holt, an evangelical Christian and logging magnate from Oregon, and his wife, Bertha, initiated the first wave of adoptions from Korea when they adopted eight Amerasian GI babies in 1955. Shortly thereafter their religiously inspired mission to save needy Korean children became a lifelong crusade, and the Holts established Holt Adoption Agency, which, now Holt International Children's Services, continues to be the leading agency for transnational adoption.

Today home study screenings are required by law of all prospective parents, yet, in the past, screenings could be, as it was for the Holt agency, as perfunctory as filling out a religious questionnaire. An incredulous Pearl S. Buck in 1964 described the questions as pertaining to "rather a primitive kind of religion. . . . what is called Fundamentalist." Buck, although highly skeptical of Holt's unorthodox adoption practices, met the legendary and somewhat notorious Harry Holt in Korea and, after seeing him in action, was quickly won over by his unwavering dedication to finding homes for the hundreds of half-Korean children in his care.

Although a humanitarian impulse lay at the heart of Holt's mission, religion alone could not guarantee a happy home. Americans wanting to adopt during the baby boom of the 1950s and sixties encountered a "shortage" of available white babies and very strict, even discriminatory, screening processes for domestic adoption. Those who may have been ineligible to adopt domestically therefore found overseas adoption to be the only other viable option. Elizabeth Kim's controversial memoir, *Ten Thousand Sorrows* (2000), describes her tortured life in Arizona as a Korean-Caucasian child raised by an evangelical couple whose abuse scarred her physically and psychologically for years. She escaped the abuse of her family, only to end up in an even more abusive marriage to a mentally ill husband, and finally set out on her own as a single mother.

Another tragic case is described by Tammy Tolle/ Chu Dong Soo in her film *Searching for Go-Hyang*. She and her twin sister were raised in Korea until the age of eight by poor parents who struggled financially to raise them and their two brothers. Her mother approached an adoption agency, hoping to send them to the U.S. for a "better life." Despite assurances given to Dong Soo's mother by the agency that she would be able to maintain contact with her children, the girls were sent abroad without notice and their Korean parents denied any information regarding their children's well-being or whereabouts. The girls endured eight years of abuse in their adoptive home, where they were "forced to forget" and even forbidden to speak Korean. They left their adoptive home at age sixteen and worked their way through high school, eventually reuniting with their Korean family after ten years' separation.

Other troubling cases on the Korean side have materialized as well. Situations in which birth mothers were coerced or deceived into surrendering their children for adoption have come to light, and accounts have surfaced of extended family members or in-laws delivering children to orphanages without knowledge of the parents. Between 1951 and 1964 the number of abandoned children at orphanages increased from 715 to 11,319, a remarkable figure that suggests to one demographer that the "presence of efficient foreign adoption facilities encouraged the abandonment of children" in Korea (Weil 1984:282). How the orphanages functioned in the postwar period as a surrogate welfare system and as conduit for foreign aid money begs further investigation. One myth of Korean adoption from the early years is that these adopted children were all "orphans," without any biological ties to Korea. In fact, most were paper "orphans" with living kin in Korea to whom, in the course of adoption, legal ties had been cut.

Deann Borshay's *First Person Plural* is a particularly telling account. She describes how, at a Korean orphanage, she was "switched" with another child whose adoption to the Borshay family in California had already been arranged. The father of that child had changed his mind and retrieved his daughter from the orphanage the day before she was scheduled to fly to the U.S. Deann was then substituted for the first child, Cha Jung Hee, given her name, passport, and documents, and sent to California. Deann's adoptive parents insisted that her memories of having a family in Korea were "bad dreams." To prove it to her they showed her the adoption agency documents stating she was an orphan and both her parents had died. Later in her life, however, she discovered that, in fact, she had a family in Korea who had been searching for her and that her real Korean name is Kang Ok Jin. Upon meeting her Korean family, she learned that her mother, struggling to raise five children alone, was convinced by a neighbor to send her daughters to a nearby orphanage to be cared for temporarily. The orphanage asked her to consider sending her last daughter, Ok Jin, the future Deann, to be adopted, and, believing that she would have a better life with a chance for an education, she agreed. Perhaps worried that Ok Jin's mother might also change her mind at the last minute, the orphanage sent her off a day early, and there was never even a chance to say goodbye.

The misinformation transmitted through the adoption agency is not unique to Borshay's story. Increasingly, adoptees are finding that information they valued as fragile clues to their personal histories was, in fact, fabricated—raising important human rights concerns. Yet adoptees in this situation have very little recourse, and adoption agency representatives, who may regret the mistakes of the past, do not hold themselves or the agencies accountable. Given the dubious circumstances under which some of these adoptions were conducted, untangling the ethics of birth family searches and reunions also proves to be a challenge. Adoption agencies follow strict policies to protect the identity and privacy of birth mothers, who may wish to remain anonymous. Agency social workers are the key mediators for adoptees who try to search for their birth families, yet in cases where birth mothers do have a desire to find their children the agency's policies can function as a barrier to a mutually desired reunion.

Of course, adoption agencies may not be intentionally deceptive, and many adoptees have experienced aboveboard and ethical adoption circumstances as well as successful reunions facilitated by adoption agency social workers. The adopted Koreans who started streaming back to Korea in the late 1980s largely took adoption agencies by surprise, and social workers were unprepared to take on the responsibility of searching for birth families. In addition, given the spotty nature of many of the adoption records of that time (records may have been misplaced, incomplete, or never collected), agency social workers do not always have the adequate resources to help adoptees who seek information about their birth families.

Faced with these obstacles, adoptees who search often resort to the Korean media, by placing announcements in newspapers or appearing on television talk shows, with hopes of reaching their biological families.[6] These methods, however, raise other ethical issues both around the exploitation of vulnerable and desperate adoptees by journalists eager to fulfill the public's fascination with melodramatic family reunion stories and around the privacy rights of birth mothers and fathers who may be adversely affected by the discovery of these "long lost" kin.

The moral complexity of these cases trouble the "success" narratives of adoption agencies such as Holt. Its advertisement for the Gathering program features an old black and white photograph of four young Asian children ("orphans"?) smiling and posing for the camera, arms across each other's shoulders. The caption reads, "We believed in you back in the fifties. And look at you now. . . . We couldn't be prouder." The paternalism in this advertisement that constructs adoptees as perennial children is prevalent in the discourses of agencies as well as of the Korean government. Like the myths encapsulated in the word *orphan,* assumptions about adoptees are also embedded in the language—the word commonly used for adoptees in Korean is *ibyanga,* literally meaning, "adopted child." Adoptee activists in Korea have sought to redress this infantalization by replacing *ibyanga* with a more appropriate term for adult adopted Koreans, *ibyangin,* meaning "adopted person."

WHOSE VOICE?

The Amerasian children of the war, fathered by U.S. and European soldiers, were adopted in the late 1950s and 1960s, and the subsequent wave of children in the 1970s was of full Korean parentage. Rather than suffering the social stigma of being half-Korean, the children of this second wave were victims of economic restructuring, extreme poverty, a lack of social service support for single mothers, and Korea's staunchly "Confucian" social values, which place paramount importance on the purity of bloodlines. Meanwhile, in American society, as local adoption opportunities decreased because of the legalization of abortion and the political censure of black-white adoptions, an increasing number of Korean children were adopted into Caucasian middle-class homes.

Adoption from Korea has proven to be extremely sensitive to economic fluctuations and concerns over the nation's international reputation. There have been periodic attempts by the government to curtail foreign adoption, most notably in the late 1970s, after North Korea criticized the South's liberal "selling" of children to "foreign marauders" (Foster-Carter 2002), and following the 1988 Seoul Olympic Games when adoption became an embarrassing subject of scrutiny for the international press. Reportedly bringing in $15 million to $20 million per year, adoption in Korea had become a cost-effective way of dealing with social welfare problems.

As recently as July 2002, in the afterglow of the successful cohosting of the 2002 World Cup Games, the government announced a series of measures to further bolster the nation's image that included a plan to end overseas adoption by 2015. It is too soon to determine whether this new plan will indeed lead to the end of international adoptions from Korea, or whether it will be set back by future economic pressures, as has been the case with other such plans over the past four decades. What is certain, however, is that Korea, with the lowest social welfare spending of any OECD country (Kim 2000:26), will have to undertake serious reform of its welfare system, especially with respect to women and children. With over seven thousand children in need of welfare intervention each year, the Korean government and adoption agencies will have to step up efforts to promote domestic adoption.

Against this problematic backdrop, adult adoptees have experienced an unparalleled welcome from the Korean government in the late 1990s. The South Korean ambassador to the U.S., in his plenary address at the Gathering, noted, "You demonstrate the capacity to transform oneself from humble beginnings to successs." Indeed, the word *success* echoed throughout the opening speeches, leading one to suspect that the class status of adoptees, as measured by their college educations and professional occupations, had something to do with how this story of success was being written. The South Korean ambassador to the U.S., in his plenary address, noted, "You demonstrate the capacity to transform oneself from humble beginnings to success." According to the Gathering survey, 70 percent graduated college, 24 percent had graduate degrees, and 15 percent were enrolled in university or postgraduate work. Adoptees thus demonstrate the same progress and development model offered by the narrative of Korea's phenomenal modernization—its meteoric rise out of a tragic colonial past, through the devastation of war, to its ascendance as a newly industrialized "Asian Tiger," boasting the world's eleventh largest economy in 1996. And, at the same time, they also reflect a classic American Horatio Alger tale of "making it" against the odds.

Yet the official narratives of success require from adoptees a certain amount of "forgetting"—and the reincorporation of Korean adoptees as

"Koreans" involves a letting go of the difficult pasts from which these adoptees lives emerged. In fact, at the Gathering, the First Lady of Korea's video address put it plainly when she asked adoptees to "forget your difficult past and renew your relations with your native country . . . based on the blood ties that cannot be severed." Yet the histories of adoptees are intimately linked to those who were left behind by Korea's economic rise and those left out of the official story of Korean modernity. Returning adoptees thus bring the darker stories behind the "miracle on the Han"—stories of poverty, divorce, rape, abandonment, and teenage pregnancy—into view. Some Koreans may believe that adoptees have fared well, having entered into a privileged Western world, with all the opportunities for education and advancement it can afford. This crude calculation, however, discounts the pain and loss of family, belonging, and history that adoptees must often cope with.

In the workshop I attended a debate ensued among some adoptees about how best to represent adoption to a wider public. Some strongly advocated that the positive aspects of transnational adoption should be promoted to counteract negative stereotypes about adoption and adoptees and build a sense of pride in the community. Another adoptee, who had a very difficult adoption experience, retorted, "Do we choose to speak in a positive or a negative way about it? It's both positive and negative and more complicated than that—it's not a simple question or statistic. . . . We need to emphasize the positive aspects, yes, but we need to allow us to acknowledge the pain and express it."

Other tensions have since arisen as well. Although the event was purportedly by and for adoptees, there were many adoption professionals in attendance (most of whom were parents of the adoptee-participants) to observe, volunteer, or facilitate the workshops. This fact suggested to some dissenting adoptees that their experiences were still being appropriated and mediated by adoption agencies, and they refused to attend because of Holt International's orchestrating role. One of the so-called minigatherings, dubbed "KADapalooza," took place in March 2001 and was set up in response to the Gathering. KADapalooza, deriving its name from the hugely popular musical event Lollapalooza, was organized by the adoptee organization a/k/a Southern California, and, according to board member SoYun Roe, was intended to provide a less structured environment than the Gathering. It focused on bringing adoptees together to hang out, have a good time, and share exclusively among themselves.

This resistance notwithstanding, the Gathering has expanded to become a recurring international event. The second Gathering was in Oslo, Norway in 2002, and the third Gathering, scheduled for 2004 in Seoul, is being planned as a major homecoming. It has proven to be a powerful force in forming a Korean adoptee global "movement" and is increasingly addressing public discourses related to the future of international adoption practice and policy, specifically around postadoption issues of cultural heritage, ethnic identity, and birth family search and reunion.

Following the first Gathering, an overwhelming number of positive letters were sent to the Gathering's Internet message board, and "mini-gatherings" and regional groups were formed around the country. The Gathering's stated goal to produce "community" seems to have been accomplished despite the wide-ranging diversity of the participants. Indeed, throughout the conference the desire to pinpoint similarities and to draw generalizations was tempered by a sensitivity to the large group's impressive diversity.

The need for research on adopted Koreans was expressed frequently during the course of the Gathering, often in the context of trying to determine the broader significance of the similarities and differences the participants were discovering among themselves. The attendees recognized that the conference itself was a form of research, but, for many, having a "scientific" or generalizable outcome study was considered a necessary and sorely lacking resource for their own self and group understanding. Yet to be the subjects of their own history, rather than having adoption agencies, psychologists, social workers—and anthropologists— making judgments about how they, as part of a daring "social experiment," have fared, is an important and unprecedented development.

The Gathering was the brainchild of Susan Soon-Keum Cox, who was adopted from Korea in 1956 and is a public policy executive at Holt International. She is also actively involved in promoting Korean and transnational adoption issues on the national stage. Her influence has made the Gathering not only a social support group event but also a political one. Despite the fact that the first conference claimed to be apolitical—as a time for celebration and sharing—it was also used as a show of support for the upcoming vote in Congress on the Hague Convention on Protection of Children and Co-operation in Respect of International Adoption.[7]

At the second Gathering another policy issue on the agenda was the drawing up of a postadoption policy declaration as a collective response

to the Hague Convention's requirement for postadoption services to secure the child's right to preservation of her "ethnic, religious and cultural background." At the close of the second Gathering the problem of
equity and access to information for adoptees who search for birth family was raised as a possible policy focus for the third Gathering. Adopted
Koreans are clearly poised to have an impact on the future of transnational adoption.

In addition to discussions of child protection and human rights policy,
there is also the ongoing contestation over the politics and ethics of Korean adoption and its future. Over the past four or five decades the demographics of birth mothers may have changed, but the compromising
effects of modernization on the lives of women and children have not di-
minished.[8] The female factory workers of the 1960s and seventies and the
unmarried college-age women of the 1980s who surrendered their children for adoption have today been replaced by teenage girls whose unplanned pregnancies currently support the supply of adopted babies. Korea's rapid industrialization, uneven economic development, and
patriarchal attitudes about women's sexuality are all factors that serve to
perpetuate the social conditions that contribute to the abandonment or
relinquishment of children in Korea. The televised search and reunion
stories, the circulation of adoptee art, and the conferences and public
events staged by adoptee activists have made adoptee stories and the con-
tinuing problem of adoption increasingly visible in Korea. Although Korea's adoption program, characterized as ethical, reliable, efficient, and
transparent, is today a model for other overseas adoption programs, critics of Korean adoption see it as a humanitarian project that quickly turned
into a profitable substitute for social welfare services. Social work scholar
Rosalind Sarri and her colleagues point out the problematic contradiction
between Korea's wealth as a nation and the adoption of its children overseas—a contradiction that also troubles many adult adopted Koreans—and
they trenchantly criticize the Korean government for its "long-term dependency on intercountry adoption programs as a major policy solution."

So, after the pomp and circumstance surrounding returning adoptees
subside, there is the realization that for every adoptee who returns as an
adult to Korea, another child is on its way to being adopted overseas. Indeed, some adult adoptees, on their way back from Korea, volunteer to
escort babies on their life-transforming journey to their new American
parents and find it very rewarding to share in the reproductive process

they themselves experienced. Others, however, find the political economic circumstances that perpetuate international adoption to be dis-
tressing and in urgent need of reform.

Whereas adoptees express desires to change "the system," these stances
are often tempered by a sense of futility, and so far more radical calls for
reform have not been made. At the first Gathering, one adoptee movingly
recounted his return trip to Korea, and his daily visits to an orphanage
where he cradled the babies and imagined that he was holding himself.
He angrily questioned why the Korean government continued to rely
upon adoption when "it has enough money to take care of its own."
Someone suggested that because of Korea's long and ancient history, cultural change would be slow, as opposed to the rapid changes that characterize American culture. The adoptee then wondered aloud: How does
culture change?

> *Adoption across political and cultural borders may simultaneously be an act of*
> *violence and an act of love, an excruciating rupture and a generous incorpora-*
> *tion, an appropriation of valued resources and a constitution of personal ties.*
> —PAULINE T. STRONG, 2001

Transnational adoption raises moral and ethical ambiguities that are difficult, if not impossible, to disentangle and run through the multifarious
experiences, histories, and circumstances of adult adoptees. As adoption
from China becomes increasingly prevalent and visible in cities and small
towns throughout the U.S., adult adopted Koreans play an important role
in educating the next generation of Asian adoptees and their parents in
the challenges of being a multiracial adoptive family.

Adult adoptees' experiences as "pioneers" of transnational adoption
have made them valuable resources for rethinking adoption policy and
practice, and some have worked as advisers and consultants to agencies
and parents or as mentors for younger adoptees. They speak to prospective and adoptive parents about the identity issues and psychological problems they faced and about what parents should expect to encounter as
their transracially adopted children mature. And some adoptees are now
adopting children from Korea themselves, thus building multigenerational
Korean adoptive families.

The social experiment of transnational adoption from Korea has been
dubbed a success by both American adoption professionals and the Kore-

an government, celebrated as a beacon of a truly global and multicultur-alist future. Yet this rosy picture is darkened by the experiences of some adoptees. The Korean state's attempts to imbue adoptees with cultural "roots" or diasporic "identities" are discredited by adoptee counternarra-tives of loss—of birth family, cultural "authenticity," psychic wholeness, personal history and memory, and legitimate citizenship. Moreover, the optimism of the official rhetoric obscures the complex political and eco-nomic contexts in which gender and class inequalities continue to place birth mothers in the difficult position of having to "choose" to give up their children for adoption.

Lacking even an "official" history, adopted Koreans are making history in both senses: not only are they writing individual and collective histories through shared stories, they are doing it for the first time. There are a num-ber of competing claims to adoptee identity—from adoption agencies and the Korean state as well as from the media and other dominant institu-tions—and by articulating their identities and producing alternative public spheres these adoptees are performing necessary and urgent cultural work.

By piecing together recovered memory and forging meaning through self-examination and narrative, these adoptees are, ultimately, engaged in a struggle for personhood. These histories are vital to understanding not only the darker side of Korean modernity but also the ongoing practice of adoption in the context of global capitalism and the conditions under which tens of thousands of children a year cross increasingly porous na-tional borders.

NOTES

Thanks first to the editors for their careful attention and enduring pa-tience through the numerous drafts of this chapter. Portions of this article have been heavily revised from material first published in "Korean Adoptee Autoethnography," *Visual Anthropology Review* 16(1) , and in "Wedding Citizenship and Culture," *Social Text* 74. I am extremely grateful to Jackie Aronson, Tobias Hubinette, Mihee Cho, Maya Weimer, Hollee McGinnis, and Me-K. Ahn for their reviewing and giving feedback on earlier drafts of this article. Any errors or omissions are certainly my own.

1. Adoptee groups have formed in the Netherlands, Belgium, Denmark, France, and Germany, in the U.S. in New York, Washington, D.C., Colorado, Washing-ton State, and California. Global Overseas Adoptees' Link (GOA'L) was established in Seoul in 1998 by six adoptees living in Korea. In addition to the Gathering, two

other inaugural conferences for adoptees and/or their families took place in 1999: the Korean American Adoptee Adoptive Family Network Conference (KAAN) and the GOA'L Conference. In conjunction with the KAAN Conference, SoYun Roe, an adoptee advocate and cofounder of adoptee organization a/k/a SoCal, curated the SNAPSHOT exhibit, a showcase of works by Korean adoptee artists at the Korean American Museum in Los Angeles.

2. Kevin Kaliher and Meaghan Uijung Dunn, two Korean adoptees, produced a Cartoon Network show, *The Kitty Bobo Show*, whose main character is a cat adopted by a dog family.

3. Mihee Cho's short film, *Adoption,* was produced in 1988 and has won festival awards in both Europe and Korea. Korean adoptee autoethnographic memoirs include Thomas Park Clement's *The Unforgotten War*, Elizabeth Kim's *Ten Thousand Sorrows*, Katy Robinson's *A Single Square Picture*, and literary anthologies *Seeds from a Silent Tree* and *Voices from Another Place.*

4. Whereas the great majority of adoptees at the conference were raised by white middle-class families, there was a great deal of diversity of color, racial identification, class, and sexuality. The earlier wave of mixed-race adoptees had very different experiences from full-Korean adoptees, especially depending on how they were positioned with respect to color and race in America.

5. The age at which adoptees emigrated certainly has much to do with their ability to recall their early experiences. Those adopted as infants or at very young ages often have little or no memory of Korea, compared with those adopted at later ages such as Borshay.

6. Adoptees who search also turn to more experienced adoptees for help. For instance, Korean-Belgian adoptee Mihee Cho has been instrumental in assisting the searches of more than six hundred adoptees since 1991.

7. The Hague Convention, a UN charter, is governed by UNICEF's Convention on the Rights of the Child and addresses the issue of children's human rights. It is intended to safeguard the "best interests of the child" and was drafted in 1993 in response to reports of baby selling and trafficking in Latin America and eastern Europe. It has been ratified by both the United States and Korea, but has not yet been legislated by the Korean government.

8. Korea's rapid industrialization between the 1960s and 1990s entailed massive shifts that transformed, within one generation, a largely rural, agricultural economy of extended family households into an industrialized, urban economy of nuclear households.

WORKS CITED

Adolfson, Nathan. 1999. *Passing Through.* Video. National Asian American Television Association.

Ahn, Me-K. [Karen Me Kyung Muckenhirn]. 1994. *living in halftones*. Video. Third World Newsreel.

Arndt, Jennifer Christine Yang Hee. 1997. *Crossing Chasms*. Video. Rainbow Films.

Bishoff, Tonya and Jo Rankin, eds. 1997. *Seeds from a Silent Tree: An Anthology by Korean Adoptees*. San Diego: Pandal.

Borshay Liem, Deann. 2000. *First Person Plural*. Video. National Asian American Television Association.

Bruining, Anne Mi Ok. 1991. "The Politics of International Adoption: Made in Korea." *Sojourner: The Women's Forum* 14(9): 18.

Buck, Pearl S. 1964. *Children for Adoption*. New York: Random House.

Clement, Thomas Park. 1998. *The Unforgotten War: Dust of the Streets*. Bloomfield: TruePeny.

Cox, Susan Soon-Keum. 2000. *Voices from Another Place: A Collection of Works from a Generation Born in Korea and Adopted to Other Countries*. St. Paul: Yeong and Yeong.

Evan B. Donaldson Adoption Institute. 1999. *Survey of Adult Korean Adoptees: Report on the Findings*. New York: Evan B. Donaldson Adoption Institute.

Foster-Carter, Aidan. 2002. "Adopting, Adapting: Korean Orphans." *Asia Times Online*. July 17. www.atimes.com/aties/Korea/DG17Dg01.html

Gathering of the First Generation of Korean Adoptees. 1999. Conference Program. September 10–12. Washington, D.C.

Kim, Eleana. 2003. "Wedding Citizenship and Culture: Korean Adoptees and the Global Family of Korea." *Social Text* 74.21(1): 57–81.

—— 2001 "Korean Adoptee Autoethnography: Refashioning Self, Family, and Finding Community." *Visual Anthropology Review* 16(1): 43–70.

Kim, Elizabeth S. 2000. *Ten Thousand Sorrows: The Extraordinary Journey of a Korean War Orphan*. New York: Doubleday.

Kim, Samuel S., ed. 2000. *Korea's Globalization*. New York: Cambridge University Press.

Progressive (January).

Robinson, Katy. 2002. *A Single Square Picture: A Korean Adoptee's Search for Her Roots*. New York: Berkeley.

Rothschild, Matthew. 1988. "Babies for Sale: South Koreans Make Them, Americans Buy Them." *Progressive* (January): 18–23.

Russell, Catherine. 1999. *Experimental Ethnography: The Work of Film in the Age of Video*. Durham: Duke University Press.

Sarri, Rosalind, Y. Baik, and M. Bombyk. 1998. "Goal Displacement and Dependency in South Korean–United States Intercountry Adoption." *Children and Youth Services Review* 20:87–114.

Strong, Pauline T. 2001. "To Forget Their Tongue, Their Name, and Their Whole Relation: Captivity, Extra-Tribal Adoption, and the Indian Child Welfare Act."

In Sarah Franklin and Susan McKinnon, eds., *Relative Values: Reconfiguring Kinship Studies*. Durham: Duke University Press.

Theiler, Kim Su. 1993. *Great Girl*. 16mm Film. Women Make Movies.

Tolle, Tammy. 1998. *Searching for Go-Hyang*. Video. Women Make Movies.

Tomes, Kimberly SaRee. 1997. *Looking for Wendy*. Video. Third World Newsreel.

Tuan, Mia. 1999. *Forever Foreigner or Honorary Whites? The Asian Ethnic Experience Today*. New Brunswick, N.J.: Rutgers University Press.

Weil, Richard. 1984. "International Adoptions: The Quiet Migration." *International Migration Review* 18(2): 276–293.

10
Activism and Exile: Palestinianness and the Politics of Solidarity

Rabab Abdulhadi

On a recent October night, over 150 people weathered the brutal cold and crowded a lecture hall at New York University. A mixed group of faculty, students, and community activists, they came to learn of Palestinian conditions under Israeli occupation and to extend support for Bir Zeit, the largest Palestinian university. Bir Zeit has been subjected to intensified and renewed closures, sieges, and widespread arrest of faculty and students since the Israeli occupation of the West Bank and Gaza Strip in 1967, which have only increased during the first and the more recent Intifada. Organized by NYU Students for Justice for Palestine (SJP) and a host of academic departments, the event featured a panel of Arab speakers: Walid Omary, senior correspondent of Al-Jazeera Satellite Station in Palestine, Carmela Armanois Omari, administrative and financial vice president of Bir Zeit University, Khaled Fahmy, associate professor of Middle East Studies, and Amahl Bishara, a graduate student in anthropology and media studies. Speakers tackled the politics of representation in the U.S. media, particularly as it pertains to the occupied Palestinian areas.

As I stood to moderate, the diverse audience and setting reminded me of events we had organized over twenty years ago in solidarity with the Palestinian people before, during, and after the breakout of the first Palestinian Intifada against the Israeli occupation. There sat Rawia, the former president of the Union of Palestinian Women's Associations in North America. Next to her sat George, a Lebanese activist and a cofounder of the Organization of Arab Students in the U.S.. Between Rawia and George were Wafa and Sana, the former an organizer on behalf of Azmi

Bishara, the Palestinian member of the Israeli Knesset whose platform demands that Israel become a country of its citizens rather than an automatic home for world Jewry; the latter a human resource specialist at NYU and a former leader of the General Union of Palestine Students.

But there were also new faces. Some came from "back home" and intended to go back: Nisreen, a Palestinian woman who came from Jordan to work with UNIFEM, and Reem, a graduate student in drama therapy and a former member of Al-Funoun, the Palestinian Popular Arts Ensemble in Ramallah, on the West Bank. Others were born and raised in the U.S.: Renda, a Palestinian American henna artist,[1] who grew up in San Francisco, was the initiator of the Williamsburg Bridges Palestine 2002 in Brooklyn, an artistic and a political project featuring the work of fifty Palestinian artists—an unimaginable dream back in the 1980s. Next to Renda sat Reem and Abbas, activists with Al-Awda, or Palestinian Right of Return Coalition. Activists for justice and peace were there as well. In the back Charles, a leader of Students for Justice in Palestine (SJP), sat next to Sherene, a cofounder of SJP and a Palestinian American doctoral student in history and Middle East studies at NYU whose parents became refugees in 1948. She was born in Beirut, Lebanon and raised in the United States.

The driving force behind this event, however, was Rich Blint, a graduate student in Africana and American Studies here at NYU. An activist for justice and peace for quite a few years, Rich organized the first teach-in on the April 2002 Israeli siege of Palestine at NYU. Thus, while the audience was not much different in its composition than past events, Palestinians no longer solely led the Palestine solidarity movement. Moreover, the transnational electronic organizing and solidarity links that Rich and our colleague at Bir Zeit, Riham Barghouti, built to realize this program underscores how activists have used various structures and mechanisms to struggle for change, for justice, and for peace.

This essay traces the development of Palestine-centered American activism and identitification (or *Palestinianness*) in the United States from the late 1960s to the present. Palestinians began immigrating to the U.S. around the turn of the century and more so in the 1930s and 1940s as the combination of colonial British rule and Zionist immigration made their lives in Palestine unbearable. I argue that, paradoxically, the development of Palestinian identification, precisely because of its transnational character, was shaped by transformations in American politics, economy, and culture as well as political and social changes in the Middle East and other parts of the world. Focusing on the period that began in the late 1960s and extending to the present, this essay traces the ways Palestinian American activism has been shaped and mediated by the following factors: 1. the Palestinian struggle for self-determination, on one hand, and U.S. Orientalist, anti-Arab, and pro-Israeli discourses and policies, on the other, 2. the experience of exile and dispersion, and 3. the politics of gender, class, and race relations in North America. As I will demonstrate, the history of Palestinian American activism, and the politics of Palestinianness in the U.S., has developed in intimate connection with, and in relationship to, other groups of U.S. activists such as African Americans, feminists, and trade unionists. At the same time, Palestinians have crafted contentious identities that reflect their experiences as exiled people.

ACTIVIST ETHNOGRAPHY

This essay represents a challenge on a personal and a political level. My data is drawn from my double capacity as a journalist and an activist. First, as an active member of the Palestinian community in the United States, I organized and participated in rallies, political events, and national demonstrations that I cite here as well as conferences that were organized by a host of local, national, and international organizations representing the interests of students, women, and labor.[2] On some occasions I bought tickets like other members of the community, but more often than not I was either a co-organizer or a featured speaker at these gatherings. Second, as a Middle East Affairs journalist at the United Nations (1984–1994), I attended events and interviewed (formally and informally) Palestinian American leaders and activists in the Palestinian community in the United States. As a journalist I frequently accessed leaflets and other gray material (records, archives, and literature) of Palestinian activism in the U.S. As an activist-journalist I helped to produce and publish community newsletters such as *Palestine Focus*, representing the Palestine Solidarity Committee, and *Voice of Palestinian Women*, the newsletter of the Union of Palestinian Women's Associations in North America.

As an activist and a scholar, then, I engage in ethnography in which I am not just an outsider looking in nor am I solely an insider to community dynamics. I continue to feel the responsibility this doubled-up-position implies. On the one hand, I feel that I must try as much as I can to express and articulate the sentiments of my comrades who participated in making this history of Palestinian activism. On the other, I realize that I cannot narrate the stories of every community activist or capture the richness, diversity, and subtlety of events' interpretations. This essay, then, must be seen as a modest attempt to tell a particular narrative of Palestinian activism as much as it is about critically reflecting upon the activist history my comrades and I collectively made.

PALESTINIAN IMMIGRATION TO THE U.S.: POLITICS, EXILE, AND IDENTITY

Before the 1960s Palestinian immigrants were mostly poor Christians from Jerusalem and its surrounding villages and towns, especially Ramallah. Men came first and peddled clothing from door-to-door to save enough money to send for their families. By 1948 they had become U.S. citizens: for this group of immigrants or, more precisely, exiles, the fall of Palestine and the establishment of the state of Israel made it impossible to dream of returning home; there was no home to return to. While strongly sensing the injustice of their reality, early generations of Palestinian immigrants did not translate their sentiments into collective action. Due to the 1950s political environment that discouraged multicultural expression and herded immigrants into a "melting pot," Palestinian Americans kept practices of their Palestinianness away from the public eye: they cooked Arabic food, spoke Arabic to their children, arranged their marriages to each other. They maintained ties to Palestine by sending money to relatives, visiting whenever they had a chance, and helping Palestinian students who came to the U.S. to earn higher degrees, especially those who became stranded and stateless in 1948 after the fall of Palestine.[3]

Furthermore, inconspicuous to the public eye, Palestinians carved their own communal spaces by organizing themselves into town associations, such as the Ramallah Federation. However, they deliberately seemed nonpolitical on the surface. Conditions in the U.S. were simply not conducive to the emergence of an overt expression of Palestinianness. On the surface the federation seemed to exemplify the Palestinian chapter of the "American" melting pot narrative: By the late 1960s its members had become fluent in English; they were naming their children Johnny, Mary, and Mike; many had joined the Lions, Shriners, and Freemason clubs; and they operated professional businesses such as banks and real estate and engineering firms. The federation continued to hold annual conventions and to act as a family reunion and matchmaking site. At the same time, while seeming to melt into Americanness, the Ramallah Federation conventions also raised funds for hospitals, schools, and scholarships for the Ramallah folks back home.

In the late 1960s, however, a new generation of immigrants fleeing to the U.S. shifted the terms of Palestinianness. The 1967 war produced a second wave of uprootedness, as residents of villages, towns, and refugee camps in certain areas of the West Bank left homes and possessions behind and contributed to a new expanding of the Palestinian diaspora. From Jordan, Egypt, and other Arab countries, Palestinian refugees migrated to what they came to define as locations of double and triple exile in Europe, Australia, New Zealand, and the United States. Palestinians who came to the U.S. after 1967 were different from the earlier Ramallah group. They were mostly peasants whose lands were confiscated by the Israeli military, thus denying them livelihood. They came from Beit Hanina, Silwan, and Silwad—suburbs of Jerusalem, which were annexed and turned into the "eternal capital of Israel" in 1967.

Palestinians arriving in the U.S. in the late 1960s found a different reality from that which earlier immigrants experienced. Business opportunities that were opened to immigrants during the New Deal were no longer available. Moreover, with U.S. support for Israel at an all-time high in the aftermath of the 1967 war, Palestinian immigrants found the U.S. white middle class predominantly hostile or at a minimum ignorant of their predicament. To earn a living, Palestinian immigrants first sold clothing and then opened their grocery stores in poor Black and Latino neighborhoods, which were more open to Arabs. Unlike their predecessors, recent Palestinian immigrants were not as eager to fully embrace what they perceived to be the "American way of life." This group of Palestinians had lost any illusions or ideal expectations of a "melting pot" society—to them U.S. citizenship meant a green card, a passport, and safety for themselves and their families. At the same time, Palestinian students enrolling in U.S. colleges were drawn by the image of the United States as "the land of opportunity," and thus they hoped to combine work and study, earn their degrees and return home. Most students, however, arrived from a Middle East in which oppositional movements in Palestine and elsewhere were struggling against neocolonialist oppressive regimes, U.S. intervention, and Israeli occupation and expansionism. Thus most Palestinian students arrived in the U.S. politically conscious, clear if not overt in their commitments and support for regional oppositional movements.

Politically, the overwhelming support Israel began to receive from the U.S. (especially during the Johnson and Nixon administrations) was offset by the growth of U.S. peace and justice movements. The 1960s United States was the arena of intense political and social mobilization against the war in Vietnam, racism, and residual McCarthyism. Spearheaded by the Black power movements and campus activism around these issues, U.S. oppositional spaces were a hospitable environment for Palestinian and other Arab political activists. Organizations began to emerge to reflect the changing political reality in both the Middle East and the United States. For example, a number of intellectuals, such as Edward Said, Ibrahim Abu-Lughod, Naseer Aruri, Abbas Nasrawi, Samih Farsoun, and Hisham Sharabi set up the Association of Arab American University Graduates (AAUG) whose mission was to counter what later became known as Orientalism (Said 1978), anti-Arab discrimination, and to promote the Palestinian cause in the U.S. academic and intellectual circles.

Students founded the Organization of Arab Students (OAS) as a platform for radical and oppositional Arab thought and politics. Irrespective of the risks of speaking out (many came from, and intended to go back to, places like Saudi Arabia, Jordan, and the Israeli-occupied Palestinian areas), student activism flourished, raising the consciousness of students and recent immigrants alike on what was going on in the Arab world. Significantly, the OAS linked up with activists from different parts of the world. These connections paralleled developments in the Palestinian and Arab liberation movements.

In the *jaliyeh,* or community (which included immigrants who were neither students, academics, or professionals), the expanded U.S. space for oppositional and alternative Arab and Palestinian expressions made it possible for Palestinian Americans to hold onto and at times display symbols of their cultural heritage. Increasingly, then, Palestinian immigrants took a semipublic mode in celebrating their religious holidays (Muslim or Eastern Orthodox Christian), teaching their children Arabic, sending them to Palestine during summer vacations, organizing village and town associations, participating in demonstrations, and donating funds to Palestinian charities back home. For instance, as it became more politically active, Ramallah Federation changed its name to Ramallah Federation–Palestine. Beit Hanina Charitable Society and El-Bireh–Palestine Society began to adopt and implement programs that supported their town folks "back" in Palestine while also providing social spaces for their youngsters to meet. In other words, Palestinians in the immigrant community were finally identifying themselves publicly as Palestinians.

THE ETHNIC TURN—SELF-DETERMINATION BACK HOME; INCLUSION AT HOME?

Activism in the 1960s thus inspired Palestinians and Palestinian Americans to take more overtly activist stances on the various issues that affected their lives. The 1980s environment of celebrating multiculturalism enabled Palestinian Americans to struggle for a more equal footing both in the Middle East and in the United States.

By the mid 1970s Palestinian Americans in U.S. cities with increasingly large Palestinian communities (eg, Detroit, Chicago, Brooklyn, San Francisco, Youngstown) had founded Arab Community Centers. These centers were also social spaces for young male activists to read Arabic newspapers from the Middle East, watch news on TV, play chess and backgammon, debate the politics of the PLO, and exchange tips on employment and ways to acquire U.S. residence and citizenship. Increasingly the centers became sites for Saturday Arabic schools and limited social gatherings that transcended village and town associations. Yet, due to the dominance of a pro-Israeli stand in U.S. policies and public culture, the centers kept political advocacy low key for the most part.

Around the same time, however, Yasser Arafat gave his 1974 "gun and olive branch" speech before the UN General Assembly. This landmark occasion culminated in recognition of the PLO as the sole and legitimate representative of the Palestinian people by a majority of UN member states. This recognition significantly shifted Palestinian politics as well as the course of Palestinian American activism. Palestinians in the U.S. began to form all-Palestine organizations. For example, three nationalist groups emerged to transcend the village- and town-based structures of organization: The Palestine Red Crescent Society (PRCS), Palestine Aid Society (PAS), and the Committee for a Democratic Palestine (CDP). The three groups formed the Palestine Congress of North America, which was modeled after the Palestine National Council, the Palestinian parliament in exile. Students at U.S. universities founded the General Union of Palestinian Students (GUPS) as well.[4] In the years following Arafat's speech the Arab Community Centers were transformed accordingly. For example, during the 1982 Israeli invasion of Lebanon the centers became sites of activism. Large numbers of Palestinians who came from refugee camps in Lebanon congregated each evening to hear the latest news of their relatives and friends. These gatherings led women, men, and youth to collectively launch campaigns to support Palestinian and Lebanese populations under the ninety days of Israeli siege in Beirut.

Palestine solidarity activism underlined the need for political engagement beyond communal boundaries and antiwar organiations. However, electoral politics was not seen as a vehicle for public claims, which was partly due to Palestinian distrust of U.S. politicians and the tilt toward Israel and partly because the majority of immigrants did not view themselves as Americans, only as Palestinians. All of this began to change during Jesse Jackson's first presidential campaign in 1984, thus marking a significant turning point in activists' strategies. For most Palestinians who never cared nor voted for any presidential candidate, this election was qualitatively different—it was the first time in U.S. history that a presidential candidate not only embraced Palestinian and other Arab Americans, welcoming them into his Rainbow Coalition campaign, but also called for the establishment of an independent Palestinian state.[5] Arab Community Centers in particular played a major role in Jackson's presidential bid: they set up town meetings, invited speakers from the Rainbow Coalition to address the membership, organized voter registration drives, and collected contributions. And while initially recruited into the campaign as foot soldiers, Palestinians, especially from the Chicago Community Center, were soon playing advisory and leading roles in the Rainbow Coalition. For example, Camilia Odeh, who two years later became the first president of the Union of Palestinian Women Association in North America, served on the board of the Rainbow Coalition and traveled from city to city to recruit volunteers and raises funds for Jackson's presidential campaign.[6]

Palestinian youth were also mobilized. Newly forming youth groups expressed greater pride in Palestinianness, and political activity around Palestine and other campuswide concerns increased. Prompted by study groups and inspired by political discussions and activism at Arab Community Centers, young Palestinian Americans who reached adulthood at the height of Palestinian activism founded Palestinian American Youth (PAY) as their collective form of expression. To second- and third-generation Palestinian Americans, identifying with their national roots was not as ostracizing as it had been for their parents' generation. The 1980s was the era of multiculturalism, pluralism, and diversity; ethnic pride was not a liability any more.[7]

The political and organizational features of Palestinian youth groups reflected their particular location as U.S. immigrants with Palestinian heritage. They mixed social activities such as picnics, Halloween celebrations, and Saturday night parties with affirmations of Palestinianness including the formation of the well-known Palestinian *Dabke* (folkloric dance) group, Al-Watan, or homeland. The competing influences of Palestinianness and Americanness as politically and socially shaped identifications led Palestinian American students to organize political events reflective of their transnationalism. For example, PAY New York members were actively involved in founding Arab and Palestinian Clubs at different CUNY colleges. These clubs' primary activities focused on organizing Palestinian educational events around Palestine, such as the Day of the Land (March 30), Palestinian Prisoners' Day (April 17), and International Day of Solidarity with the People of Palestine (November 29). Palestinian students also formed coalitions with other international students and students of color to celebrate Black History Month and International Women's Day; to honor Malcolm X; and to protest CUNY tuition increases. The character of these events wove elements from Palestinian political culture "back home" as much as it drew from the repertoire of other U.S.-based collective action (see Tilly 1978). Palestinian youth-based organizing thus epitomizes 1980s-era Palestine-centered activism, where asserting *Palestinianness* meant identifying with the struggle of other nationally and racially marginalized groups.

INTERNATIONAL SOLIDARITY

The 1980s also broadened Palestinian-American international alliances. The UN's recognition of the PLO in the mid-1970s conferred international legitimacy to the Palestinian cause. Such recognition enabled Palestinian Americans to strengthen their ties with other communities of color and to participate in justice movements in Palestine and across the globe. At the same time, as alliances with radical organizations, including anti-Zionist Jewish groups, multiplied, the lack of support that Palestinians could expect from U.S. (middle-class and white) liberals also became apparent. For example, in 1981 Palestinian activists organized the November 29th Coalition for Palestine. Taking its name from November 29, the international day of solidarity with the Palestinian people, the coalition organized a demonstration of eight thousand people at the United Nations. The list of endorsements reflected the breadth of support for Palestinian rights on an international as well as on a domestic level: internationally, endorsers included Granada's ambassador to the UN (before the U.S. invasion in 1983), the African National Congress, FDR/FMLN of El Salvador, CISPES (Committee in Solidarity with the People of El Salvador), and a large number of oppositional groups from Asia, Africa, and Latin America. On the U.S. front, with the exception of anti-Zionist Jews and militant peace and justice groups, the list of participants was striking in that supporters were almost exclusively from groups of color. Sponsors included African American and Caribbean groups such as Patrice Lumumba Coalition, the Caribbean People's Alliance, *Haiti Progress*, Black United Front, and the National Conference of Black Lawyers. Latino groups included the Puerto Rican Committee, Center for Puerto Rican Studies, Puerto Rican Socialist Party, Casa de Las Americas (a Cuban group based in New York), and a number of Chilean, Argentine, Guatemalan, and Honduran groups. Native American groups such as the Committee to Defend Leonard Peltier, the International Indian Treaty Council, and the American Indian Movement were also among the endorsers. Importantly, anti-Zionist Jewish groups and a number of militant peace and justice groups made up of predominantly white members further supported the event.

The list of supporters thus reveals the peculiar limitations of support for Palestinian causes in the U.S. Support for Israel or ambivalence toward Israeli violations of Palestinian rights kept left-liberal groups from extending to Palestinians the same backing or empathy they had offered to Central American liberation movements. George, a Lebanese activist directly involved in the coalition's planning, attributed this failure to the character of the U.S. political system:

> While the Republicans and the Democrats are divided over U.S. policy in Central America, for example, no such division exists insofar as Middle

East policy goes. Both Parties are united around Israel. And the liberals, the mainstream of the U.S. peace movement, are allied with the Democratic Party.

The connection between the liberal leadership of the U.S. peace movement and the Democratic Party is one reason for withholding criticism of Israeli military occupation. Another reason, according to an activist with the Palestine Solidarity Committee, had to do with the refusal of the peace movement leadership to do the intellectual labor necessary to break away from the Zionist mythology that equates criticism of Israel with anti-Semitism. A year later the challenge to reach liberal peace activists was revisited as Israel invaded Lebanon. With the exception of the left-leaning U.S. Peace Council, which was affiliated with the Communist Party of the United States (CPUSA), the leadership of major peace groups refused to get involved in what it called "the divisive politics of the Middle East conflict" and demand Israeli withdrawal from Lebanon (see Meyer 1993).

As Israeli troops advanced to Beirut, Palestinian and Lebanese activists realized that they had no option but to seize the initiative and revive the November 29th Coalition. The summer of 1982 thus witnessed a whirlwind of MiddleEast–centered activities, such as demonstrations, picket lines, petitions, teach-ins, and town meetings. Media outreach was set up in different cities across the United States. Support was garnered from university professors, churches, and community centers. Newly founded Jewish groups, such as JAIMIL (Jews Against the Israeli Massacre in Lebanon) also joined the coalition as well as Israeli peace groups in exposing Israel's complicity in the Sabra and Shatila massacres (during which right-wing Lebanese militias slaughtered hundreds of Palestinians while Israeli forces, led by Ariel Sharon, turned on flood lights to facilitate the killing).

Denying the validity of the Palestinian cause by the liberal leadership of the peace movement has consolidated Palestinian identification with other marginalized groups in the U.S. Interactions with activists of color sharpened Palestinian understanding of the U.S. racial system and enabled them to see their struggle as a part of a transnational context of domination and subordination. For example, in her first collection of poems *Born Palestinian, Born Black*, twenty-three-year-old Palestinian American Suheir Hamad explains that defining herself as both Palestinian and black was inspired by the words of the late African American poet June Jordan. In "Moving Towards Home" Jordan expresses the way she felt upon her return from a trip to a Palestinian refugee camp in Lebanon: "I was born a Black woman / and now I am become a Palestinian / against the relentless laughter of evil / there is less and less living room / and where are my loved ones? / It is time to make our way home" (as cited in Hamad 1996:ix).

The mid-1980s heightened visibility of the anti-apartheid movement further and accentuated Palestinian alliances with other struggles for justice. Palestinian intellectuals such as the late Northwestern University professor Ibrahim Abu Lughod, active in the United Holy Land Fund along with Suhail Mi'ari, executive director of the United Holy Land Fund, were regular protestors at anti-apartheid rallies in Chicago, where the two were arrested in civil disobedience actions on more than one occasion. At Columbia University Palestinian students joined their African Americans peers in staging protests to demand the Ivy League college's divestment from companies that did business with South Africa.[8] The Palestine Solidarity Committee (PSC) organized an educational speaking tour of Palestinians and members of the African National Congress of South Africa (ANC) in twenty U.S. cities under the heading "Israel and South Africa: The Apartheid Connection?" In anticipation of the tour, PSC put out a special issue of its newsletter, *Palestine Focus*, published brochures, and enlisted the expertise of specialized scholars. Organized in the midst of intensive antiapartheid campaigning, the tour was instrumental in educating college students and a wide array of grassroots groups about Palestinian and South African struggles. Most significantly, as a Palestinian activist put it:

> More significant was the fact that the tour educated Palestinians about the colonial conditions of other people and the struggles waged for freedom elsewhere in the world. Because we were organizing joint activities, the relations between us and the ANC were no longer limited to formal meetings and official interactions; we started attending and participating in each other's events, including social and personal occasions. This helped younger Palestinians understand, on a personal level, that they were not the only oppressed people on the face of the earth.

Thus, while predominantly white and middle-class liberal groups shunned Palestinian activists in the early 1980s, during this period Palestinians built more networks with African American groups and broadened their understandings of global racial dynamics. The 1980s, then, was an intense period during which Palestinian Americans identified more closely with other groups of color, both in the U.S. and internationally. Not accidently, this period also highlighted the degree to which Palestinian-centered activism raised questions of gender, class, and immigration that were similar and yet distinct from those struggles waged by other communities of color.

UPWA: CARVING A SPACE FOR PALESTINIAN WOMEN

The development of Palestine-centered feminist activism further illustrates the distinctive politics and practices of Palestinianness as a transnational and radical identification. This goes back to the early 1980s when Palestinian women in several U.S. cities began to form associations. Palestinian Women's Associations emerged to carve out a women's space that the mostly male Arab Community Centers could not provide. The associations also arose in response to U.S. liberal feminists who refused to take Palestinian women seriously, insisting on labeling Palestinian women as "nationalists" and barring them from feminist activities and celebrations. In this sense dominant U.S. women's groups were not different from other leading organizations in the peace movement who considered any mention of Palestine or Palestinians a "divisive" issue and unfit for inclusion. For example, after our requests for inclusion in international women's day celebrations in March 1983 were denied, a number of women got together in Brooklyn and formed the Palestinian Women's Association.

By 1986 Palestinian women's associations were active in fifteen U.S. and Canadian cities. Women's networking with each other led to the formation of the Union of Palestinian Women's Associations in North America (UPWA). A site of support and solidarity, UPWA enabled members to participate in decision making, engage in educational activities,, and feel empowered. Camilia Odeh, the first elected president of UPWA explained:

> You know how hard it is for a woman to get away from her home, persuade her husband to buy her a plane ticket, give her money for food and lodging, and take care of the children while she is gone. When this woman

has been able to do so and get to the convention, she has more right than me or you to run for leadership. So our board members are not only representatives of the associations which elected them; some actually felt empowered at the convention and decided to run for the board. This is wonderful. Besides, how could we implement rigid rules and claim that we are for women's liberation?

Odeh's words were shared by most union members, thus reflecting a deep commitment to feminist thought and practices. However, as an organization, UPWA was not unified on questions of sexuality, reproduction, or arranged marriages. As a Palestinian community organization, UPWA was made up of female members who carved democratic spaces for women's action. At the same time, as the sole nationally based organization of the Palestinian community that represented women at the grassroots, UPWA activities reflected the needs of its membership. Thus, while attracting a limited number of "professional" women who were gainfully employed, the membership was mostly made up of community homemakers and young student activists.[9] UPWA's priorities of reaching out to and meeting the needs of women in the community were lost on middle-class, white liberal feminists. Interpreting women's participation in cookouts for large Palestinian communal events as evidence of the workings of patriarchy, U.S. liberal feminists failed to understand the different ways in which Palestinian women enacted their Palestinianness and feminism by contributing to the success of community events while simultaneously refusing to allow activist politics to be the sole domain of men. Likewise, wearing Palestinian embroidered dresses, which was a source of pride for Palestinian women in the face of cultural degradation at the hands of the Israeli occupiers, especially for those women who could not return "back home," was seen by liberal feminists not as an assertion of Palestinianness, to which women were as entitled as men were, but as a commitment to a "patriarchal" and "tribal" display of "backward" and "traditional" culture. The limited and narrow understanding of what feminism (including Palestinian feminism) was all about isolated Palestinian women and other women of color in the dominant women's movement. Replicating the peace movement in labeling anti-occupation politics a "divisive" issue, the women's movement has also ostracized Palestinian women.

COMMUNITY IN DANGER: THE L.A. 8 CASE AND THE DEMONIZATION OF PALESTINIANS

Such elitist characterizations, of course, were not limited to liberal feminists—stereotypes of Arabs were prevalent in U.S. dominant and popular culture. As an activist-imbued expression, *Palestinianness* also emerged in direct response and opposition to xenophobia and Orientalism. The case of the L.A. 8 in particular demonstrates the ways in which Palestinian American activists countered their demonization in part by eliciting support from the allies they had established throughout the 1980s. It is necessary here to note that while Palestinianness emerged in response to a specific context, it has also shaped and influenced the context in which it played out.

By the end of 1986 this particular Palestinian immigrant community had been settled in North America for almost three decades. The immigrants of the 1960s had become citizens; women, youth, student, and community organizations were in place; ties were solidified with other communities of color; the solidarity movement was making inroads; and plans were underway to commemorate twenty years of Israeli occupation of the West Bank and Gaza Strip. However, 1987 was also an election year in which the Reagan-Bush team intended to win their second term bid. Peace and justice activists against U.S. intervention in Central America and Southern Africa were especially vocal in opposing the reelection. Having failed to intimidate solidarity groups through illegal spying, such as in the case of CISPES, and other forms of harassment, the Reagan administration resorted to targeting Palestinian activists–or what they saw as the weakest link in the anti-intervention movement.

On January 26, 1987, 250 agents of the FBI, Secret Service, LAPD, and the INS raided the homes of seven Palestinian men and a Kenyan woman married to one of the seven, handcuffed and shackled them, and brought them to a maximum security prison. The Reagan administration used the McCarren-Walter Act, a relic of the McCarthy era witch-hunt, which excludes Communists and Communist sympathizers from entry into U.S., to initiate deportation proceedings on the grounds that the Los Angeles 8 posed a threat to the national security of the United States. At first, it seemed as if the administration's plan worked. The headlines in a Los Angeles local paper announced that "War on Terrorism Hits L.A."

Reagan's popularity ratings were climbing, and the example made of the L.A. 8 had a chilling effect on Palestinian and Arab American activists who shuddered at the possibility that their legal residence might be revoked should they speak up for Palestinian rights. Other peace and anti-intervention groups also feared that their solidarity with the struggles waged by leftist guerillas in El Salvador or Angola would immediately label them as Communist.

The administration's plot, however, was foiled by two unanticipated reactions. First, upon hearing the news, over 150 Palestinians from the Los Angeles area rented buses and drove to the prison where the L.A. 8 were held to demand their immediate release on bail. This spontaneous action forced activists to get over their initial shock and initiated the organization of a campaign around the L.A. 8 case. The second was the response of American civil libertarians. The American Civil Liberties Union, Center for Constitutional Rights, the National Lawyers Guild, and the National Conference of Black Lawyers joined with prominent attorneys such as Bill Kunstler and Lennie Weinglass to defend the Palestinian detainees because, as Weinglass put it, "This had nothing to do with safeguarding against 'terrorism.' It was a clear attack on the right to freedom of speech and association—a First Amendment right." The position of Weinglass, Kunstler, and others was echoed by other prominent Jews, including the actor Ed Asner and *New York Times* columnist Anthony Lewis. Further frustrating the efforts of the Reagan administration, mainstream Jewish groups, such as the American Jewish Congress, the American Jewish Committee, and the American-Israeli Civil Liberties Coalition also rose in defense of the L.A. 8. Moreover, the revelation that the Vice-President's Task Force on Terrorism had devised a contingency plan to round up "undesirable aliens" and legal residents from seven Arab countries as well as Iran and hold them in internment camps prompted Chicanos and Japanese Americans to join the campaign to support the L.A. 8.

The demonization of Palestinians by the U.S. government had both negative and positive effects. As it solidified the label *terrorist* in connection with Palestinians, it also broadened alliances with liberal groups and raised the stakes of what being a Palestinian meant. While some Palestinians carried on business as usual, it was no longer sufficient or safe for most to identify with the cause back home, to teach the kids Arabic, or to participate in community events. In addition to pro-Palestinian activism, being Palestinian in U.S. society now necessitated involvement in domestic struggles over constitutional rights, immigration legislation, antiracist campaigns, women's rights, and gay and lesbian liberation. However, sharper struggles over what *Palestinianness* meant were looming on the horizon.

THE PALESTINIAN INTIFADA: A TURNING POINT

Involvement in a social justice agenda does not necessarily or automatically produce a unified sense of the "we"; Palestinianness is not an exception. This was no more evident than in the Palestinian Intifada, which began on December 9, 1987, and deepened the contradictions over defining *Palestinianness* in U.S. exile. On one level, back home in the West Bank and Gaza, Palestinians sought to protect the national unity forged against the Israeli occupation irrespective of differences in class, gender, religion, or political affiliation. Similar politics emerged among Palestinians who were literally and euphemistically "outside" the major arena of the conflict and felt they had to play an active role in protecting the rights of their people back home. For example, devout Palestinian Muslims in New York had no qualms about holding a midnight candlelight vigil outside the St. Patrick's Cathedral on Christmas Eve to ask passersby to "pray for peace in the Holy Land." Activists from competing political organizations collectively organized daily demonstrations and picket lines across from Israeli missions, embassies, and government offices. During community national events, wealthy Palestinian merchants queued side by side with undocumented workers as well as students and solidarity activists to pledge financial support to Palestinian grassroots projects of survival under the Israeli occupation. For example, in 1988 support was pouring into Beit Sahur, the Palestinian town that declared civil disobedience against the occupation authorities and raised the slogan "no taxation without representation."

Such unity, however, eventually eroded. Harsh Israeli measures intent on destroying the Intifada raised intense disagreements over strategy and tactics in occupied Palestine. These disagreements also interlocked with the specific ways that different groups of Palestinian Americans understood the place of gender, class, and race and gender and sexuality and shaped the ways in which different organizations expressed their solidarity with the Palestinian Intifada. For example, reports of poisonous tear gas used by the Israeli military to break up Palestinian demonstrations affected solidarity activists differently than it did Palestinian women.[10] The Midwest chapters of Palestine Solidarity Committee organized an elaborate campaign against Federal Labs, the U.S. pharmaceutical company that manufactured the gas, including a civil disobedience action in which activists chained themselves to the gates of the company's headquarters in Pittsburgh, Pennsylvania.[11]

Palestinian women's solidarity with their "sisters" under occupation took a different form.[12] Suspicion that hundreds of Palestinian women suffered miscarriages after exposure to the poisonous tear gas highlighted a predicament for the Union of Palestinian Women's Associations in North America (UPWA)—how to articulate a stand that balanced our desire to expose Israeli brutality and to publicly address the issues of reproductive rights without misrepresenting Palestinian sentiments. Thus, on the eve of the national march for abortion rights, UPWA came out with a carefully worded statement that spoke to different audiences at once and reflected our tenuous position as transnationally connected, locally active, and communally grounded. Couching our statement in the liberal vocabulary of individual rights, we asserted women's right to choose whether or not to have children. In this way the UPWA sought to reach out to both liberal feminist organizers of the march while clearly locating itself amidst groups of feminists of color who opposed the march's narrow focus on abortion rights, opting instead to demand a comprehensive framework of reproductive freedoms.[13] By calling for a reduction in U.S. funding of the Israeli occupation and for a diversion of financial resources to social programs, and by further insisting that reproductive rights not only implied abortion rights, Palestinian women positioned themselves in the camp of class-conscious feminists of color without alienating NOW and other liberal women's groups.

Just as the Intifada opened possibilities for alliances between Palestinian women and U.S. feminists, it also consolidated Palestinian Americans' ties with other activists of color. Palestinian identification with activism in antiracist struggles in particular seemed only "natural," given the unwavering solidarity African Americans expressed with the Palestinian Intifada. For example, African American activists organized the Days of Rage campaign to protest escalating police racist attacks in the New York area and to coincide with November 29, the international day of solidarity with the Palestinian people. On that cold evening hundreds of African

Americans, wearing *kafiyyahs* (Palestinian scarves), linked hands across the United Nations demanding justice for both peoples.

At the same time, the Intifada also brought class differences among Palestinian Americans to the fore. While the Palestinian American middle class was most concerned with advocating support for Palestinian national rights, Palestinians workers in Palestinian-owned grocery stores were as conscious of their class location as they were of their Palestinianness. For them being Palestinian did not prevent their employers from exploiting their illegal alien status by forcing them to work long hours; paying them below-minimum wages; offering them no health insurance or job security; and expecting them to behave as if everyone belonged to one big happy family—as workers in Brooklyn and Manhattan put it. The experiences of these Palestinian workers suggests that culture and class identities do not "displace each other"(Aronowitz 1992:8) but that they can and do coexist simultaneously. Palestinian workers thus expressed their solidarity with the Intifada by attempting to network with U.S. trade unions. Yet the majority of activists among Palestinian American workers were newcomers who did not speak English fluently. Nor did they have the resources of middle-class Palestinian left intellectuals to engage leftists and labor advocates in the academy. They also lacked the political clout to reach out to the U.S. labor movement, which was heavily influenced by its ties to the Israeli labor federation. To express their solidarity with Palestinian workers back home, they joined the initiative to create the Palestine Labor Action Network (PLAN).

Developments in Palestine and North America contributed to the formation of PLAN. On one hand, Israeli treatment of Palestinian daily workers was being exposed in reports of the International Labor Organization, the International Federation of Free Trade Unions, and in the Israeli press.[14] Palestinian trade unionists and their international supporters were responsible for the exposure, including Marty Rosenbluth, a U.S. labor activist who volunteered his time and expertise with the Palestinian human rights group Al-Haq, the West Bank Affiliate of the International Commission of Jurists. Trade unionists of color who could not afford to take a leave of absence from their jobs to volunteer in Palestine joined fact-finding missions to visit Palestine during their vacations and were among the initiators of PLAN.

While Palestinian-centered activism during the Intifada also expanded the network of support for Palestinian rights, it also exposed the inherent contradictions of a national mobilization. The Intifada can be seen as a historic moment during which different groups with different interests and positions contested the master narrative of Palestinianness. Subsequent developments, especially the Gulf war and the Israel–PLO Accords of 1993, finally shattered any illusion of a homogenized Palestinian identity.

OSLO ACCORDS AND BEYOND: IMPLICATIONS AND COMPLICATIONS

The Israel–PLO Oslo Accords of 1993 and the emergence of Palestinian self-rule in parts of the West Bank and Gaza raised as never before questions about Palestinian identity. A new definition of Palestinianness diluted by the terms of Oslo was much different from the inclusive vision of the Palestinian Declaration of Independence adopted at the Palestinian National Council meeting in Algiers in 1988. Instead of making Palestinianness available as a euphemistic home for all Palestinians, the Palestinian Authority now offered a narrow definition of citizenship that was limited to the areas under its control (most clearly seen in the 1996 elections of the Palestinian Legislative Council). This construct of the inside versus the outside had initially reinforced Palestinian unity across all kinds of borders, but it excluded and silenced the criticism of those on the "outside."[15]

As a result of the signing of the Oslo Accords, most Palestine-centered activism in the U.S. collapsed: U.S. solidarity activists could not maintain their organizing efforts when the impression given by the media, the U.S., and the Israeli governments as well as the Palestinian Authority suggested that the Middle East conflict was resolved. North American solidarity activists decided that their energies could be better exerted elsewhere. It was time for Palestinians to regroup and take stock. This regrouping, of course, changed how Palestinian identity was constructed. No longer viewed as part of inclusive Palestinianness, Palestinians on the outside (of the areas controlled by the Palestinian Authority) were now seen as marginal to the Palestinian collectivity. The 1996 Palestinian Legislative Council elections considered Palestinians not registered with the Palestinian Authority and the Israeli government (under the Oslo Accords) ineligible to vote. Thus Palestinians in the diaspora felt excluded and betrayed by the Palestinian leadership. For Palestinian activists in the

U.S. who created a solidarity movement, invested their energies and the best years of their lives in political activism, Oslo signaled a need to re-configure what Palestinianness meant to displaced Palestinians.

Enacting their identity, young Palestinian Americans founded Al-Awda, the Palestinian Right of Return Coalition, in 1998, to both mark the fifty years of Nakbah, or dispossession, and to demand the right of re-turn for Palestinian refugees. The creation of Al-Awda reaffirmed the in-divisibility of Palestinianness and thus created the environment for the emergence of new forms of activism among Palestinian Americans and their allies. The Jerusalem Intifada that began in September 2000 opened anew possibilities for the rearticulation of *Palestinianness* among exiled ac-tivists. The Israeli reoccupation of Palestinian areas in March-April 2001 has rendered the Oslo Accords obsolete and thus narrowed the distance between Palestinians on the outside and those inside areas under Israeli occupation. Palestinians on the outside now felt more entitled to speak out against the brutalities of the Israeli occupation while insisting on the non-negotiable right of return, thus promoting the indivisibility of the Palestinian quest for justice and peace. Simultaneously, the escalating gov-ernment campaign against U.S. immigrants of Arab and Muslim descent, especially since the 9/11 attacks, reposed to Palestinians and Palestinian Americans the question of the character of the alliances they needed to build and the particular communities to which they imagined belonging.

Just as the Jerusalem Intifada has narrowed the gap on the inside/out-side divide of *Palestinianness,* the U.S. war against all things Arab and Mus-lim (the latest episode of which is the war against and occupation of Iraq), has in fact widened the distance between Palestinians in the U.S. and their Americanness. At the same time, the targeting of Arabs and Muslims has objectively renewed the potential for alliance building between Palestin-ian and other communities of color, seen throughout these pages and most recently enacted at the NYU event in support of Bir Zeit Univer-sity with which this essay opened.

This essay has attempted to delineate the general conditions as well as the specific historical moments at which a Palestinian identification and ac-tivism in the North American exile emerged. As I have demonstrated, my attempt to define Palestinianness in the U.S. must necessarily be grounded in a transnational perspective in which gender, class, and race relations are understood in the limited context of the U.S., and they must be dialectically linked in ways that account for the complexity of the geography of exile. In particular, I argue that a people dispossessed will continue to anchor their lives in two places—the native land and the diaspora of exile—simultaneously, not here (U.S.) and there (Palestine) but here and here.

In other words, throughout their history in the U.S. displacement has remained a central organizing principle for Palestinian Americans, and so has a politics of justice and identification with the marginalized. The event to support Bir Zeit University that was organized by an African American activist seems to be the best place with which to open and close this essay. Attended by Palestinians and non-Palestinians of different activist generations, the event symbolized the dialectics of inside and outside, scholarship and academia, community and students as well as the centrality of Palestine to broader questions of justice for Palestinians here and there.

Perhaps the most fitting way to conclude this essay is not to conclude it at all. As I have argued, sociopolitical conditions in the Middle East as well as the U.S. have together steered the course of Palestinian American activism and shaped Palestinianness. Thus, in the turbulent times that characterize both the Middle East and the U.S. today, only two things are certain: Palestinian American identities and activism are in flux, and they will continue to shift as they interact with the multiple contexts in which they emerged and to which they responded in the first place.

NOTES

1. This essay draws a distinction between Palestinianness and Palestinian Americanness in that the former defines the identification and practices of Palestinians in the U.S. while the latter refers specifically to the Palestinian American experience as a hyphenated and ethnic mode.

2. These groups included, for example, the American Arab Anti-Discrimination Committee, the Arab American Institute, the Association of Arab-American University Graduates, the General Union of Palestine Students, the Union of Palestinian Women in North America, the Palestinian Academic Freedom Network, the Palestine Labor Action Network, the Palestine Solidarity Committee, Ramallah Federation–Palestine, Beit Hanina Federation–Palestine, and El-Bireh Federation–Palestine.

3. My father, who passed away in December 2002, was one of those students. Had

it not been for the help offered by a particular Harb family in Knoxville, Tennessee, he would not have survived the harsh reality of exile and displacement.

4. Founded in the early 1950s by a group of Palestinian students in Cairo and Kuwait, GUPS represented Palestinian students the world over, except for those living under Israeli occupation where membership in any Palestinian mass institution was considered a crime against Israeli security punishable by a prison sentence.

5. The fact that Jesse Jackson's popularity in the Black community was uneven at best escaped the attention of the Palestinian leadership, whose eagerness to build support for the Palestinian struggle blinded them/us from seeing the diversity of thought and practice within other communities.

6. Odeh's husband, the late Samir Odeh, was a major figure in both the Jackson presidential bid and later in Harold Washington's sucessful mayoral campaign.

7. As for racial politics, that was another matter.

8. Were it not for stopping their status as foreign students, they too would have been arrested.

9. This discussion, obviously, does not capture the richness, complexity, or the shortcomings of UPWA. These issues will be expanded upon in a forthcoming book on Palestinian feminist action.

10. This was investigated and confirmed by Physicians for Human Rights, an organization of medical doctors based in Boston, Massachusetts.

11. The highly publicized (and preorchestrated) arrests of tens of activists demonstrated the extent to which the Palestine solidarity movement was becoming sensitized to the image it projected in the U.S. media. See Gitlin 1980.

12. I am using *sisters* in this context for a lack of a better term and not to imply agreement with the essentialist notion put forth by Morgan 1984 implying all women are the same across time, space, and experiences.

13. Because the march protested Reagan's attempt to ban legal abortions, Palestinian women intimated in their statement that the forces seeking to deny U.S. women the right to decide whether or not to have children were the same forces that sought to deny Palestinian women the right to have children. Since the right wing in both cases sought to deny women the right to control their bodies, Palestinian women thought it logical that a strategic alliance should unite the efforts of Palestinian and American women.

14. For example, Israelis demeaned Palestinian labor, referring to the sites at which Palestinian daily-workers gathered as "slave markets" and to Palestinian labor as "Black labor."

15. Not all Palestinians on the outside suffered, however. The lure of a new territory for money-making was attracting Palestinian American businessmen who sought to invest in new markets by setting up industrial parks of export free zones such as Blimpies, Pizza Hut, and other U.S.-based food chains.

Works Cited

Aronowitz, Stanley. 1992. *The Politics of Identity: Class, Culture, Social Movements.* New York: Routledge.

Gitlin, Todd. 1980. *The Whole World Is Watching: Mass Media in the Making and Unmaking of the New Left.* Berkeley: University of California Press.

Hamad, Suheir. 1996. *Born Palestinian, Born Black.* New York: Harlem River.

Meyer, David. 1993. *A Winter of Discontent: The Nuclear Freeze and American Politics.* New York: Praeger.

Morgan, Robin, ed. 1984. *Sisterhood Is Global: The International Women's Movement Anthology.* New York: Doubleday.

Said, Edward. 1978. *Orientalism.* New York: Vintage.

Tilly, Charles. 1978. *From Mobilization to Revolution.* New York: McGraw-Hill.